14 ENTER CATHY

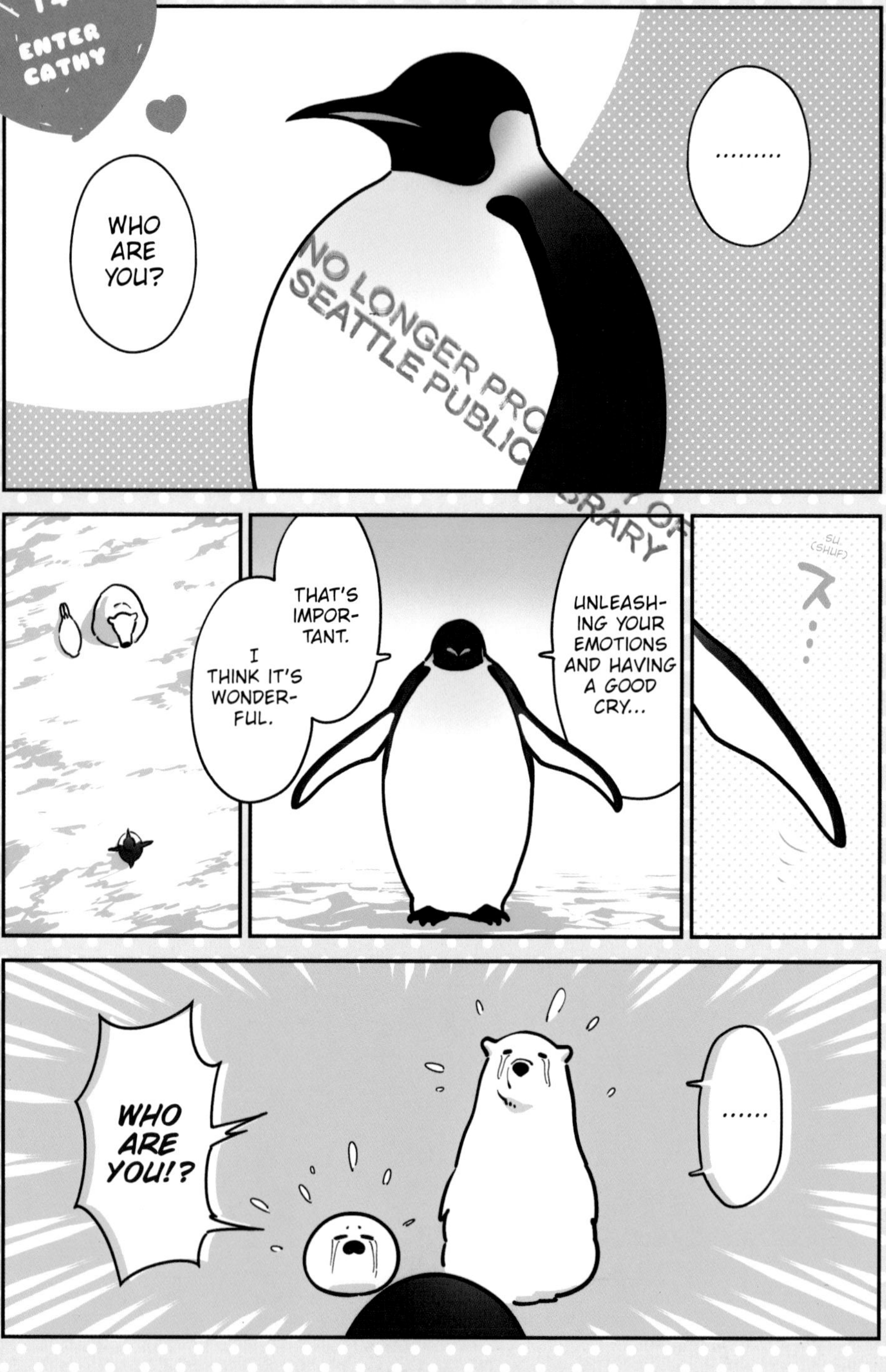
....
WHO ARE YOU?
SU (SHUF)
UNLEASHING YOUR EMOTIONS AND HAVING A GOOD CRY...
THAT'S IMPORTANT.
I THINK IT'S WONDERFUL.
......
WHO ARE YOU!?

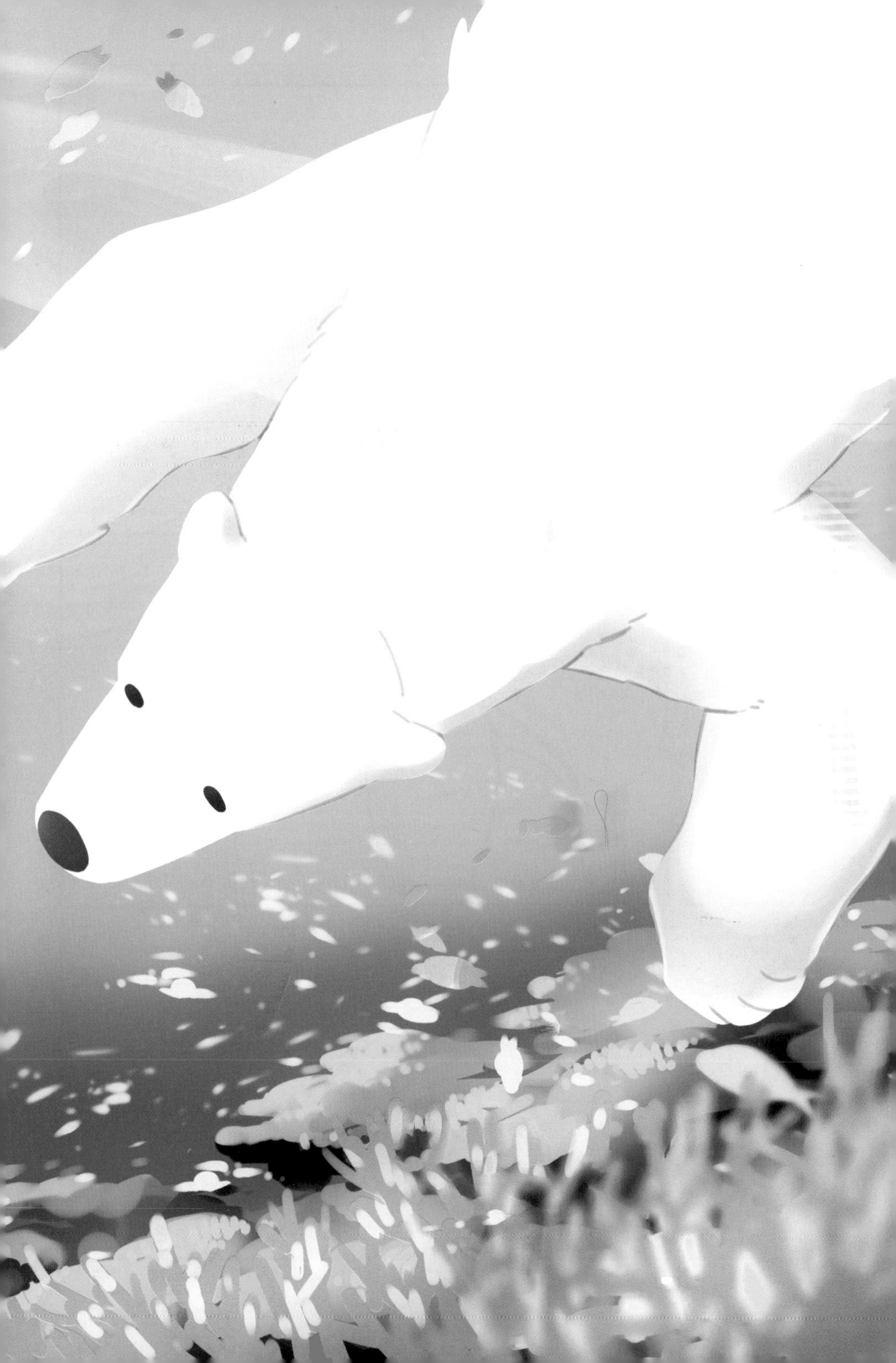

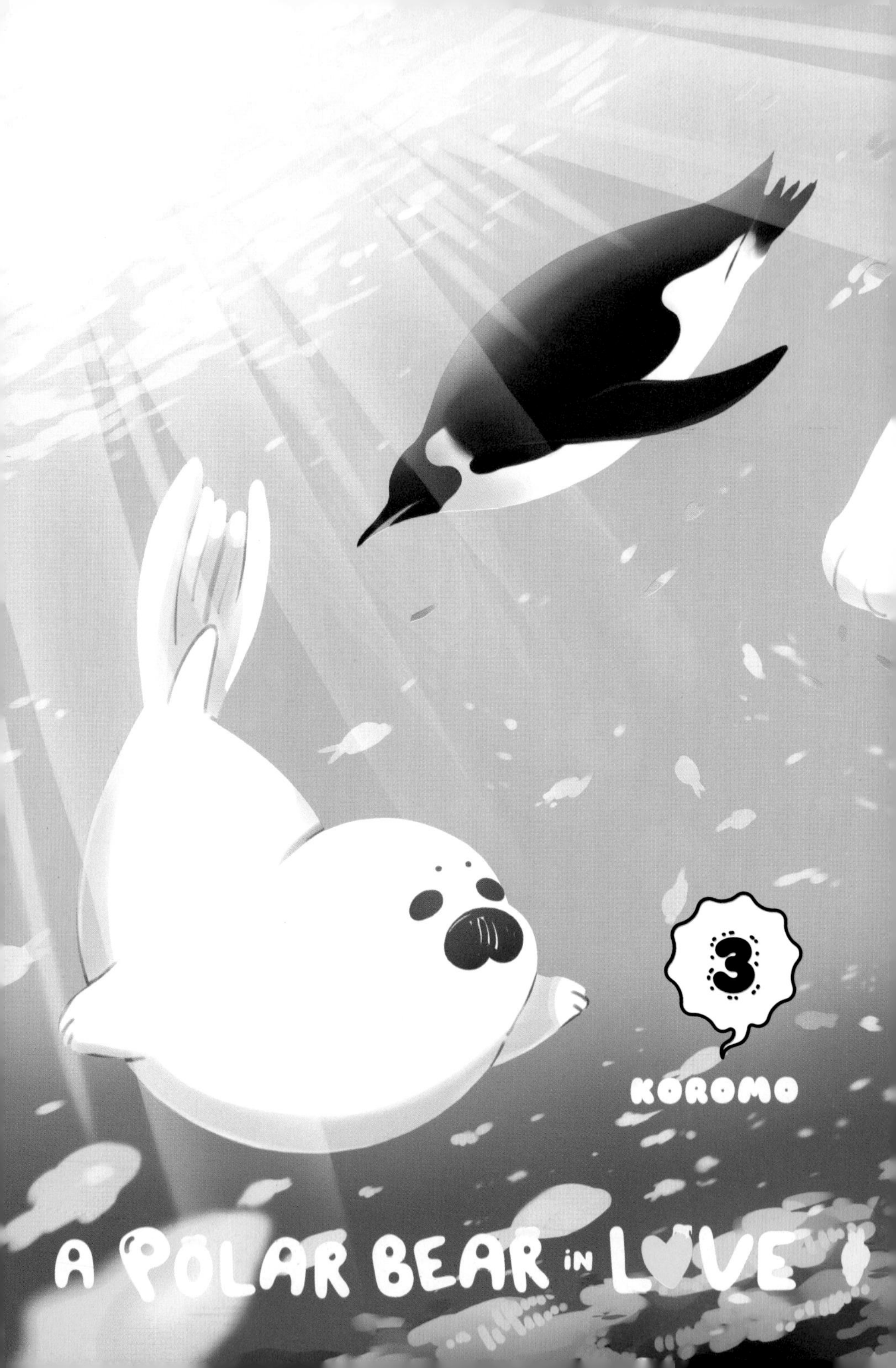
3
KOROMO
A POLAR BEAR in LOVE

c o n t e n t s

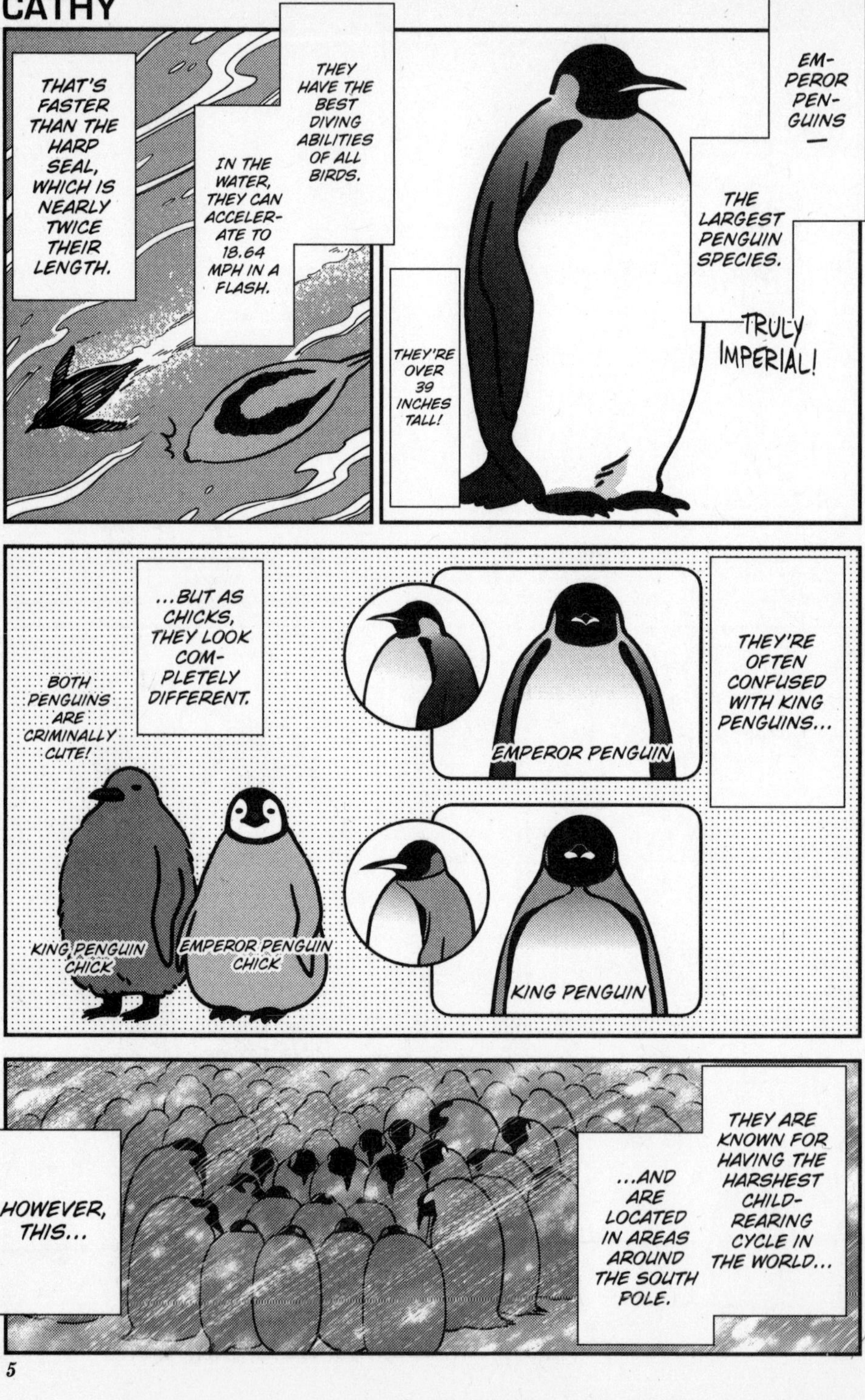
EMPEROR PENGUINS—
THE LARGEST PENGUIN SPECIES.
TRULY IMPERIAL!
THEY'RE OVER 39 INCHES TALL!
THEY HAVE THE BEST DIVING ABILITIES OF ALL BIRDS.
IN THE WATER, THEY CAN ACCELERATE TO 18.64 MPH IN A FLASH.
THAT'S FASTER THAN THE HARP SEAL, WHICH IS NEARLY TWICE THEIR LENGTH.
THEY'RE OFTEN CONFUSED WITH KING PENGUINS...
EMPEROR PENGUIN
KING PENGUIN
...BUT AS CHICKS, THEY LOOK COMPLETELY DIFFERENT.
BOTH PENGUINS ARE CRIMINALLY CUTE!
EMPEROR PENGUIN CHICK
KING PENGUIN CHICK
THEY ARE KNOWN FOR HAVING THE HARSHEST CHILD-REARING CYCLE IN THE WORLD...
...AND ARE LOCATED IN AREAS AROUND THE SOUTH POLE.
HOWEVER, THIS...

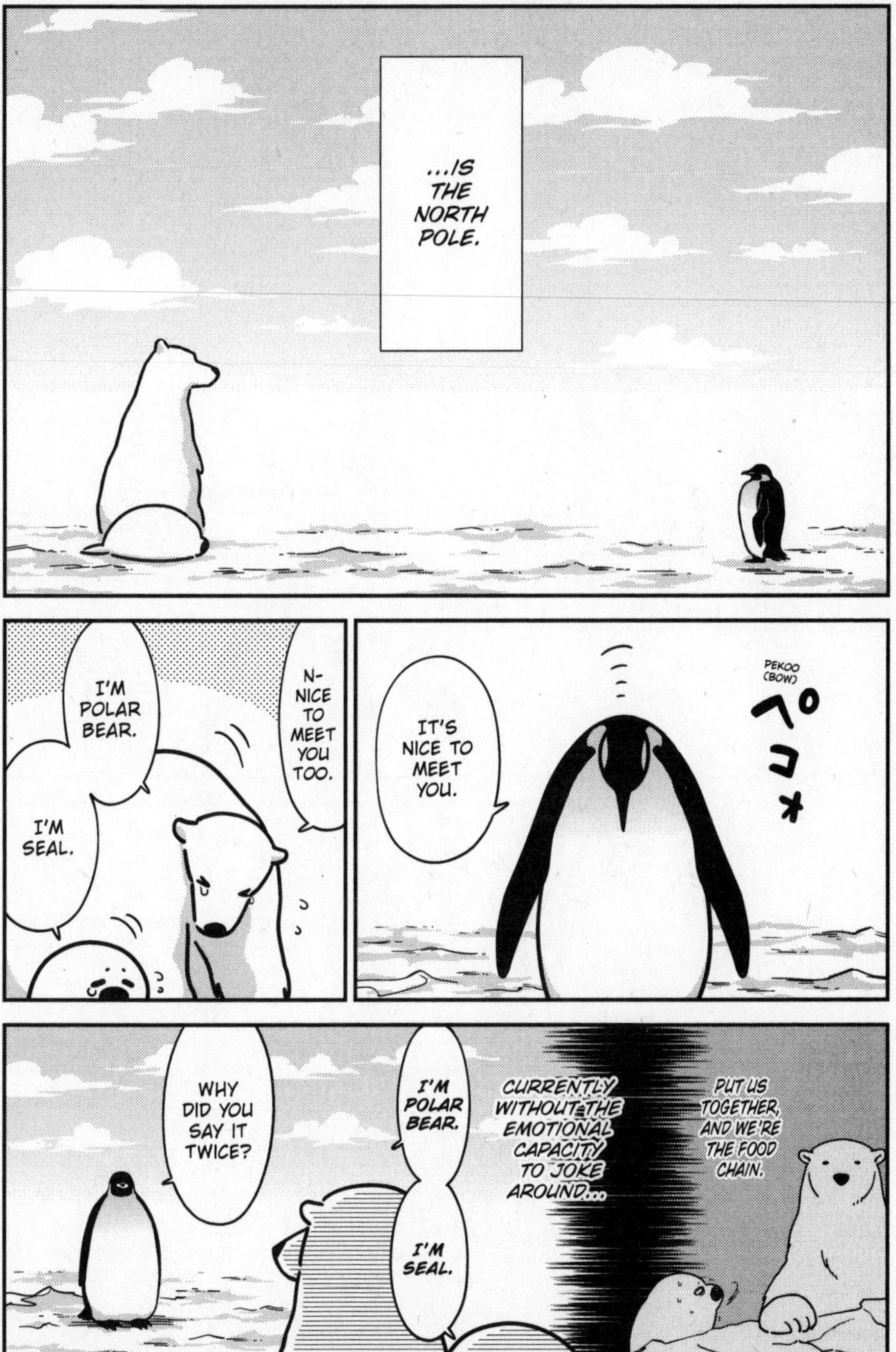
...IS THE NORTH POLE.
PEKOO (BOW)
ペコォ
IT'S NICE TO MEET YOU.
N- NICE TO MEET YOU TOO.
I'M POLAR BEAR.
I'M SEAL.
PUT US TOGETHER, AND WE'RE THE FOOD CHAIN.
CURRENTLY WITHOUT THE EMOTIONAL CAPACITY TO JOKE AROUND...
I'M POLAR BEAR.
I'M SEAL.
WHY DID YOU SAY IT TWICE?

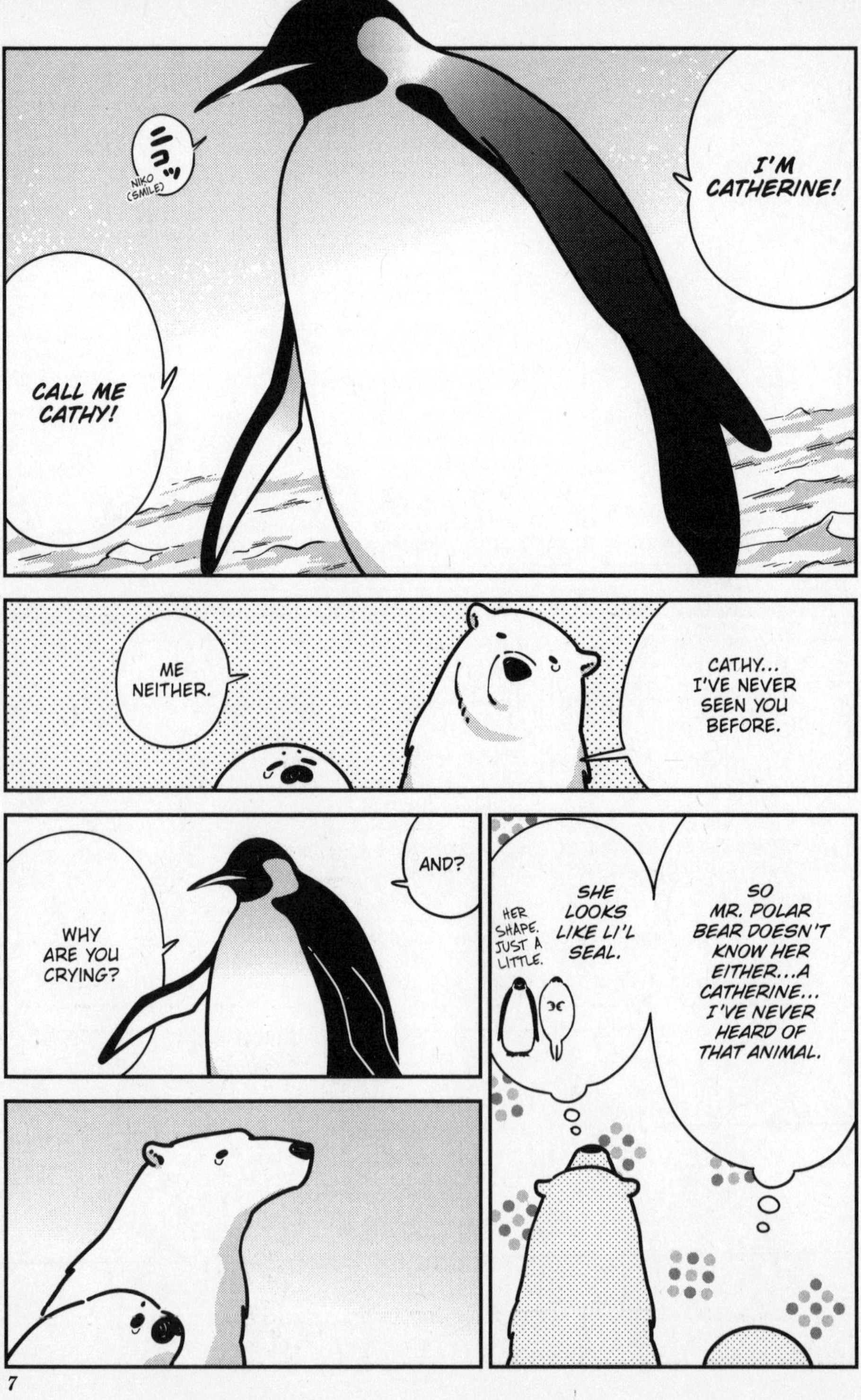
I'M CATHERINE!
ニコッ
NIKO (SMILE)
CALL ME CATHY!
CATHY... I'VE NEVER SEEN YOU BEFORE.
ME NEITHER.
SO MR. POLAR BEAR DOESN'T KNOW HER EITHER...A CATHERINE... I'VE NEVER HEARD OF THAT ANIMAL.
SHE LOOKS LIKE LI'L SEAL.
HER SHAPE. JUST A LITTLE.
AND?
WHY ARE YOU CRYING?

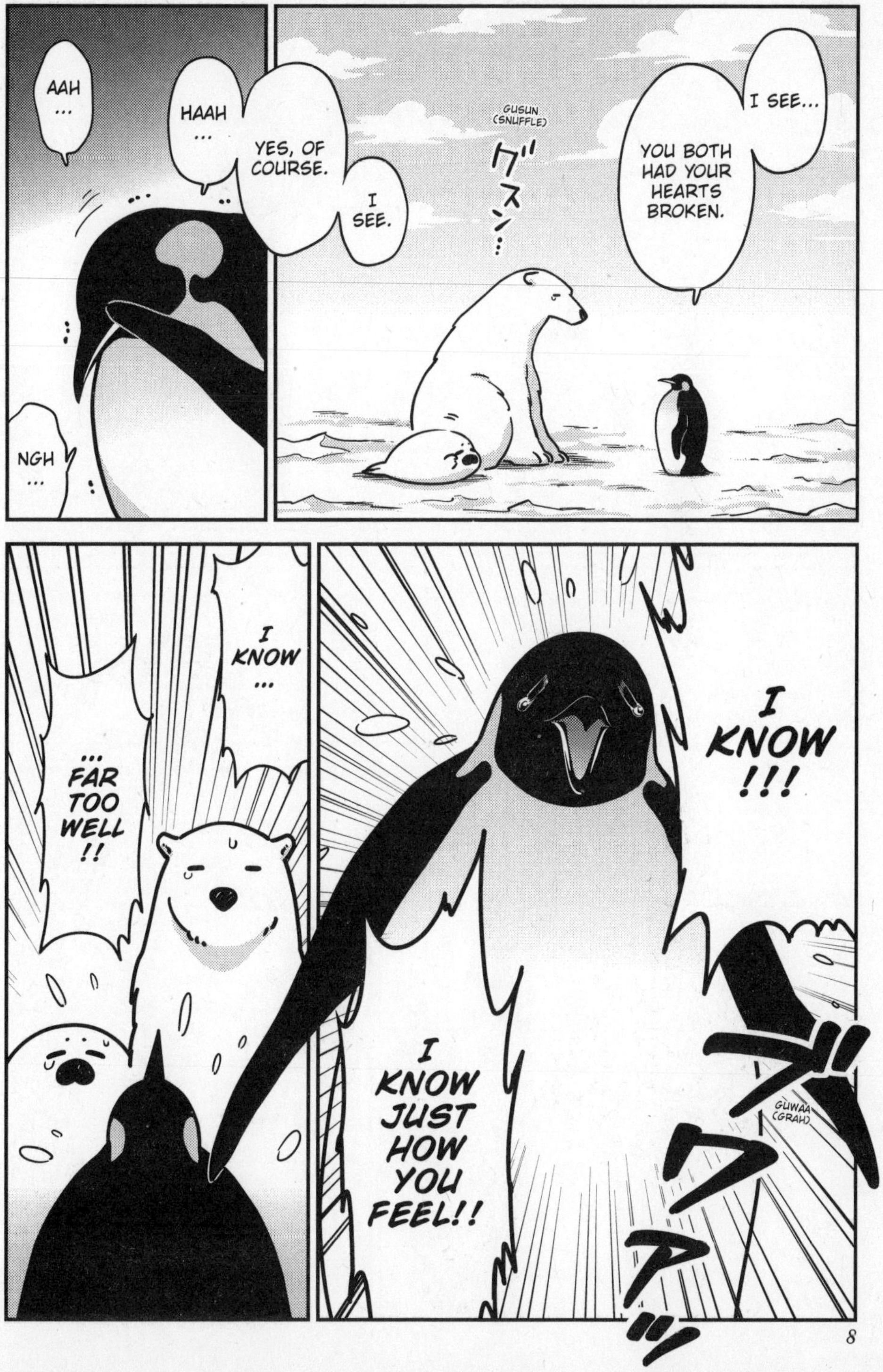
I SEE...
YOU BOTH HAD YOUR HEARTS BROKEN.
GUSUN (SNUFFLE)
グスン…
YES, OF COURSE.
I SEE.
HAAH ...
AAH ...
NGH ...
I KNOW !!!
GUWAA (GRAH)
I KNOW JUST HOW YOU FEEL!!
I KNOW ...
... FAR TOO WELL !!

LOVE IS THE WORLD

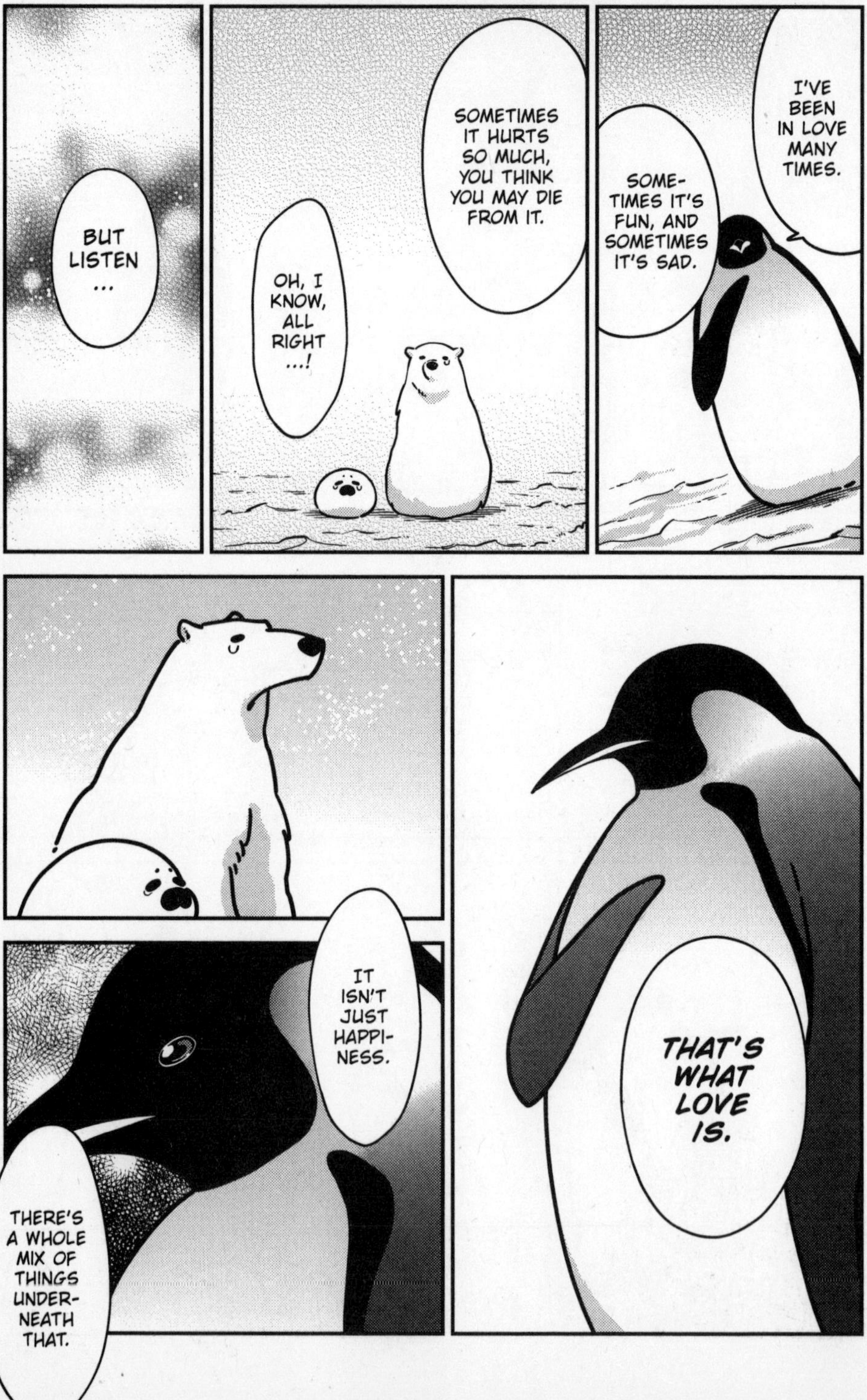

I'VE BEEN IN LOVE MANY TIMES.
SOME-TIMES IT'S FUN, AND SOMETIMES IT'S SAD.
SOMETIMES IT HURTS SO MUCH, YOU THINK YOU MAY DIE FROM IT.
OH, I KNOW, ALL RIGHT ...!
BUT LISTEN ...
THAT'S WHAT LOVE IS.
IT ISN'T JUST HAPPI-NESS.
THERE'S A WHOLE MIX OF THINGS UNDER-NEATH THAT.

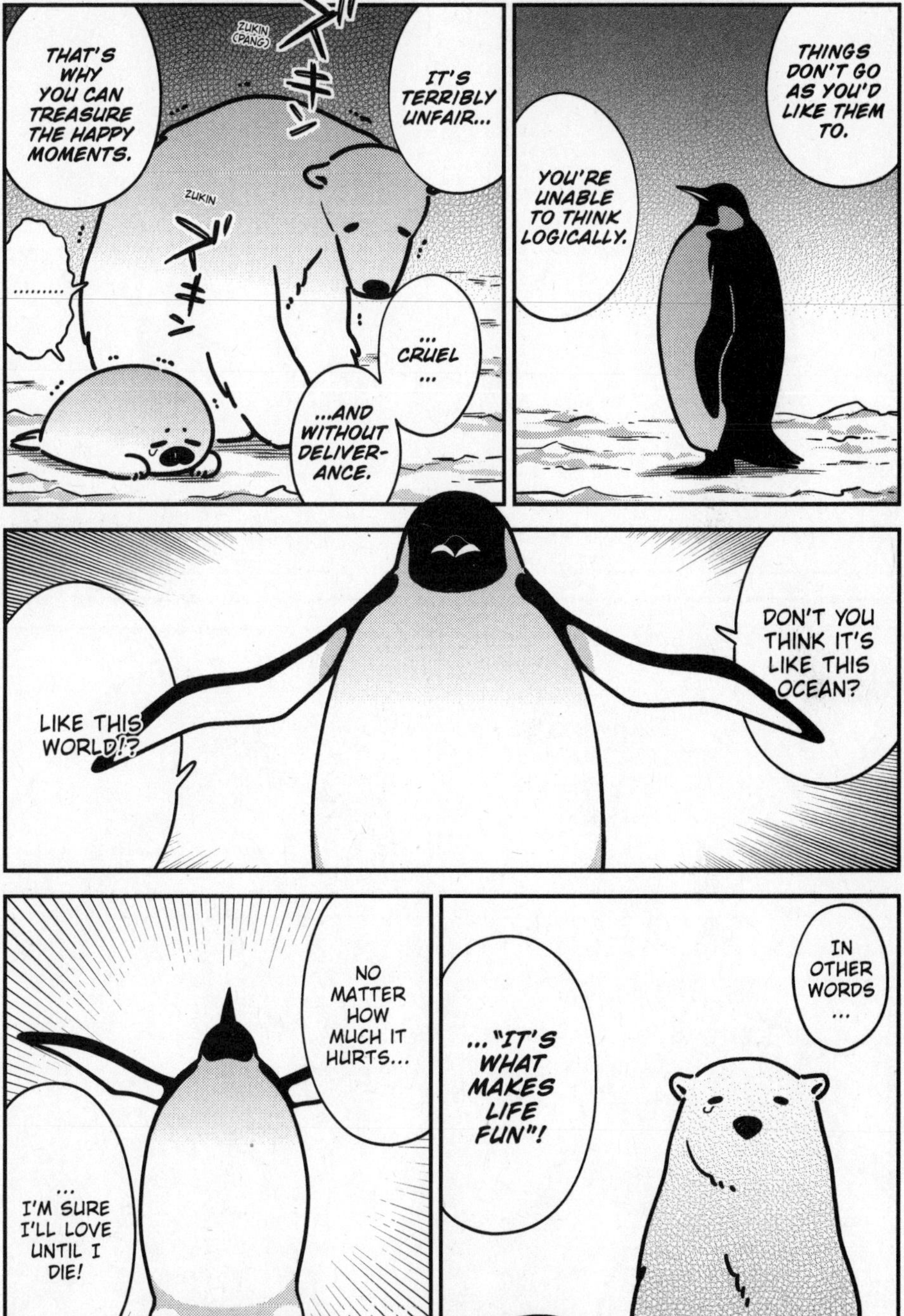
THINGS DON'T GO AS YOU'D LIKE THEM TO.
YOU'RE UNABLE TO THINK LOGICALLY.
IT'S TERRIBLY UNFAIR...
ズキン
ZUKIN (PANG)
ズキン
ZUKIN
...CRUEL...
...AND WITHOUT DELIVERANCE.
THAT'S WHY YOU CAN TREASURE THE HAPPY MOMENTS.
....
DON'T YOU THINK IT'S LIKE THIS OCEAN?
LIKE THIS WORLD!?
IN OTHER WORDS...
..."IT'S WHAT MAKES LIFE FUN"!
NO MATTER HOW MUCH IT HURTS...
...I'M SURE I'LL LOVE UNTIL I DIE!

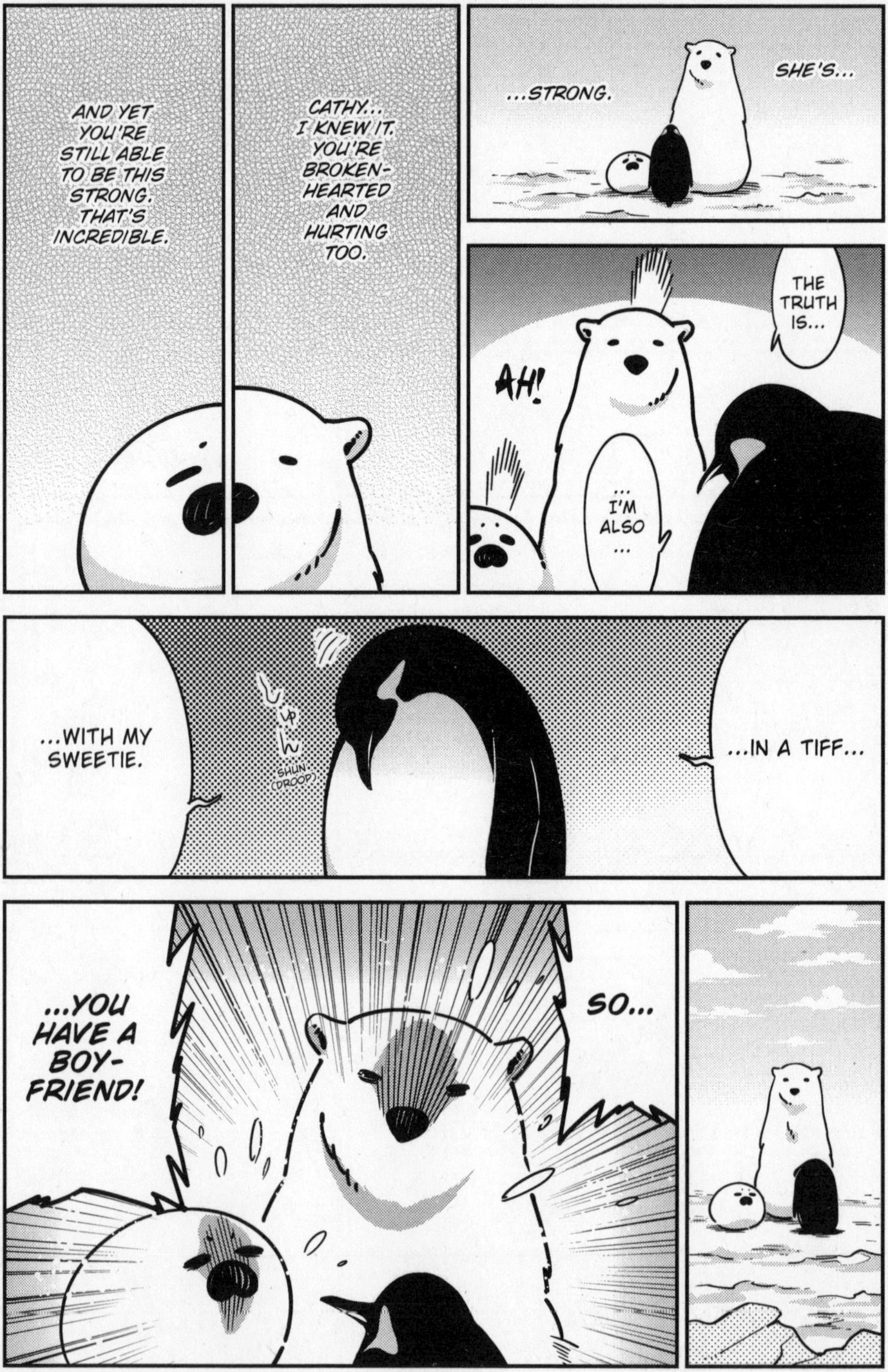

SHE'S...
...STRONG.
THE TRUTH IS...
AH!
...I'M ALSO...
CATHY... I KNEW IT. YOU'RE BROKEN-HEARTED AND HURTING TOO.
AND YET YOU'RE STILL ABLE TO BE THIS STRONG. THAT'S INCREDIBLE.
...IN A TIFF...
しゅん
SHUN (DROOP)
...WITH MY SWEETIE.
SO...
...YOU HAVE A BOY-FRIEND!

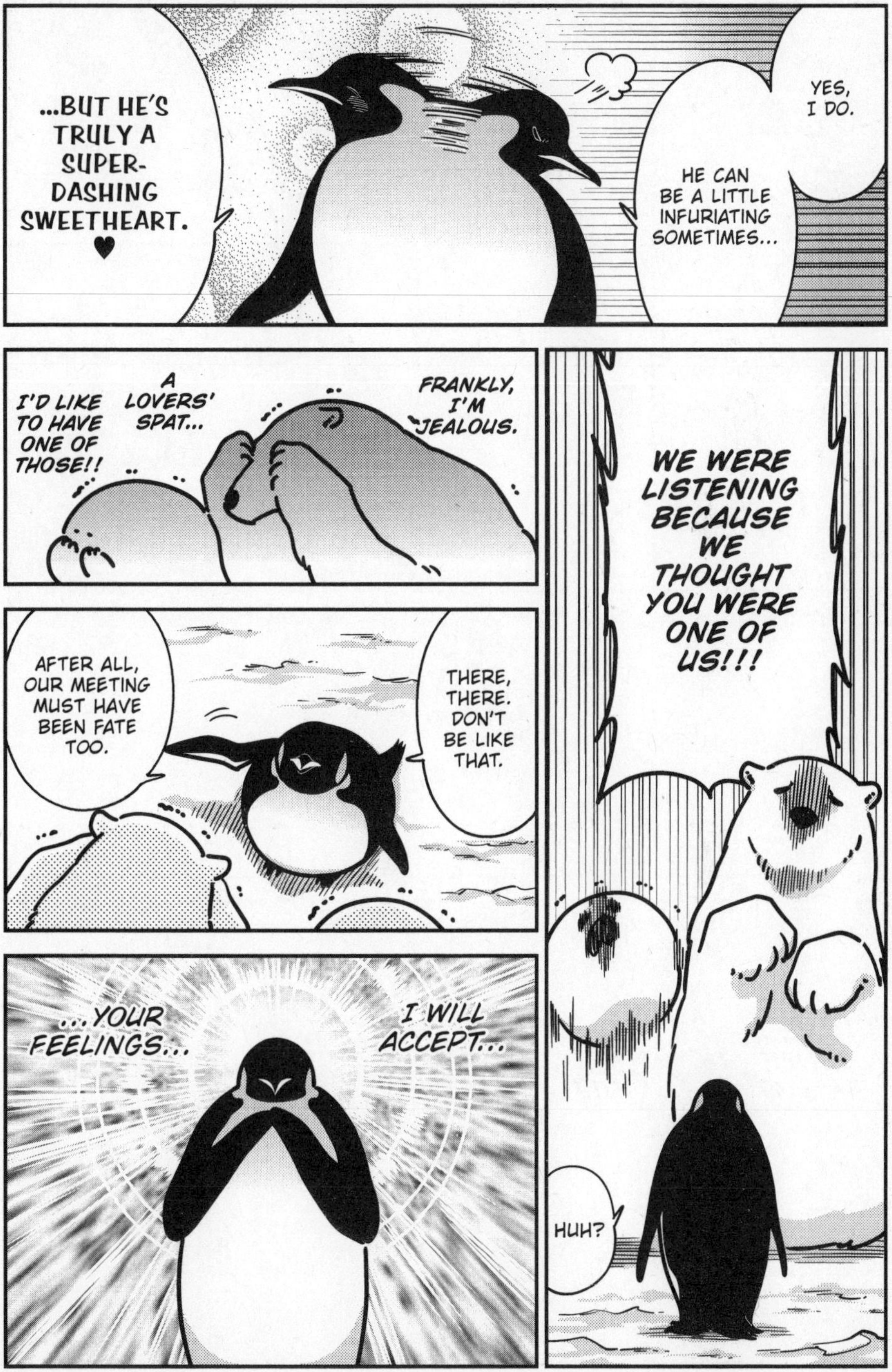
YES, I DO.
HE CAN BE A LITTLE INFURIATING SOMETIMES...
...BUT HE'S TRULY A SUPER-DASHING SWEETHEART. ♥
WE WERE LISTENING BECAUSE WE THOUGHT YOU WERE ONE OF US!!!
HUH?
FRANKLY, I'M JEALOUS.
A LOVERS' SPAT...
I'D LIKE TO HAVE ONE OF THOSE!!
THERE, THERE. DON'T BE LIKE THAT.
AFTER ALL, OUR MEETING MUST HAVE BEEN FATE TOO.
I WILL ACCEPT...
...YOUR FEELINGS...

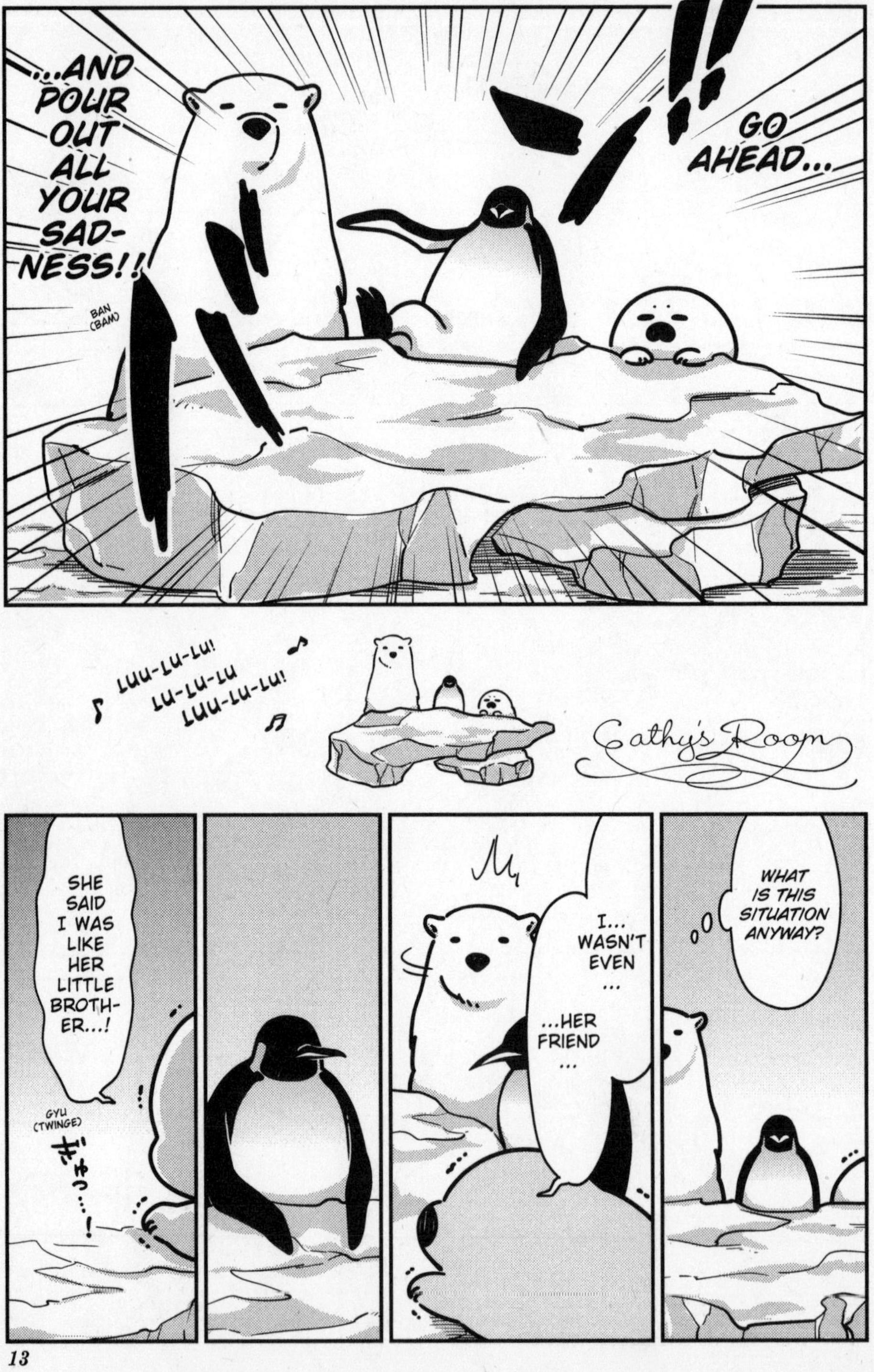
GO AHEAD...
!!
...AND POUR OUT ALL YOUR SADNESS!!
BAN (BAM)
Cathy's Room
LUU-LU-LU! LU-LU-LU LUU-LU-LU!
WHAT IS THIS SITUATION ANYWAY?
I... WASN'T EVEN ...
...HER FRIEND ...
SHE SAID I WAS LIKE HER LITTLE BROTHER...!
GYU (TWINGE)
ぎゅっ…!

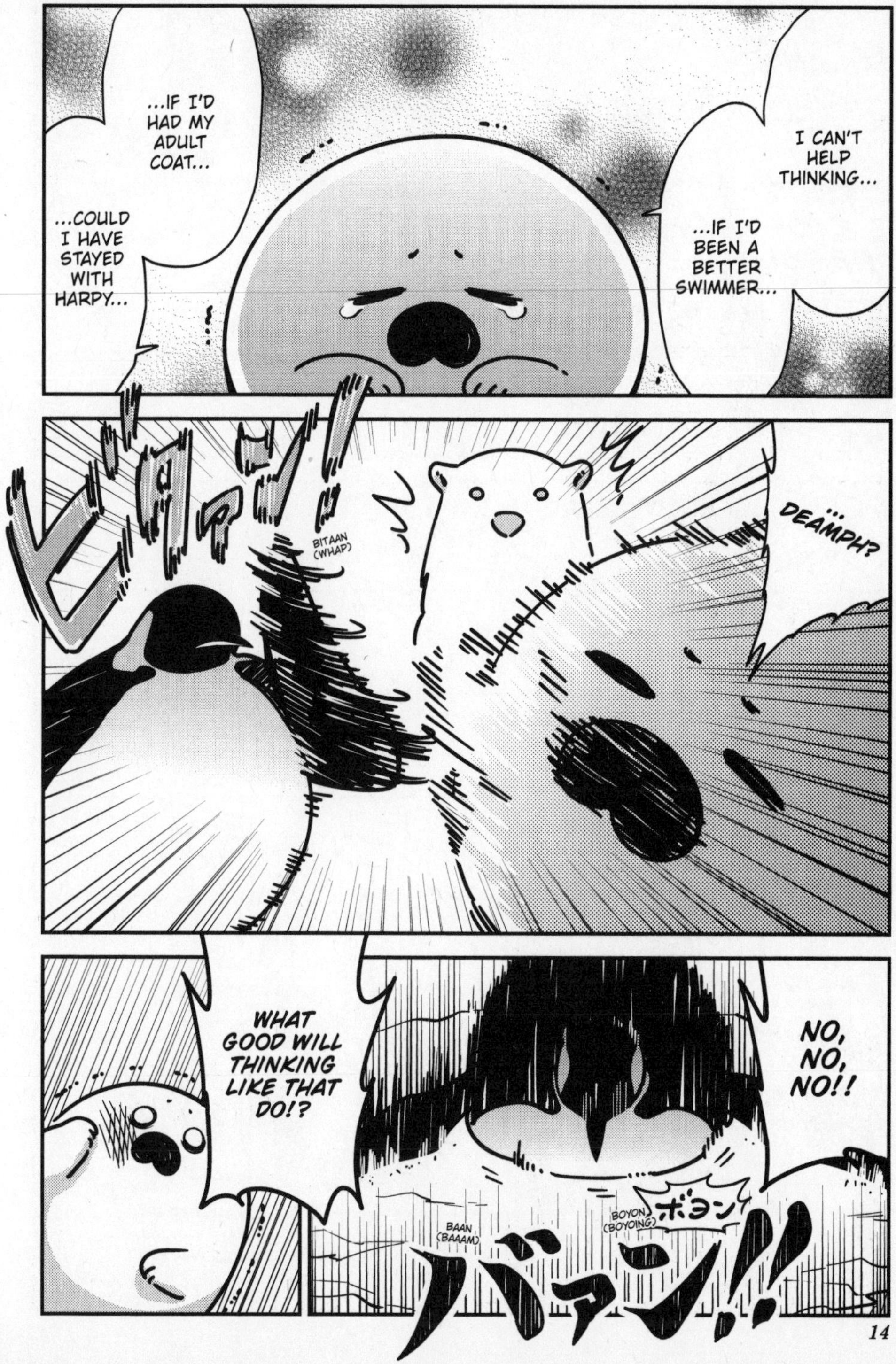

I CAN'T HELP THINKING...
...IF I'D BEEN A BETTER SWIMMER...
...IF I'D HAD MY ADULT COAT...
...COULD I HAVE STAYED WITH HARPY...
...DEAMPH?
BITAAN (WHAP)
NO, NO, NO!!
ボヨン
BOYON (BOYOING)
BAAN (BAAAM)
WHAT GOOD WILL THINKING LIKE THAT DO!?

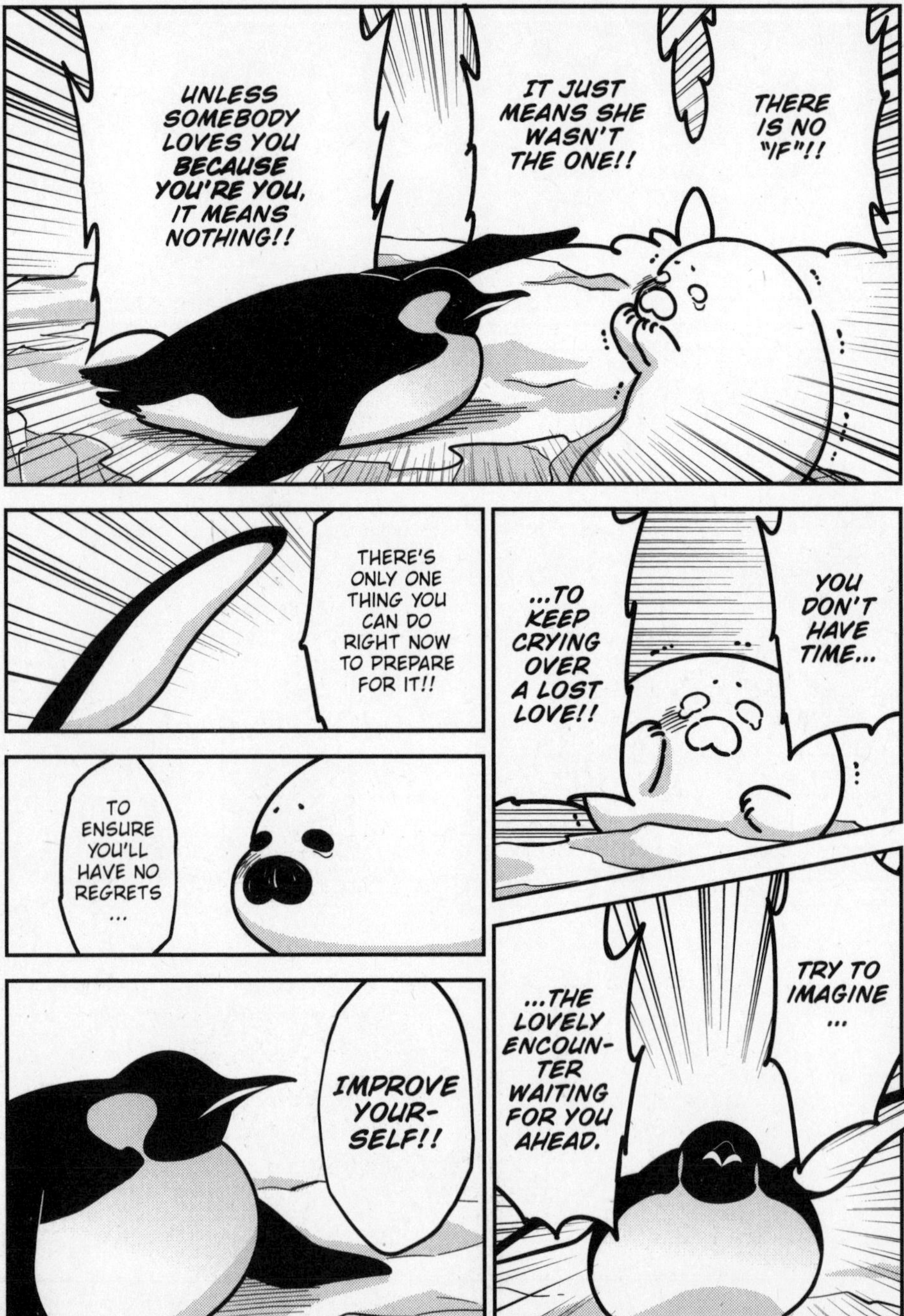
THERE IS NO "IF"!!
IT JUST MEANS SHE WASN'T THE ONE!!
UNLESS SOMEBODY LOVES YOU BECAUSE YOU'RE YOU, IT MEANS NOTHING!!
YOU DON'T HAVE TIME...
...TO KEEP CRYING OVER A LOST LOVE!!
TRY TO IMAGINE...
...THE LOVELY ENCOUNTER WAITING FOR YOU AHEAD.
THERE'S ONLY ONE THING YOU CAN DO RIGHT NOW TO PREPARE FOR IT!!
TO ENSURE YOU'LL HAVE NO REGRETS...
IMPROVE YOURSELF!!

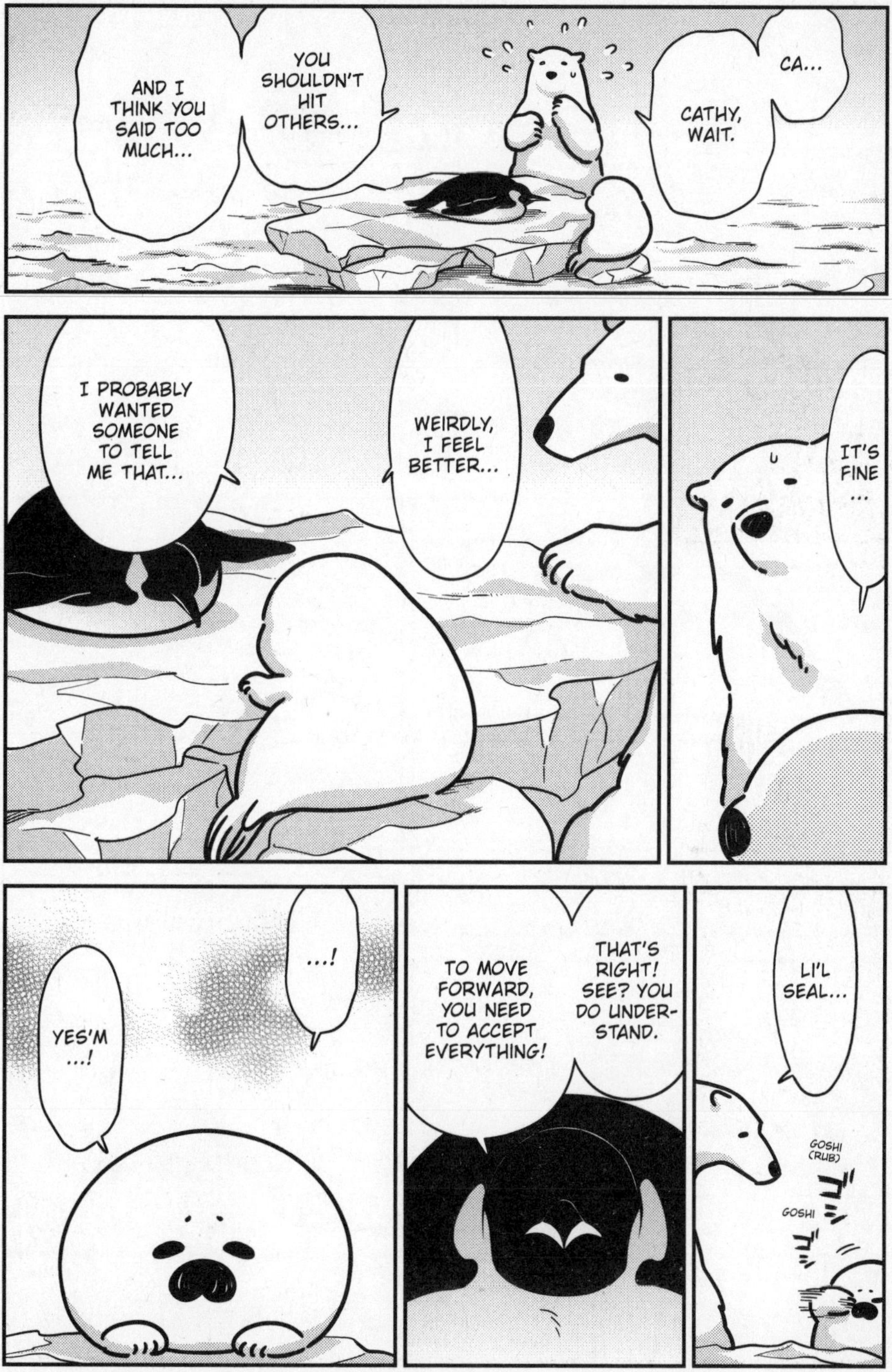
CA...
CATHY, WAIT.
YOU SHOULDN'T HIT OTHERS...
AND I THINK YOU SAID TOO MUCH...
IT'S FINE ...
WEIRDLY, I FEEL BETTER...
I PROBABLY WANTED SOMEONE TO TELL ME THAT...
LI'L SEAL...
GOSHI (RUB)
GOSHI
THAT'S RIGHT! SEE? YOU DO UNDER-STAND.
TO MOVE FORWARD, YOU NEED TO ACCEPT EVERYTHING!
...!
YES'M ...!

OF COURSE IT'S NOT ALL RIGHT

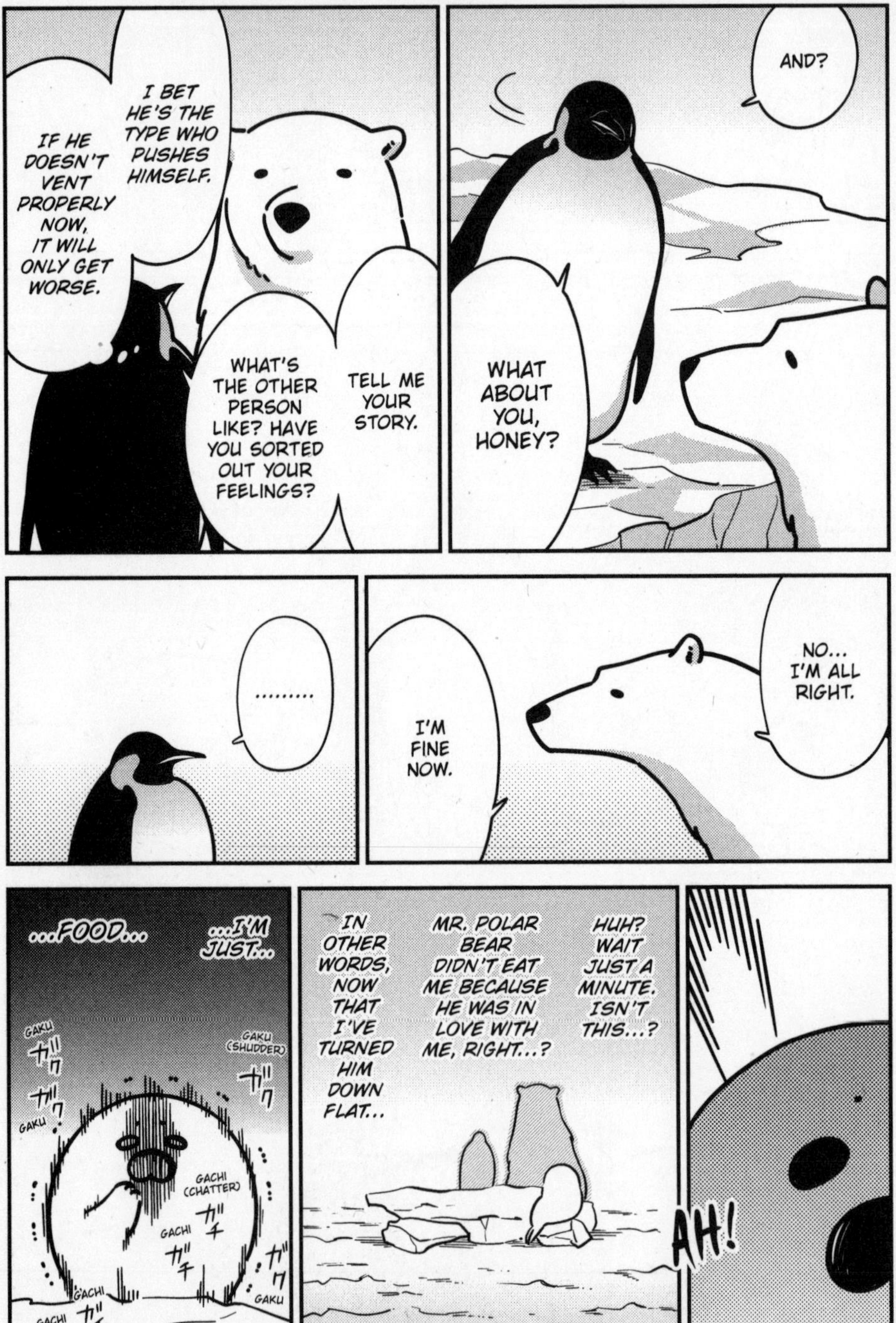

AND?
WHAT ABOUT YOU, HONEY?
I BET HE'S THE TYPE WHO PUSHES HIMSELF.
IF HE DOESN'T VENT PROPERLY NOW, IT WILL ONLY GET WORSE.
TELL ME YOUR STORY.
WHAT'S THE OTHER PERSON LIKE? HAVE YOU SORTED OUT YOUR FEELINGS?
NO... I'M ALL RIGHT.
I'M FINE NOW.
....
AH!
HUH? WAIT JUST A MINUTE. ISN'T THIS...?
MR. POLAR BEAR DIDN'T EAT ME BECAUSE HE WAS IN LOVE WITH ME, RIGHT...?
IN OTHER WORDS, NOW THAT I'VE TURNED HIM DOWN FLAT...
...I'M JUST...
...FOOD...
GAKU (SHUDDER) ガク
GAKU ガク
GAKU ガク
GAKU ガク
GACHI (CHATTER) ガチ
GACHI ガチ
GACHI ガチ
GACHI ガチ

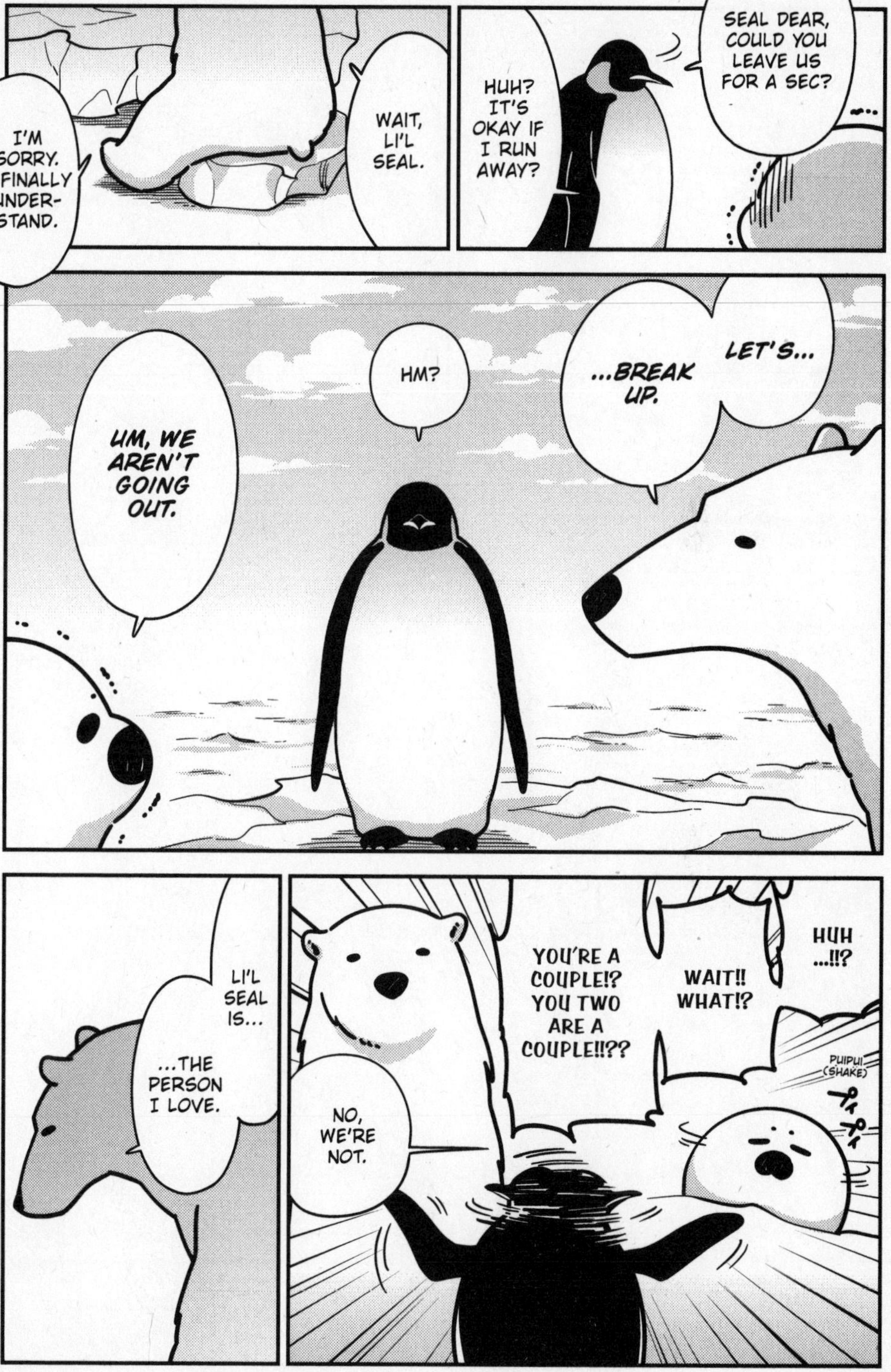
SEAL DEAR, COULD YOU LEAVE US FOR A SEC?
HUH? IT'S OKAY IF I RUN AWAY?
WAIT, LI'L SEAL.
I'M SORRY. I FINALLY UNDER-STAND.
LET'S...
...BREAK UP.
HM?
UM, WE AREN'T GOING OUT.
HUH ...!!?
WAIT!! WHAT!?
YOU'RE A COUPLE!? YOU TWO ARE A COUPLE!!??
PUIPUI (SHAKE)
NO, WE'RE NOT.
LI'L SEAL IS...
...THE PERSON I LOVE.

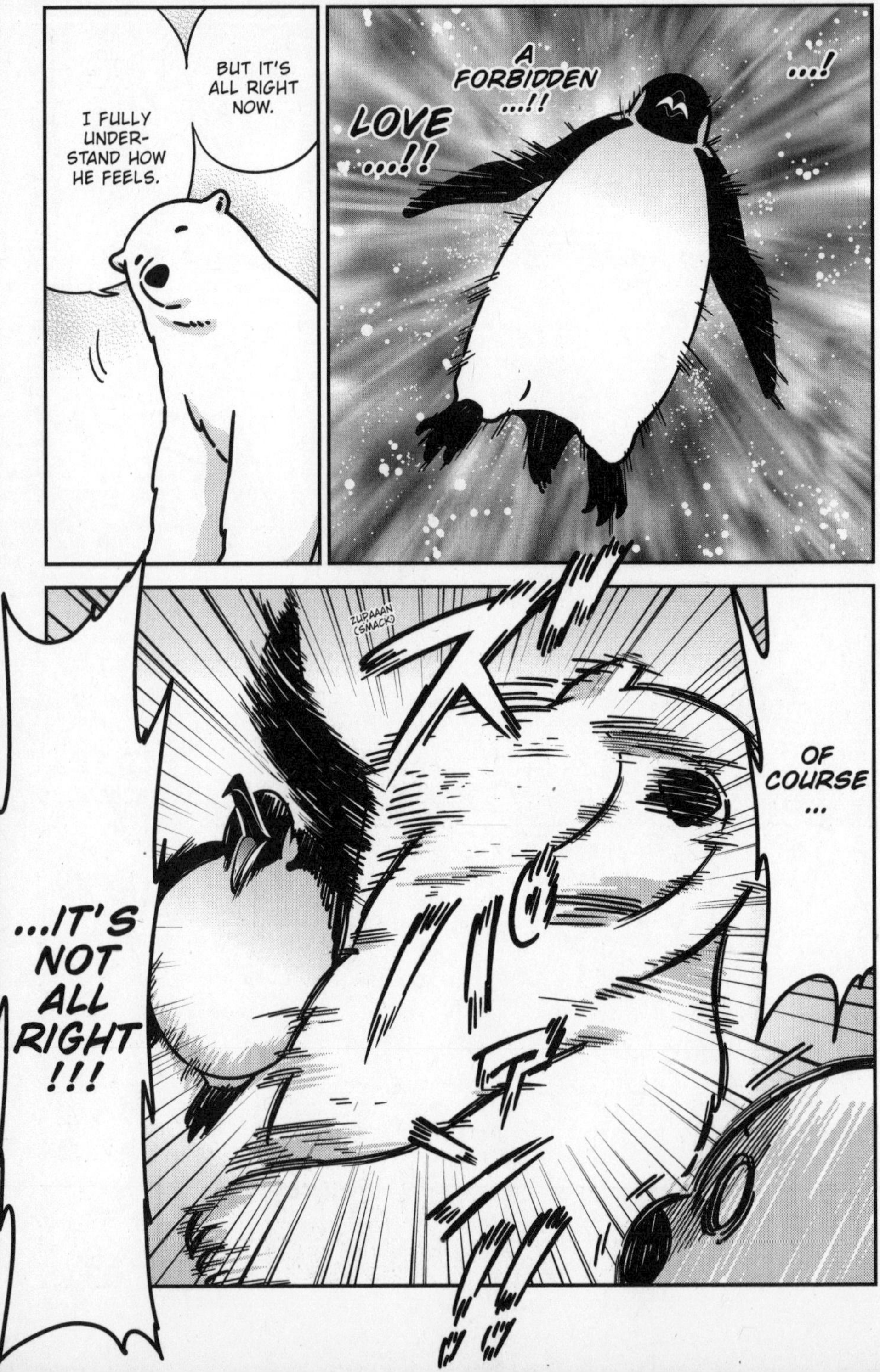
...!
A FORBIDDEN ...!!
LOVE ...!!
BUT IT'S ALL RIGHT NOW.
I FULLY UNDER-STAND HOW HE FEELS.
ZUPAAAN (SMACK)
OF COURSE ...
...IT'S NOT ALL RIGHT !!!

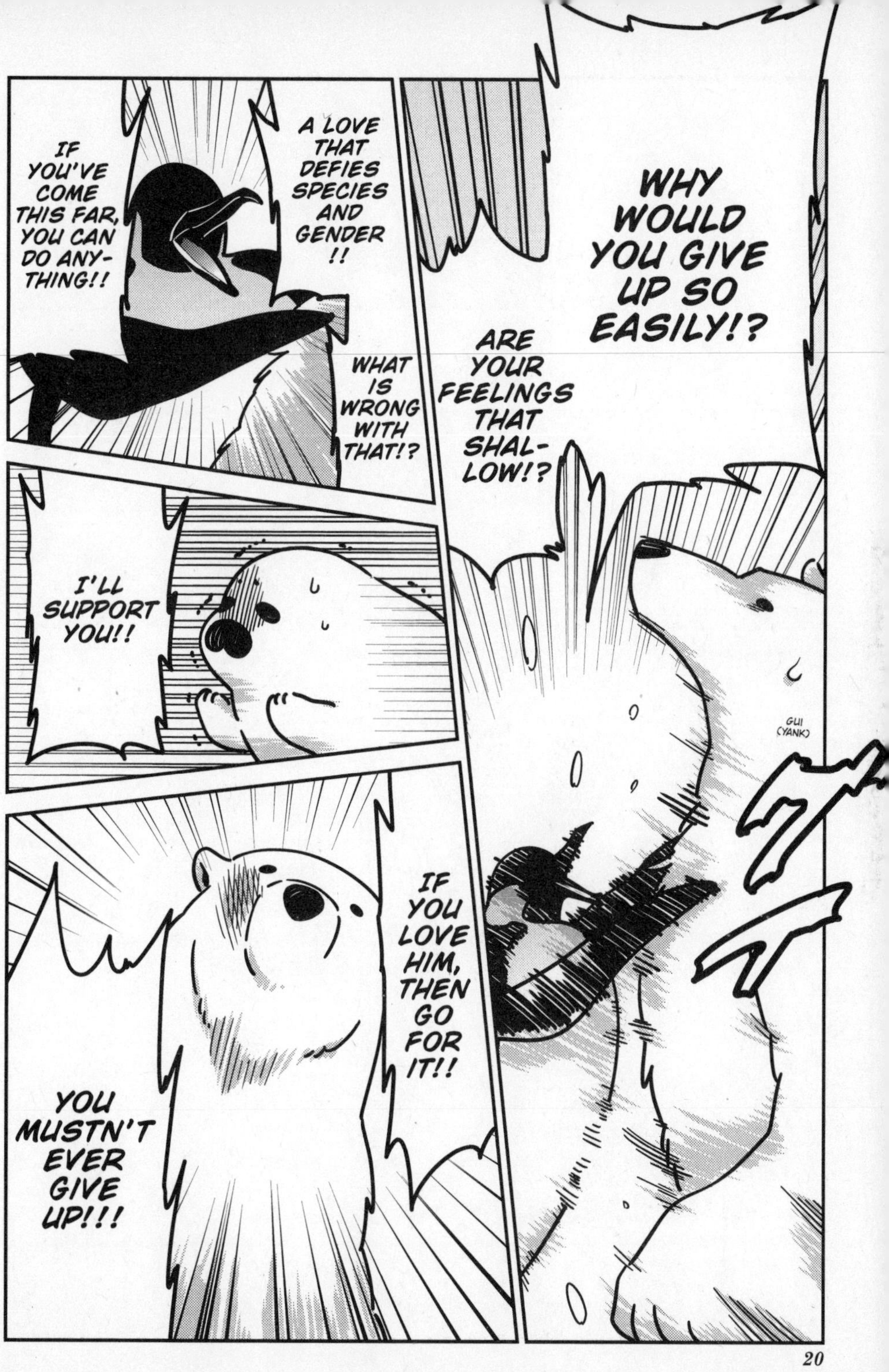
WHY WOULD YOU GIVE UP SO EASILY!?
ARE YOUR FEELINGS THAT SHALLOW!?
GUI (YANK)
A LOVE THAT DEFIES SPECIES AND GENDER!!
WHAT IS WRONG WITH THAT!?
IF YOU'VE COME THIS FAR, YOU CAN DO ANYTHING!!
I'LL SUPPORT YOU!!
IF YOU LOVE HIM, THEN GO FOR IT!!
YOU MUSTN'T EVER GIVE UP!!!

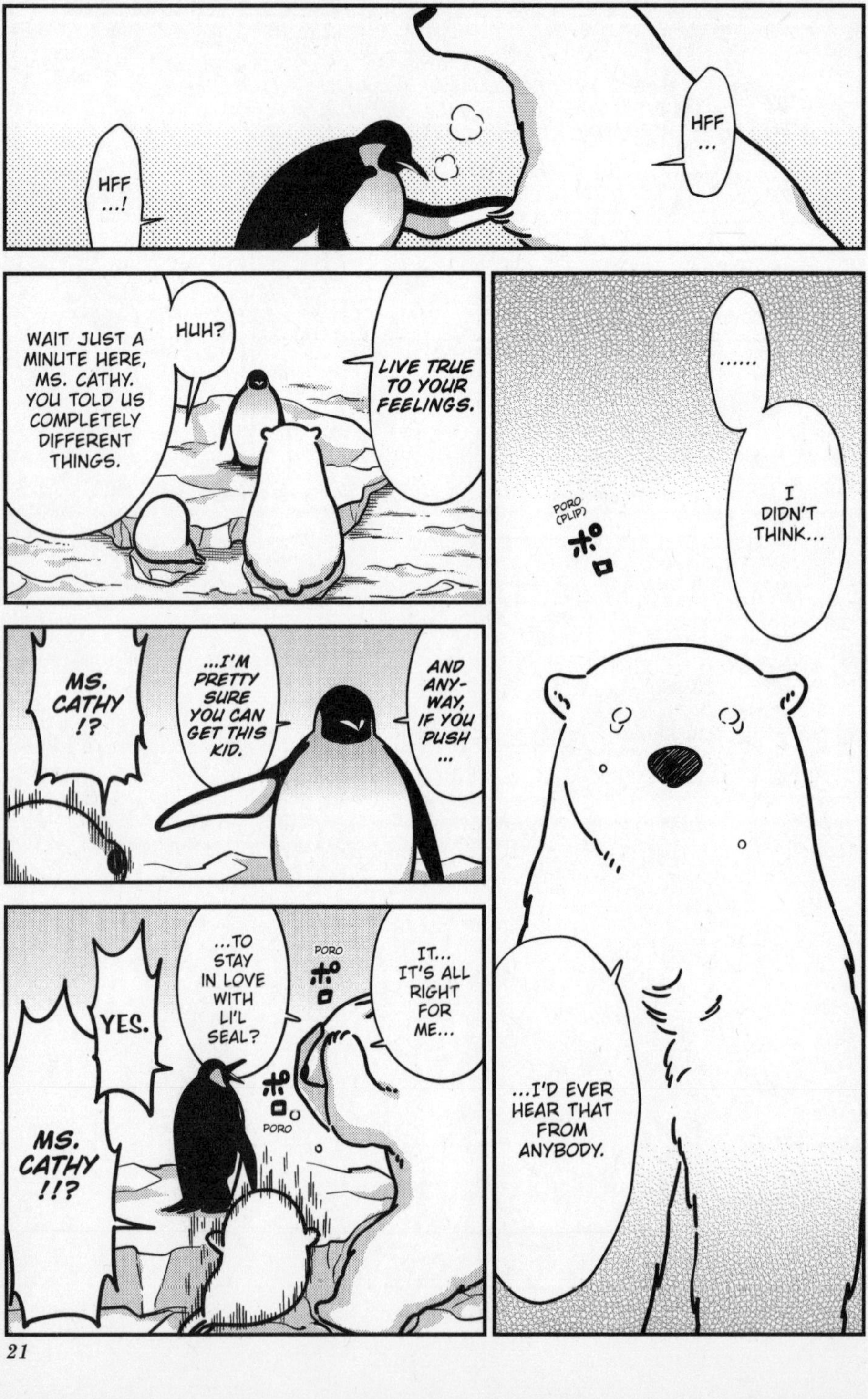
HFF ...
HFF ...!
......
I DIDN'T THINK...
PORO (PLIP)
ポロ
...I'D EVER HEAR THAT FROM ANYBODY.
LIVE TRUE TO YOUR FEELINGS.
HUH?
WAIT JUST A MINUTE HERE, MS. CATHY. YOU TOLD US COMPLETELY DIFFERENT THINGS.
AND ANY-WAY, IF YOU PUSH ...
...I'M PRETTY SURE YOU CAN GET THIS KID.
MS. CATHY !?
IT... IT'S ALL RIGHT FOR ME...
PORO
ポロ
...TO STAY IN LOVE WITH LI'L SEAL?
ポロ
PORO
YES.
MS. CATHY !!?

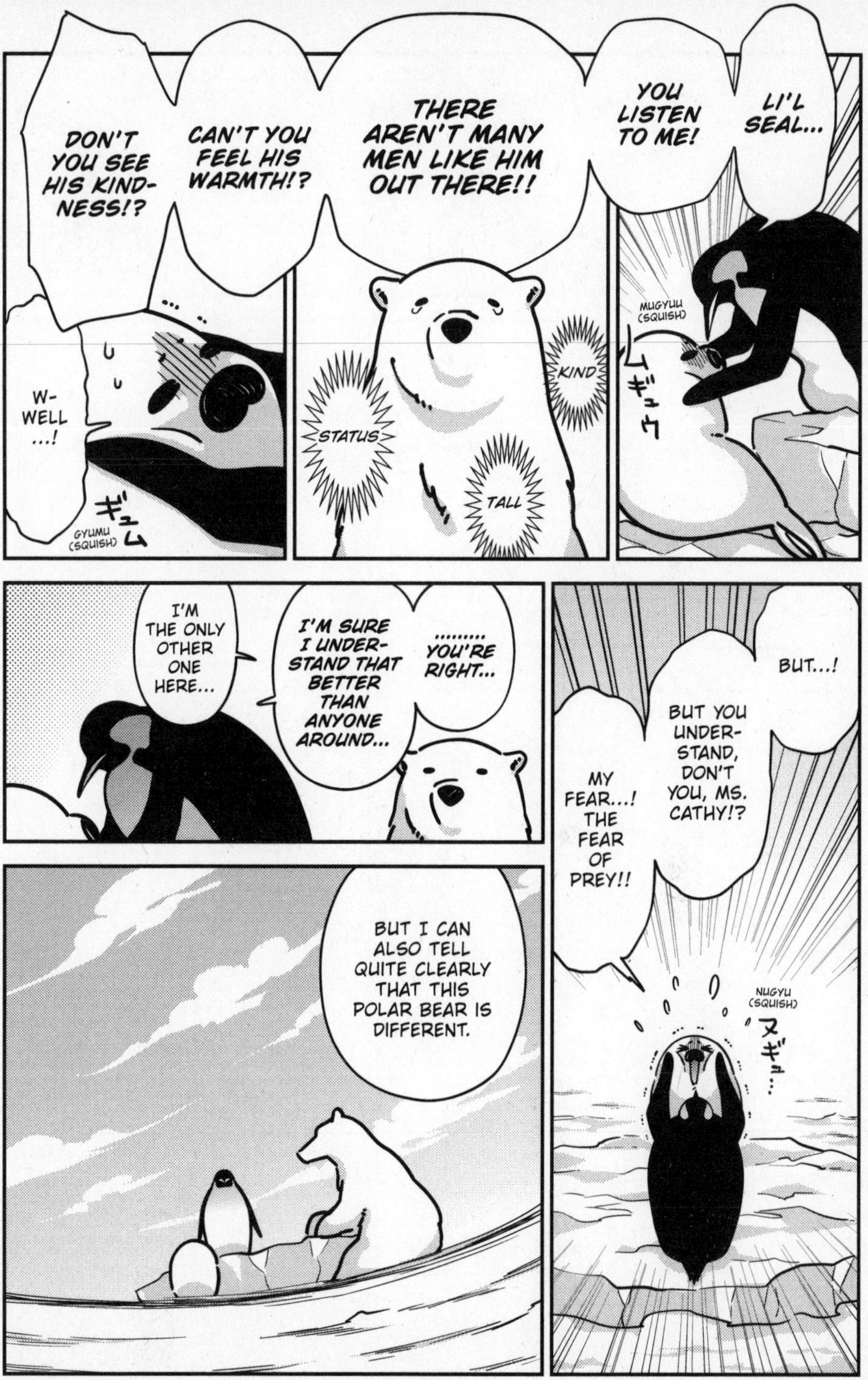
LI'L SEAL...
YOU LISTEN TO ME!
MUGYUU (SQUISH)
ムギュウ
THERE AREN'T MANY MEN LIKE HIM OUT THERE!!
KIND
STATUS
TALL
CAN'T YOU FEEL HIS WARMTH!?
DON'T YOU SEE HIS KINDNESS!?
...
W-WELL ...!
ギュム
GYUMU (SQUISH)
BUT...!
BUT YOU UNDERSTAND, DON'T YOU, MS. CATHY!?
MY FEAR...! THE FEAR OF PREY!!
NUGYU (SQUISH)
ヌギュ...
.... YOU'RE RIGHT...
I'M SURE I UNDERSTAND THAT BETTER THAN ANYONE AROUND...
I'M THE ONLY OTHER ONE HERE...
BUT I CAN ALSO TELL QUITE CLEARLY THAT THIS POLAR BEAR IS DIFFERENT.

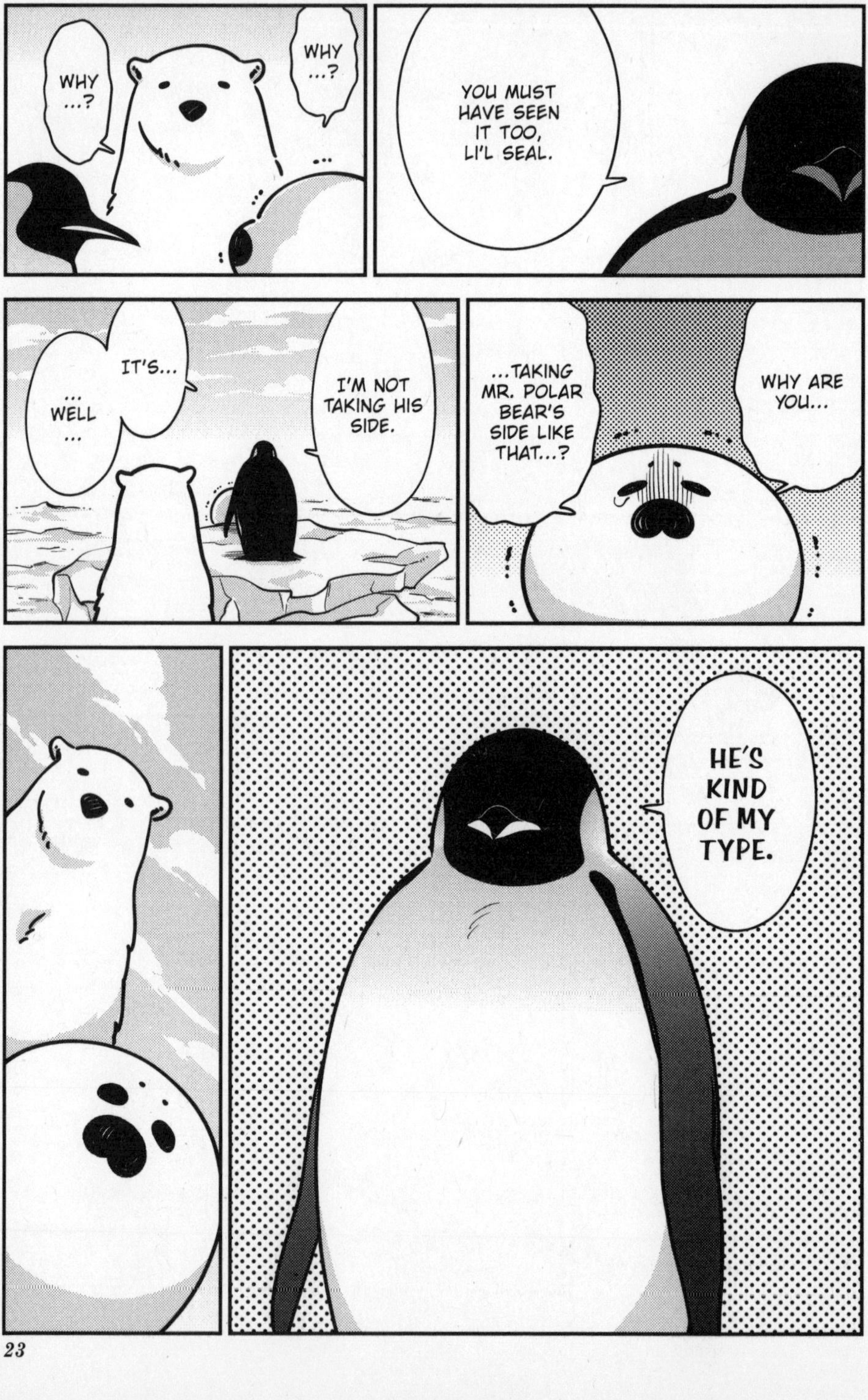
YOU MUST HAVE SEEN IT TOO, LI'L SEAL.
WHY ...?
WHY ...?
...
WHY ARE YOU...
...TAKING MR. POLAR BEAR'S SIDE LIKE THAT...?
I'M NOT TAKING HIS SIDE.
IT'S...
... WELL ...
HE'S KIND OF MY TYPE.

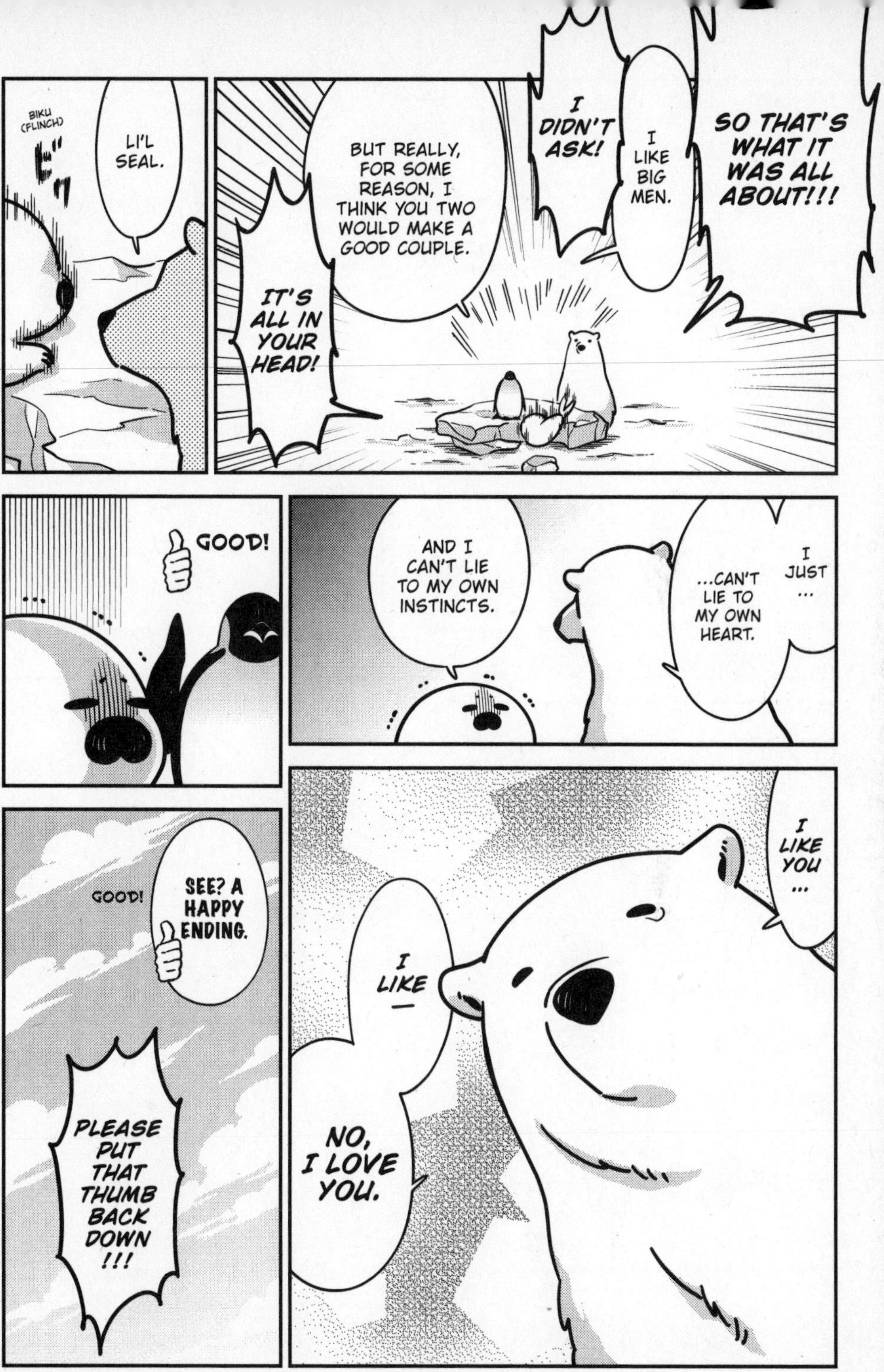
SO THAT'S WHAT IT WAS ALL ABOUT!!!
I LIKE BIG MEN.
I DIDN'T ASK!
BUT REALLY, FOR SOME REASON, I THINK YOU TWO WOULD MAKE A GOOD COUPLE.
IT'S ALL IN YOUR HEAD!
LI'L SEAL.
BIKU (FLINCH)
I JUST ...
...CAN'T LIE TO MY OWN HEART.
AND I CAN'T LIE TO MY OWN INSTINCTS.
GOOD!
I LIKE YOU ...
I LIKE —
NO, I LOVE YOU.
SEE? A HAPPY ENDING.
GOOD!
PLEASE PUT THAT THUMB BACK DOWN!!!

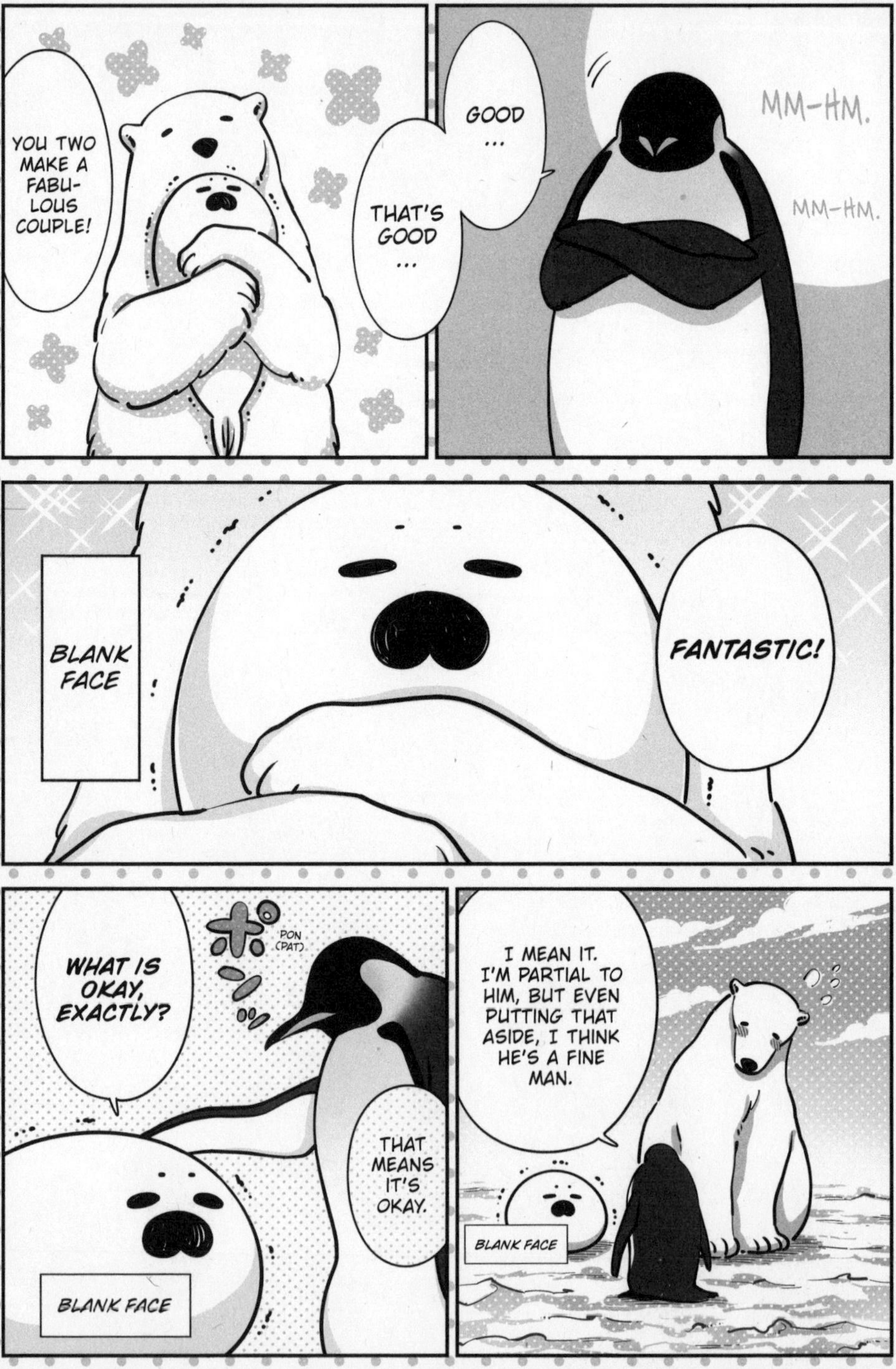
MM-HM.
GOOD ...
MM-HM.
THAT'S GOOD ...
YOU TWO MAKE A FABU-LOUS COUPLE!
FANTASTIC!
BLANK FACE
I MEAN IT. I'M PARTIAL TO HIM, BUT EVEN PUTTING THAT ASIDE, I THINK HE'S A FINE MAN.
BLANK FACE
PON (PAT)
WHAT IS OKAY, EXACTLY?
THAT MEANS IT'S OKAY.
BLANK FACE

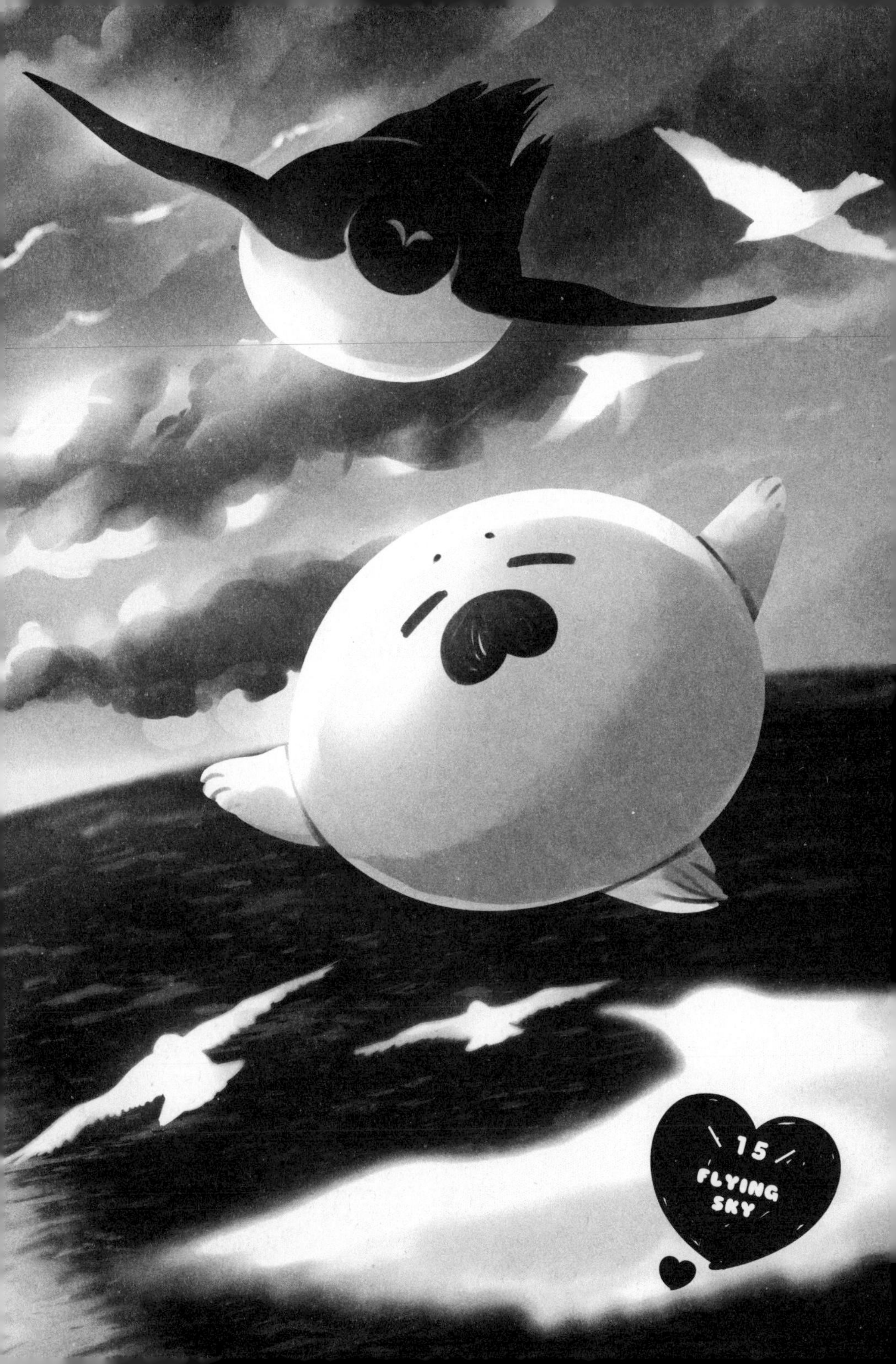
15
FLYING SKY

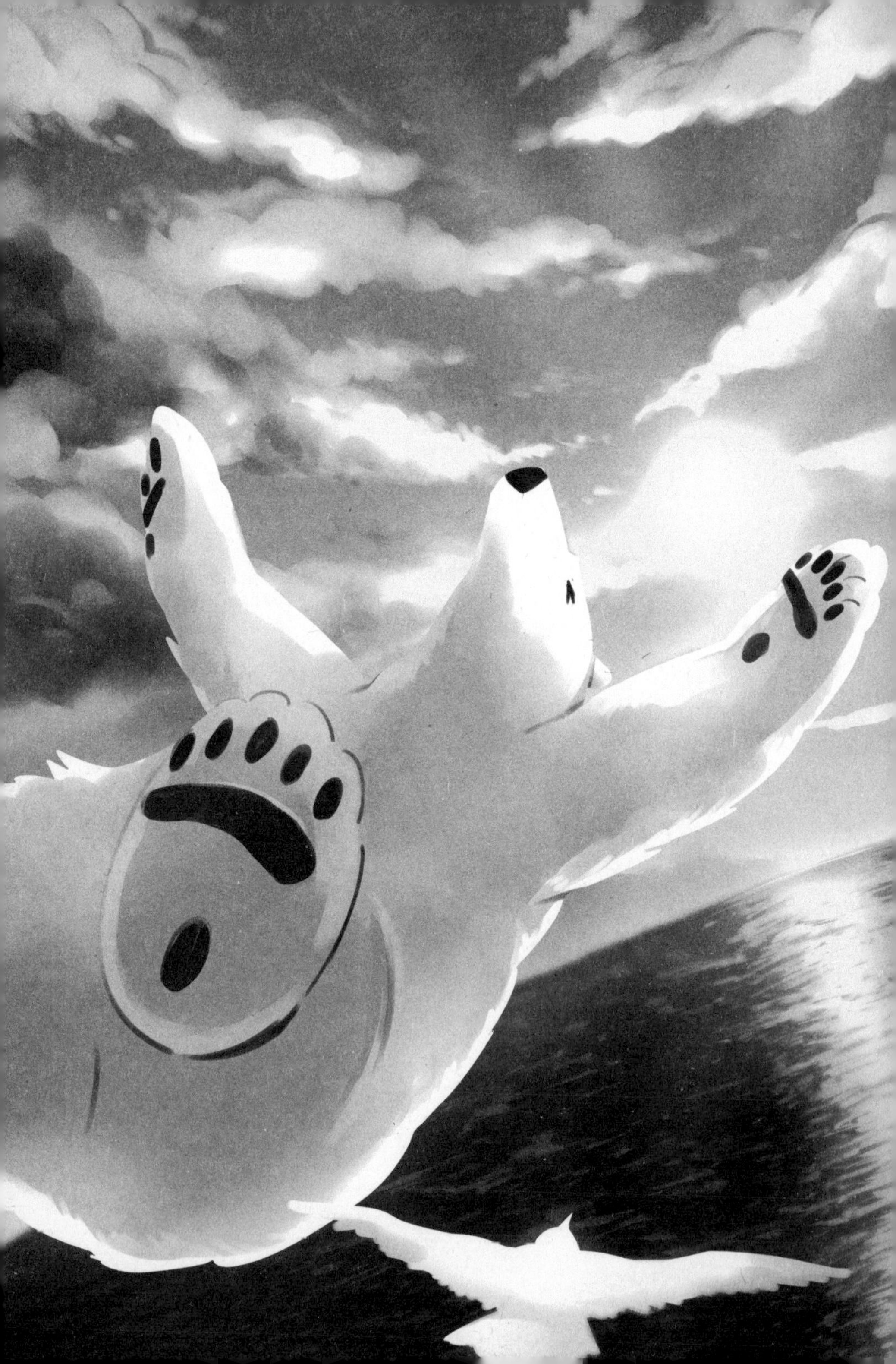

PEOPLE ARE ALWAYS ALONE

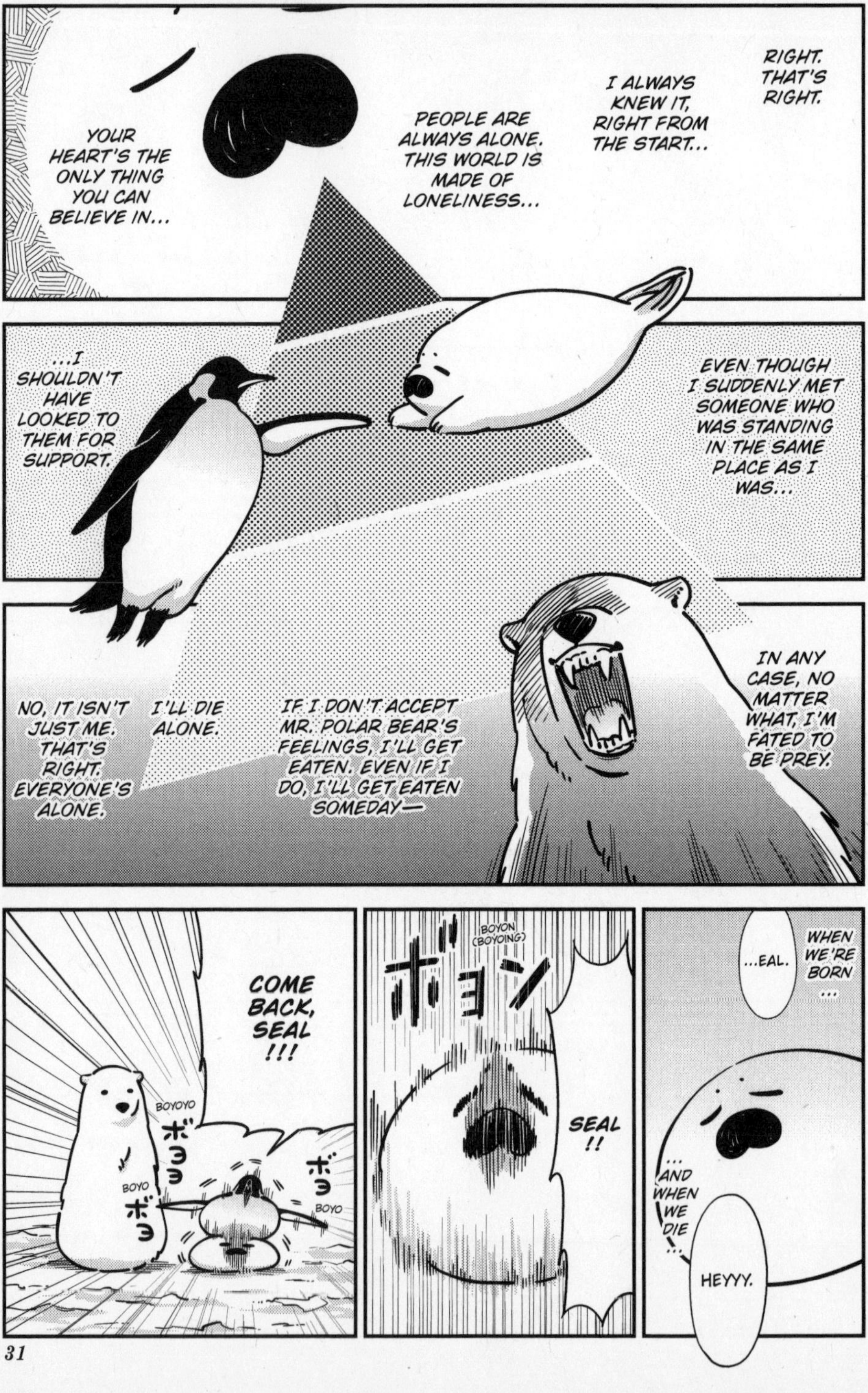
RIGHT. THAT'S RIGHT.
I ALWAYS KNEW IT, RIGHT FROM THE START...
PEOPLE ARE ALWAYS ALONE. THIS WORLD IS MADE OF LONELINESS...
YOUR HEART'S THE ONLY THING YOU CAN BELIEVE IN...
EVEN THOUGH I SUDDENLY MET SOMEONE WHO WAS STANDING IN THE SAME PLACE AS I WAS...
...I SHOULDN'T HAVE LOOKED TO THEM FOR SUPPORT.
IN ANY CASE, NO MATTER WHAT, I'M FATED TO BE PREY.
IF I DON'T ACCEPT MR. POLAR BEAR'S FEELINGS, I'LL GET EATEN. EVEN IF I DO, I'LL GET EATEN SOMEDAY—
I'LL DIE ALONE.
NO, IT ISN'T JUST ME. THAT'S RIGHT. EVERYONE'S ALONE.
WHEN WE'RE BORN...
...EAL.
...AND WHEN WE DIE...
HEYYY.
BOYON (BOYOING)
ボヨン
SEAL!!
COME BACK, SEAL!!!
BOYOYO
ボヨヨ
BOYO
ボヨ
ボヨ
BOYO

CATHY'S SPECIAL TRAINING

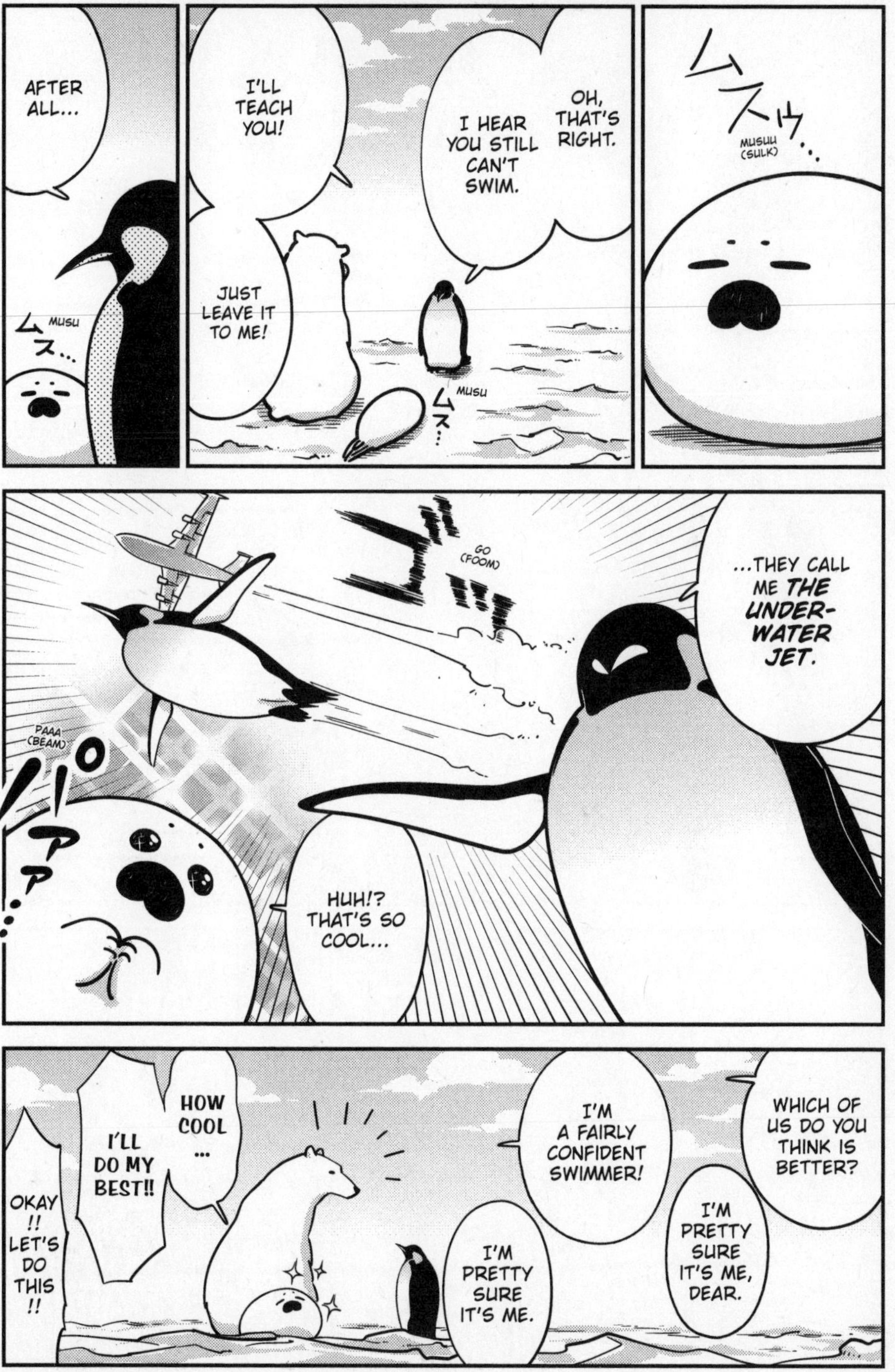

ムスゥ…
MUSUU (SULK)
OH, THAT'S RIGHT.
I HEAR YOU STILL CAN'T SWIM.
I'LL TEACH YOU!
JUST LEAVE IT TO ME!
ムス…
MUSU
AFTER ALL...
MUSU
ムス…
...THEY CALL ME *THE UNDER-WATER JET*.
ゴッ
GO (FOOM)
パアァ…
PAAA (BEAM)
HUH!? THAT'S SO COOL...
WHICH OF US DO YOU THINK IS BETTER?
I'M A FAIRLY CONFIDENT SWIMMER!
I'M PRETTY SURE IT'S ME, DEAR.
I'M PRETTY SURE IT'S ME.
HOW COOL ...
I'LL DO MY BEST!!
OKAY!! LET'S DO THIS!!

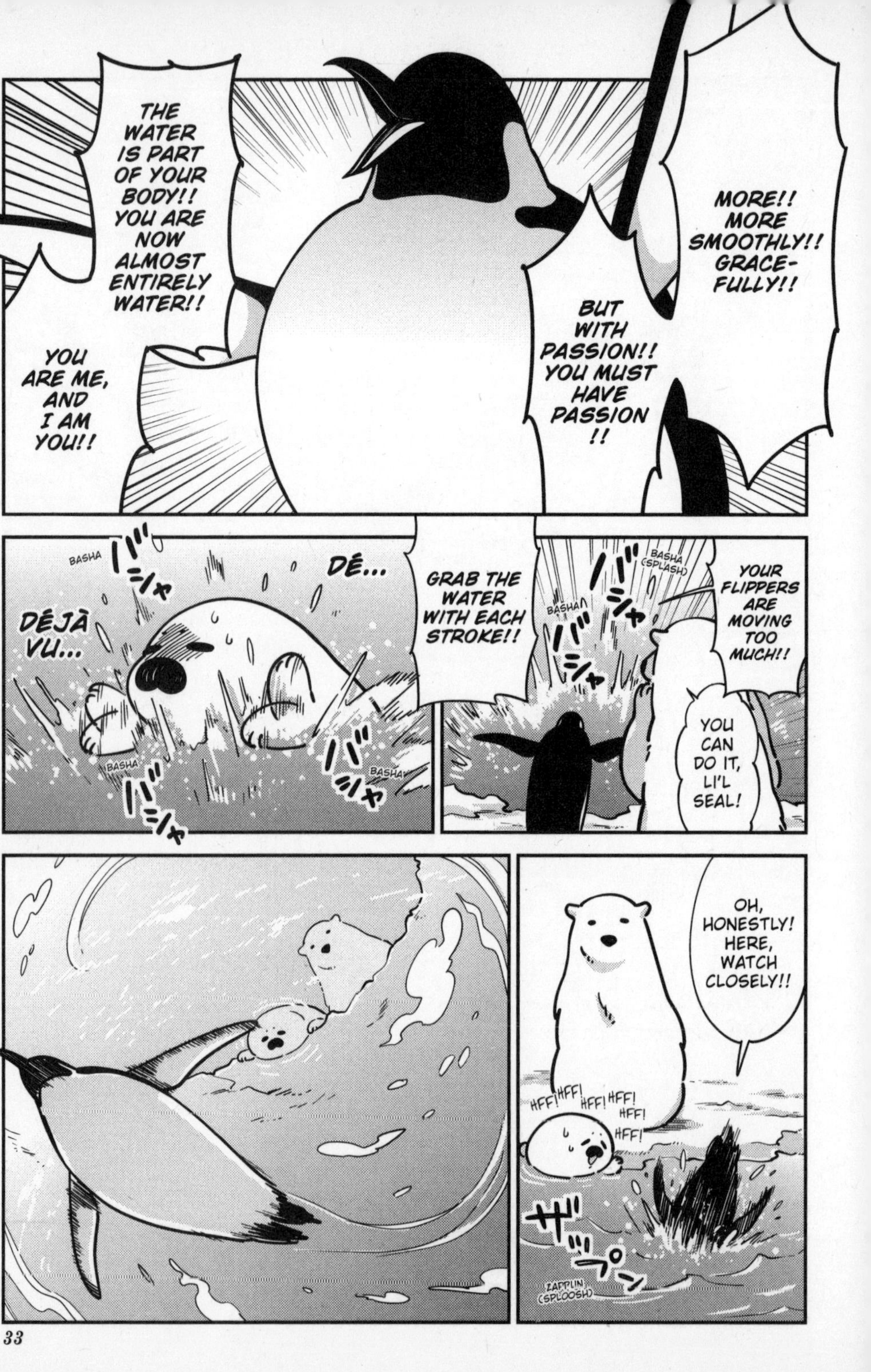
MORE!! MORE SMOOTHLY!! GRACEFULLY!!
BUT WITH PASSION!! YOU MUST HAVE PASSION!!
THE WATER IS PART OF YOUR BODY!! YOU ARE NOW ALMOST ENTIRELY WATER!!
YOU ARE ME, AND I AM YOU!!
YOUR FLIPPERS ARE MOVING TOO MUCH!!
BASHA (SPLASH)
BASHA
YOU CAN DO IT, LI'L SEAL!
GRAB THE WATER WITH EACH STROKE!!
DÉ...
BASHA
DÉJÀ VU...
BASHA
BASHA
OH, HONESTLY! HERE, WATCH CLOSELY!!
HFF! HFF! HFF! HFF! HFF! HFF!
ZAPPUN (SPLOOSH)

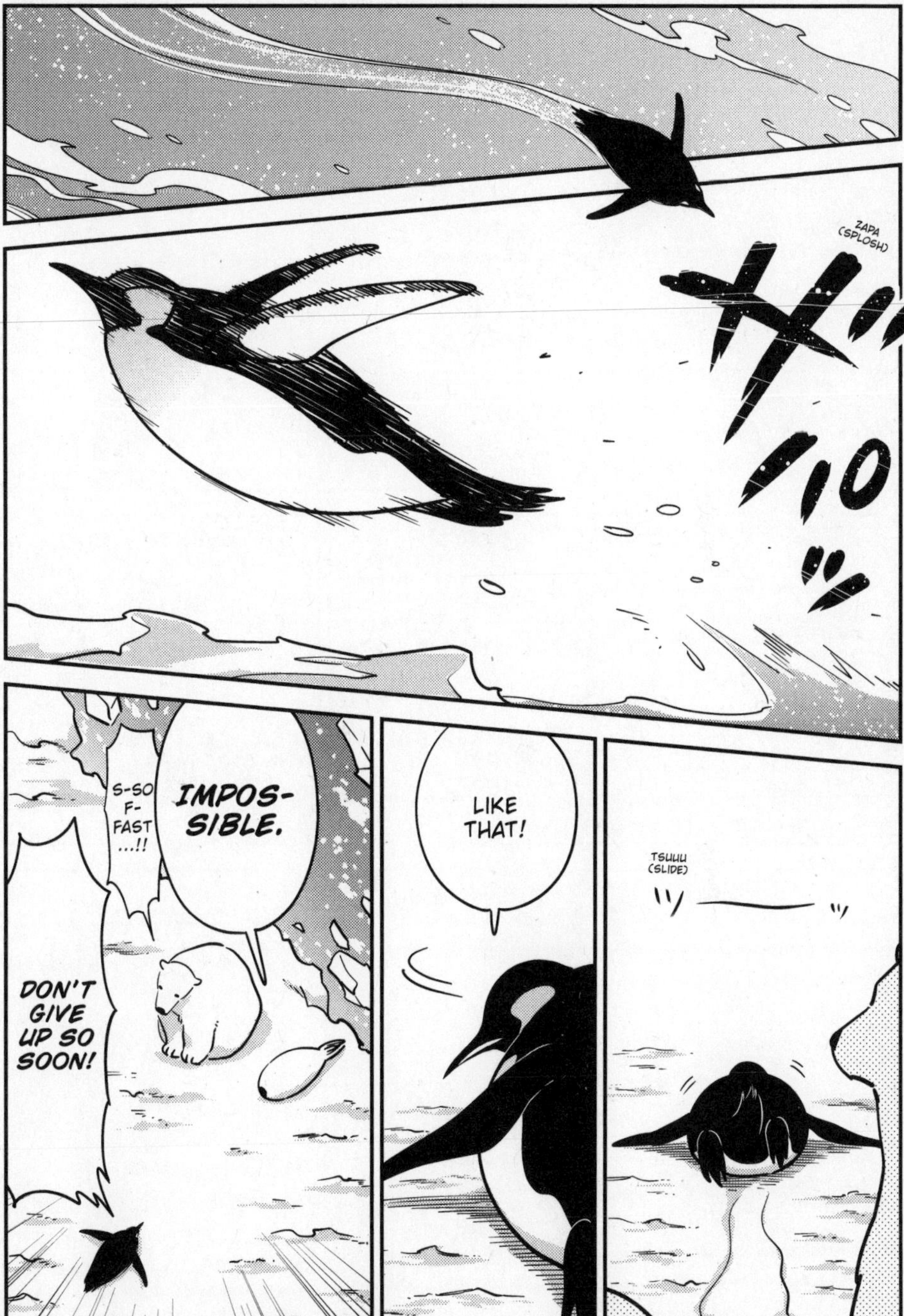
ZAPA
(SPLOSH)
TSUUU
(SLIDE)
LIKE THAT!
IMPOS-SIBLE.
S-SO F-FAST ...!!
DON'T GIVE UP SO SOON!

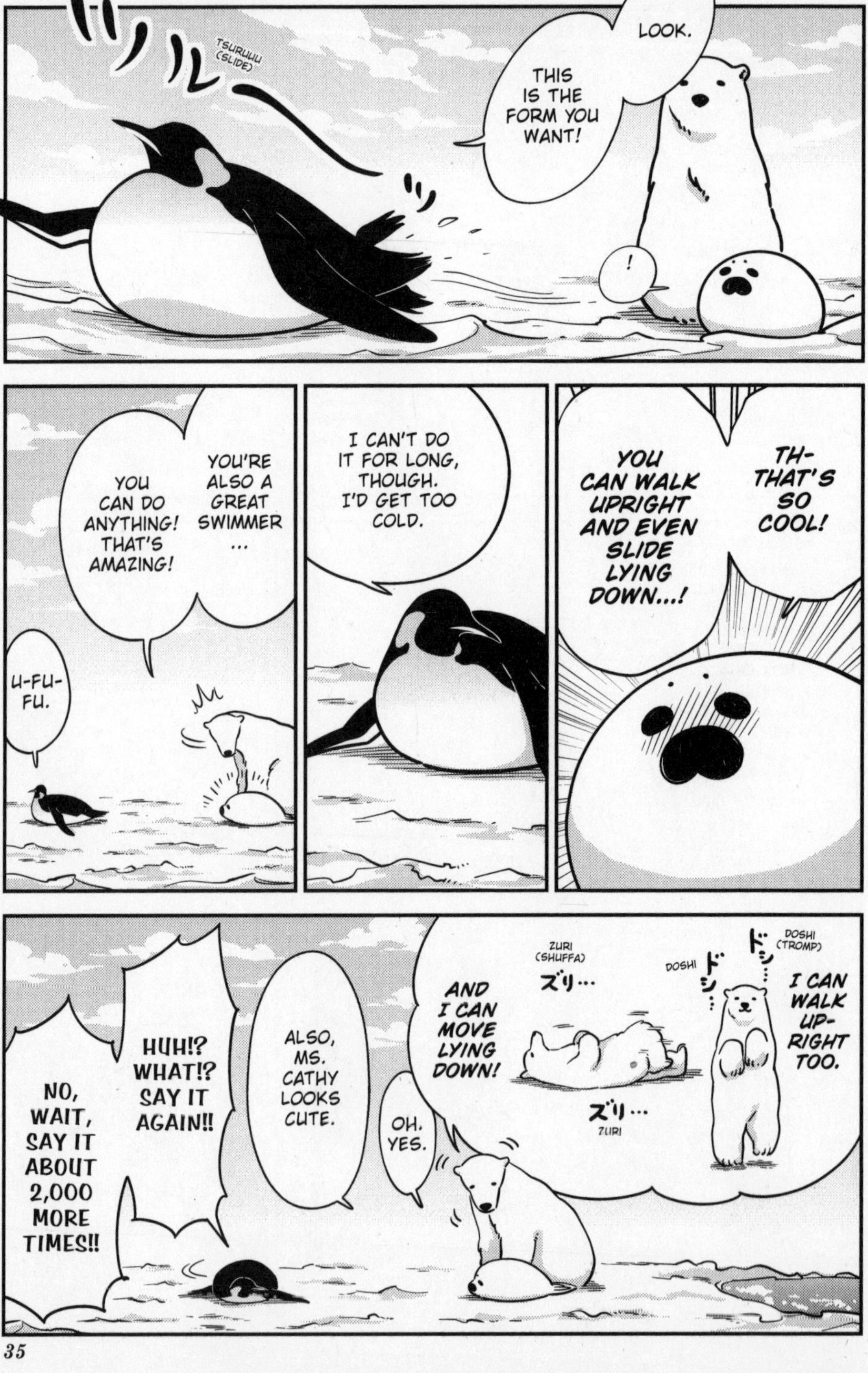
LOOK.
THIS IS THE FORM YOU WANT!
TSURUUU (SLIDE)
!
TH-THAT'S SO COOL!
YOU CAN WALK UPRIGHT AND EVEN SLIDE LYING DOWN...!
I CAN'T DO IT FOR LONG, THOUGH. I'D GET TOO COLD.
YOU'RE ALSO A GREAT SWIMMER ...
YOU CAN DO ANYTHING! THAT'S AMAZING!
U-FU-FU.
DOSHI (TROMP)
ドシ…
I CAN WALK UP-RIGHT TOO.
DOSHI
ドシ…
ZURI (SHUFFA)
ズリ…
AND I CAN MOVE LYING DOWN!
ズリ…
ZURI
OH. YES.
ALSO, MS. CATHY LOOKS CUTE.
HUH!? WHAT!? SAY IT AGAIN!!
NO, WAIT, SAY IT ABOUT 2,000 MORE TIMES!!

THE STRANGENESS OF STRENGTH

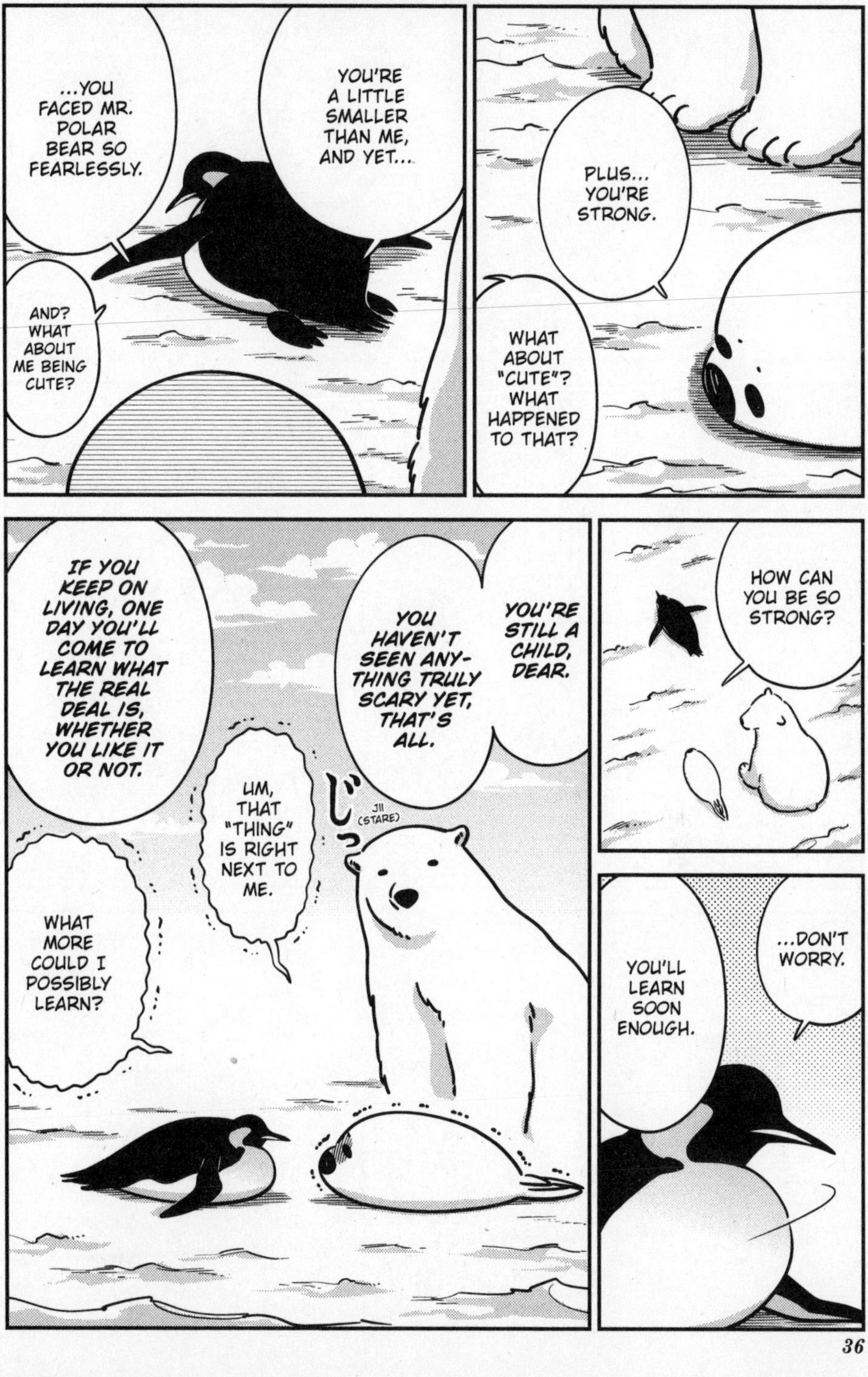
PLUS... YOU'RE STRONG.
WHAT ABOUT "CUTE"? WHAT HAPPENED TO THAT?
YOU'RE A LITTLE SMALLER THAN ME, AND YET...
...YOU FACED MR. POLAR BEAR SO FEARLESSLY.
AND? WHAT ABOUT ME BEING CUTE?
HOW CAN YOU BE SO STRONG?
...DON'T WORRY.
YOU'LL LEARN SOON ENOUGH.
YOU'RE STILL A CHILD, DEAR.
YOU HAVEN'T SEEN ANY-THING TRULY SCARY YET, THAT'S ALL.
IF YOU KEEP ON LIVING, ONE DAY YOU'LL COME TO LEARN WHAT THE REAL DEAL IS, WHETHER YOU LIKE IT OR NOT.
じっ
JII (STARE)
UM, THAT "THING" IS RIGHT NEXT TO ME.
WHAT MORE COULD I POSSIBLY LEARN?

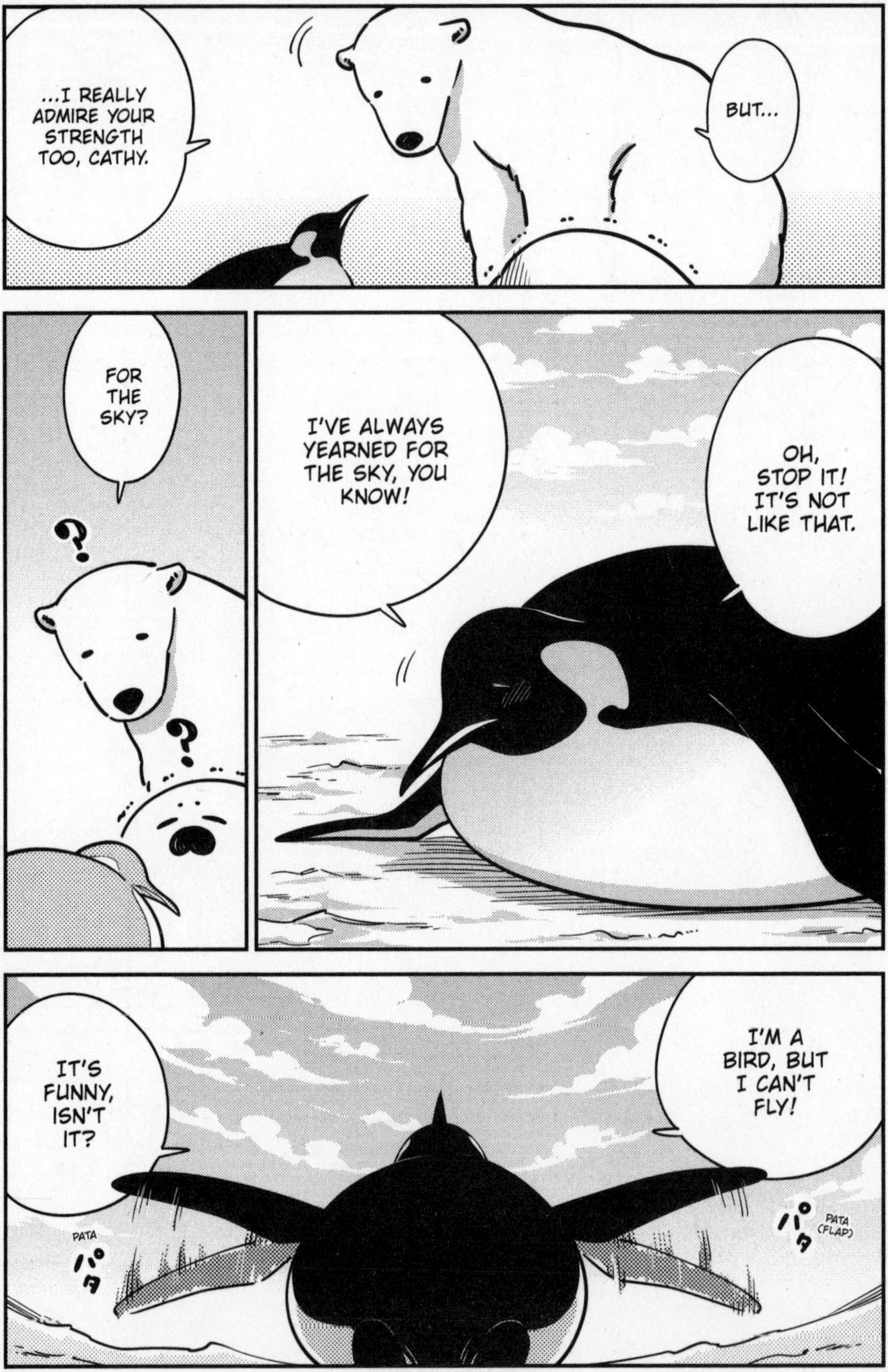
BUT...
...I REALLY ADMIRE YOUR STRENGTH TOO, CATHY.
OH, STOP IT! IT'S NOT LIKE THAT.
I'VE ALWAYS YEARNED FOR THE SKY, YOU KNOW!
FOR THE SKY?
?
?
I'M A BIRD, BUT I CAN'T FLY!
パタ
PATA (FLAP)
IT'S FUNNY, ISN'T IT?
PATA
パタ

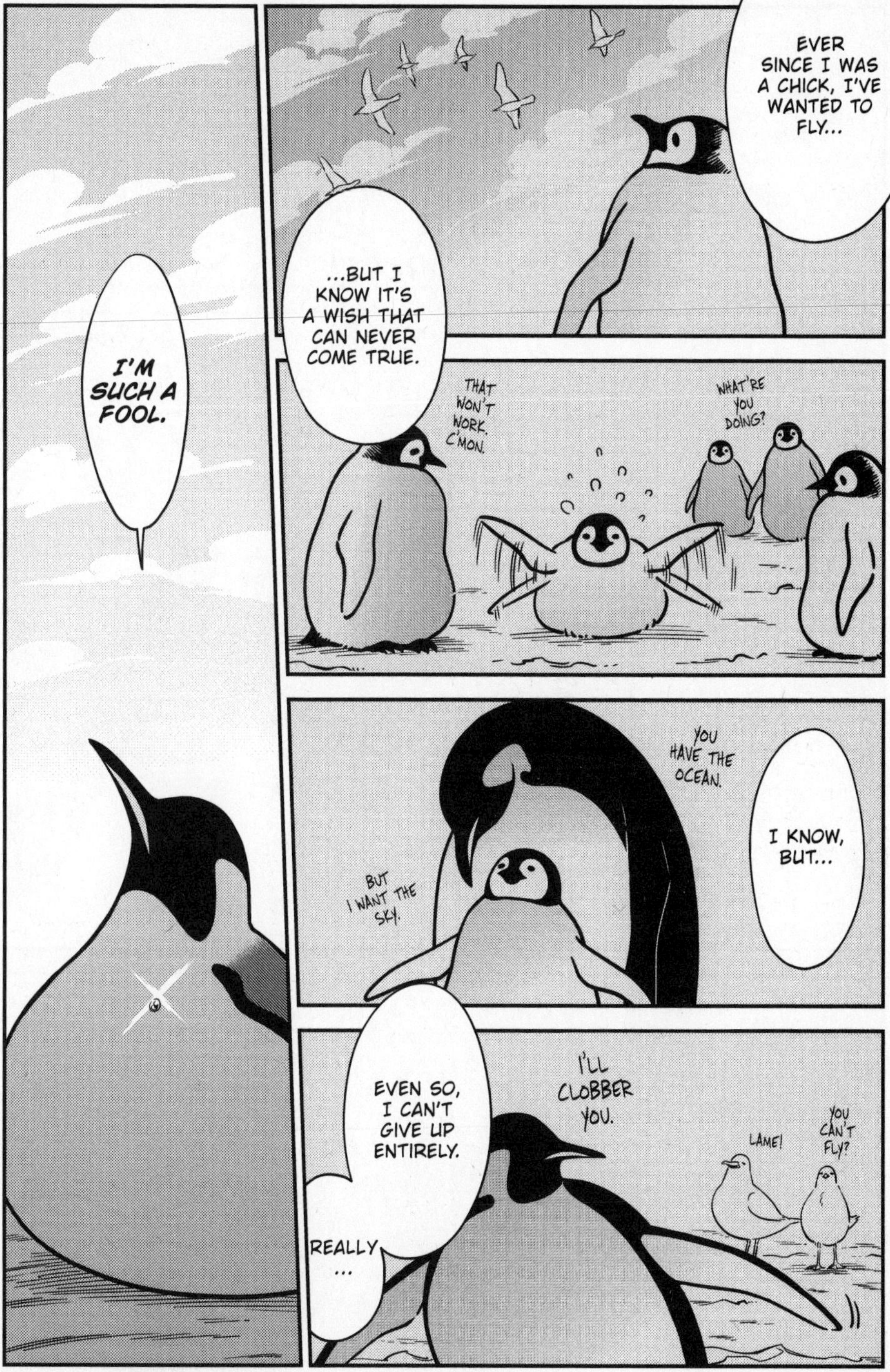
EVER SINCE I WAS A CHICK, I'VE WANTED TO FLY...
...BUT I KNOW IT'S A WISH THAT CAN NEVER COME TRUE.
WHAT'RE YOU DOING?
THAT WON'T WORK. C'MON.
I KNOW, BUT...
YOU HAVE THE OCEAN.
BUT I WANT THE SKY.
YOU CAN'T FLY?
LAME!
I'LL CLOBBER YOU.
EVEN SO, I CAN'T GIVE UP ENTIRELY.
REALLY ...
I'M SUCH A FOOL.

FLYING SKY

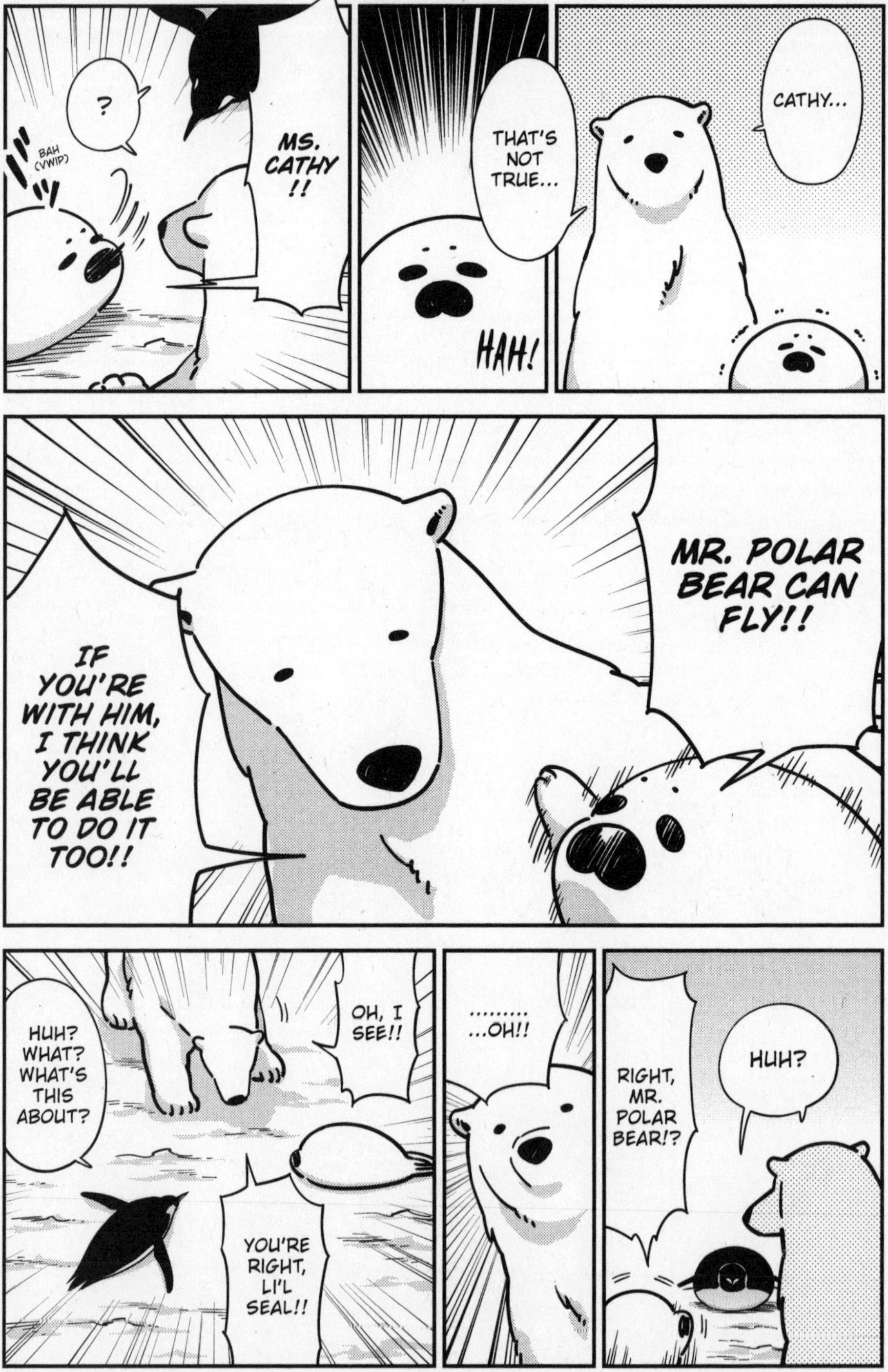

CATHY...
THAT'S NOT TRUE...
HAH!
MS. CATHY!!
?
BAH (VWIP)
MR. POLAR BEAR CAN FLY!!
IF YOU'RE WITH HIM, I THINK YOU'LL BE ABLE TO DO IT TOO!!
HUH?
RIGHT, MR. POLAR BEAR!?
....OH!!
OH, I SEE!!
HUH? WHAT? WHAT'S THIS ABOUT?
YOU'RE RIGHT, LI'L SEAL!!

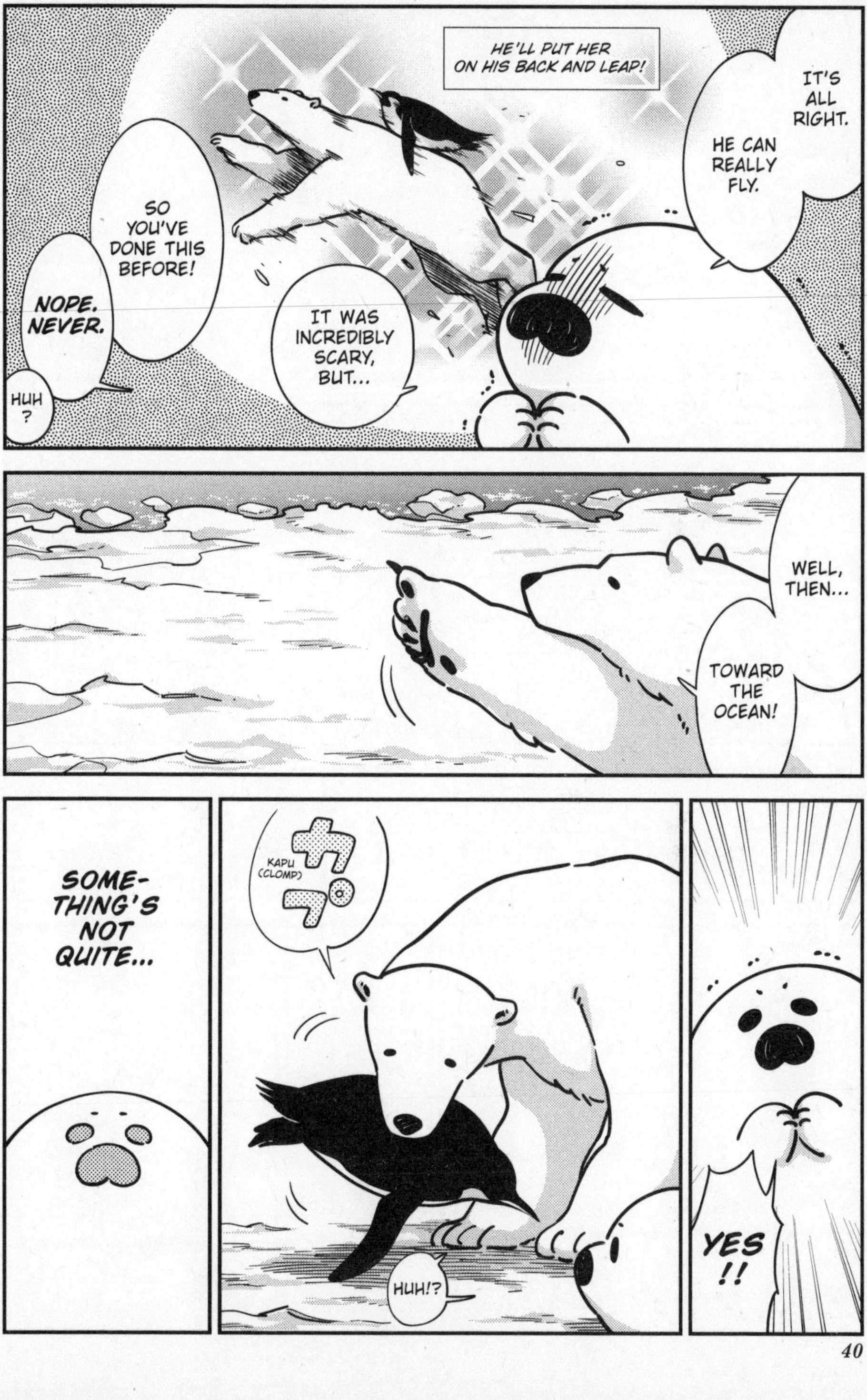
HE'LL PUT HER ON HIS BACK AND LEAP!
IT'S ALL RIGHT.
HE CAN REALLY FLY.
SO YOU'VE DONE THIS BEFORE!
IT WAS INCREDIBLY SCARY, BUT...
NOPE. NEVER.
HUH?
WELL, THEN...
TOWARD THE OCEAN!
YES!!
KAPU (CLOMP)
HUH!?
SOME-THING'S NOT QUITE...

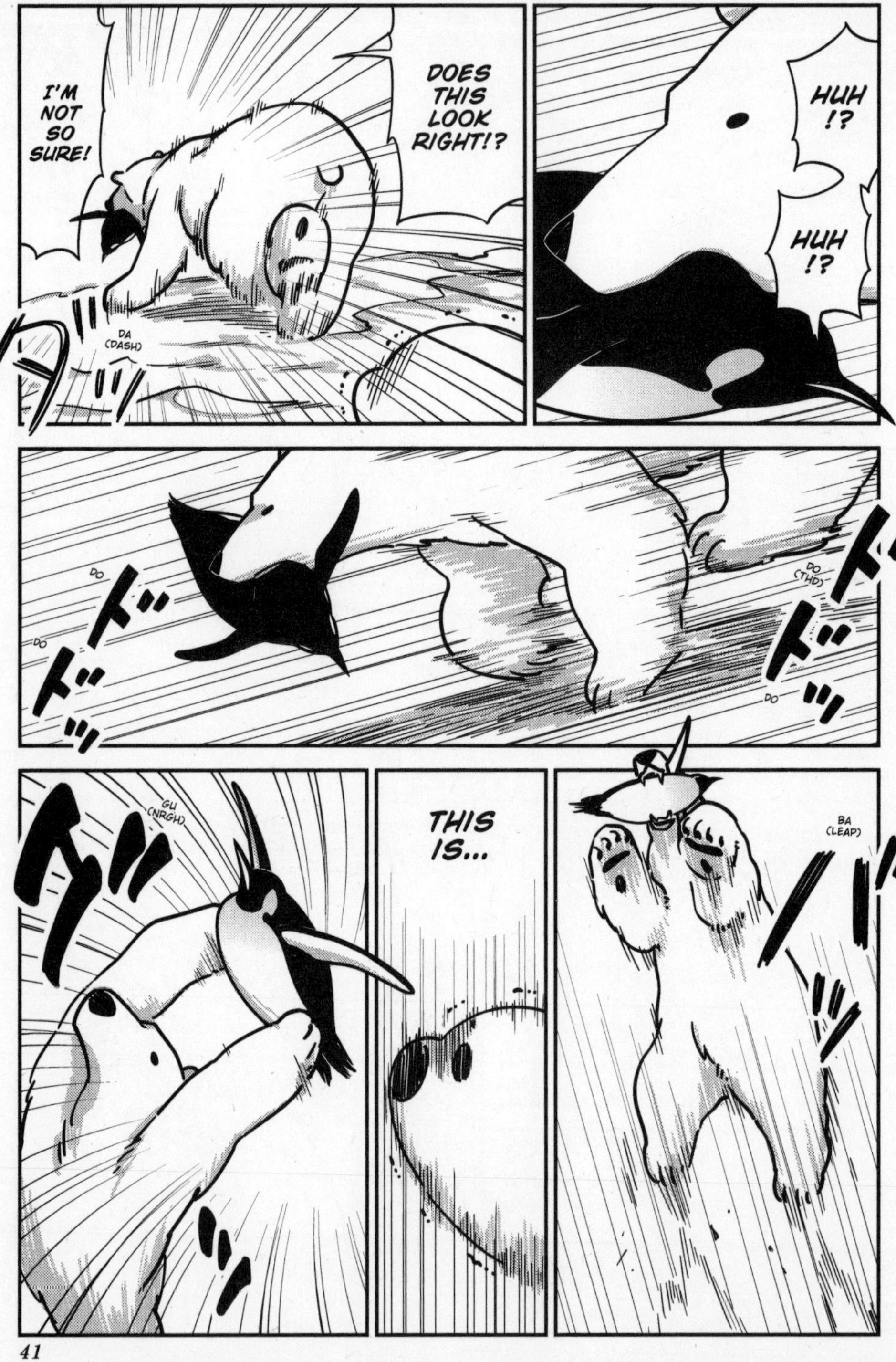
HUH!?
HUH!?
DOES THIS LOOK RIGHT!?
I'M NOT SO SURE!
DA (DASH)
DO (THD)
DO
DO
DO
BA (LEAP)
THIS IS...
GU (NRGH)

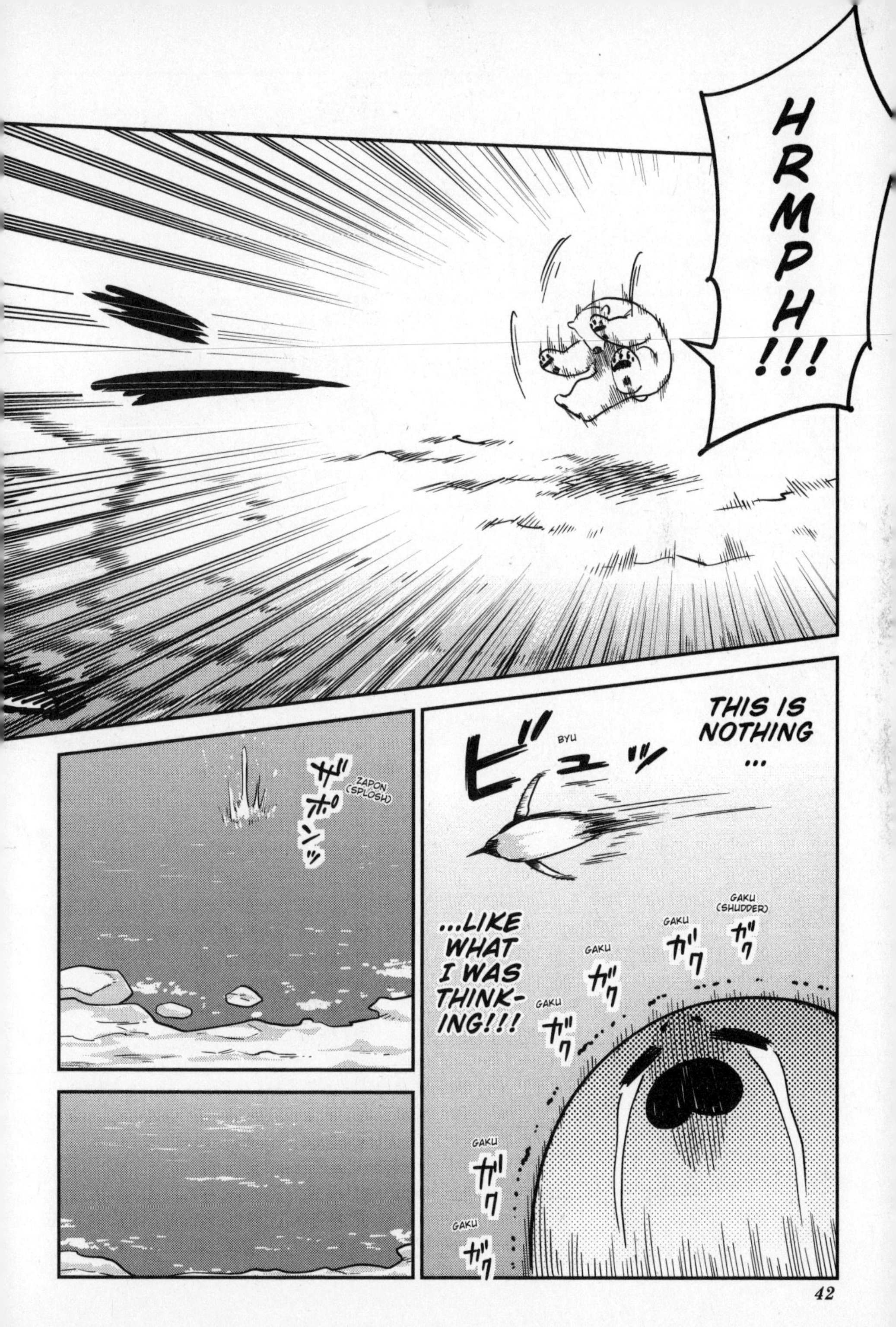
HRMPH!!!
THIS IS NOTHING ...
ビュッ
BYU
GAKU (SHUDDER)
ガク
GAKU
ガク
GAKU
ガク
...LIKE WHAT I WAS THINK-ING!!!
GAKU
ガク
GAKU
ガク
GAKU
ガク
ザポンッ
ZAPON (SPLOSH)

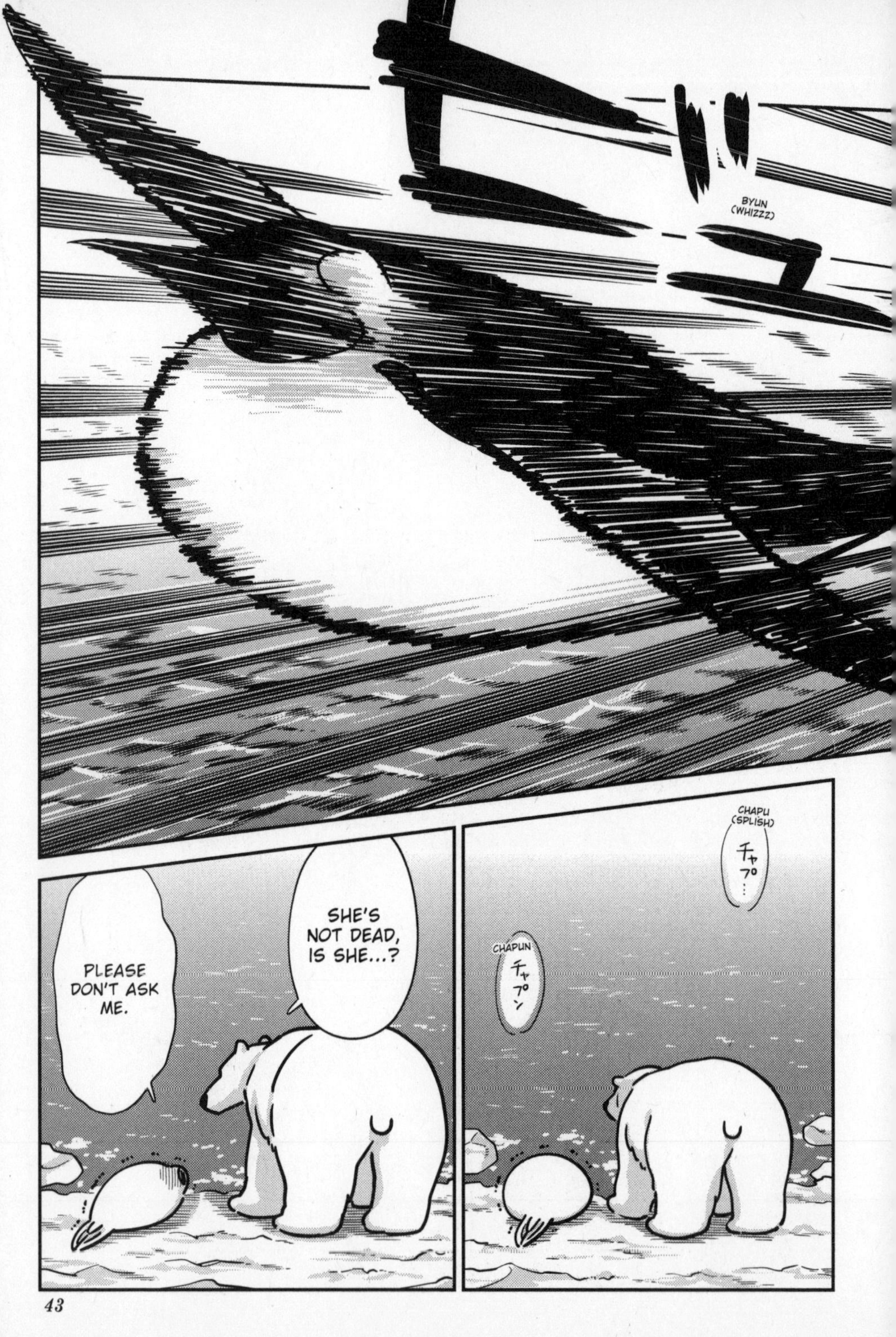
BYUN (WHIZZZ)
CHAPU (SPLISH)
チャプ…
CHAPUN
チャプン
SHE'S NOT DEAD, IS SHE...?
PLEASE DON'T ASK ME.

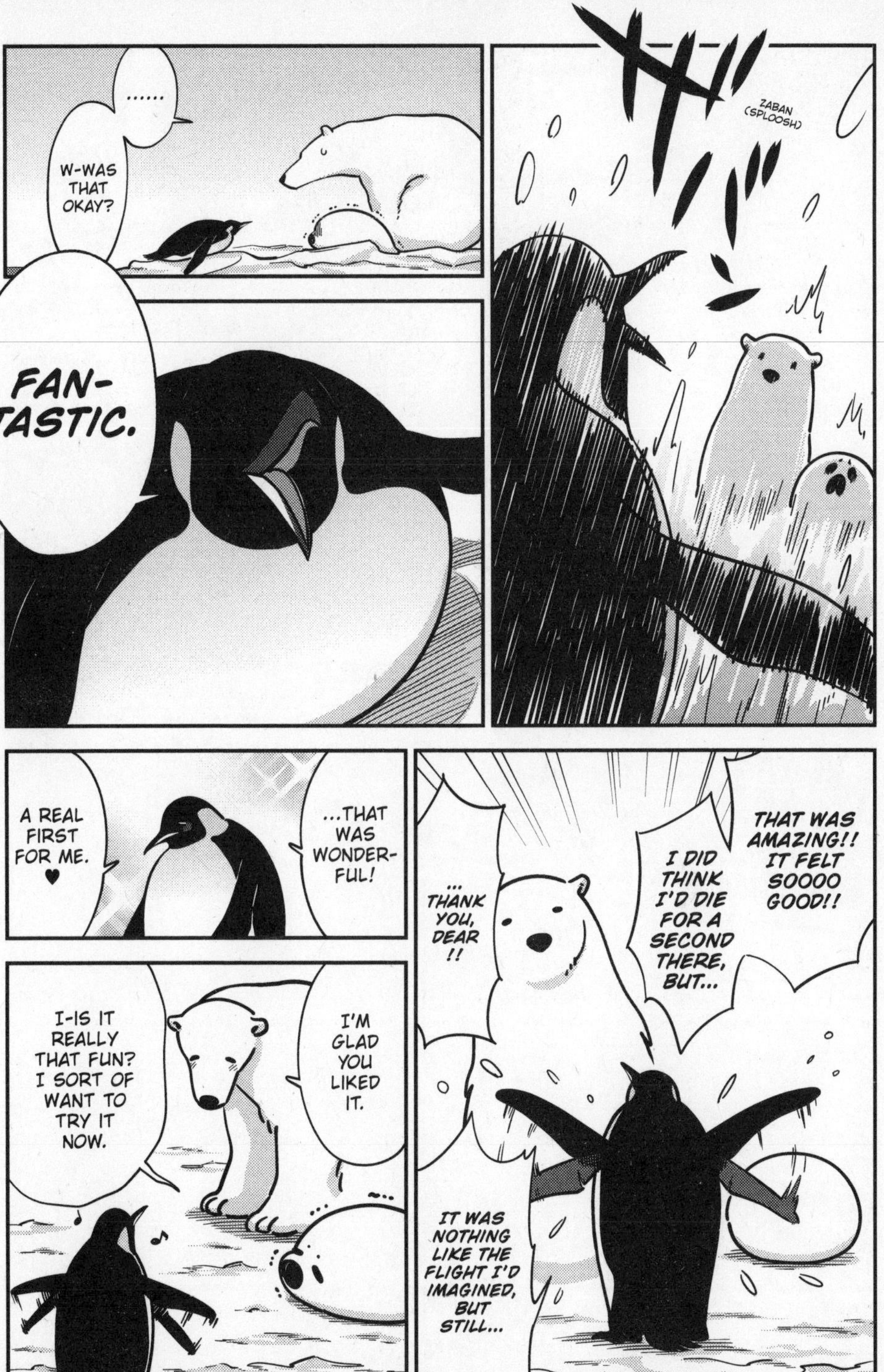
ZABAN (SPLOOSH)
......
W-WAS THAT OKAY?
FAN-TASTIC.
THAT WAS AMAZING!! IT FELT SOOOO GOOD!!
I DID THINK I'D DIE FOR A SECOND THERE, BUT...
...THANK YOU, DEAR!!
IT WAS NOTHING LIKE THE FLIGHT I'D IMAGINED, BUT STILL...
...THAT WAS WONDERFUL!
A REAL FIRST FOR ME. ♥
I'M GLAD YOU LIKED IT.
I-IS IT REALLY THAT FUN? I SORT OF WANT TO TRY IT NOW.

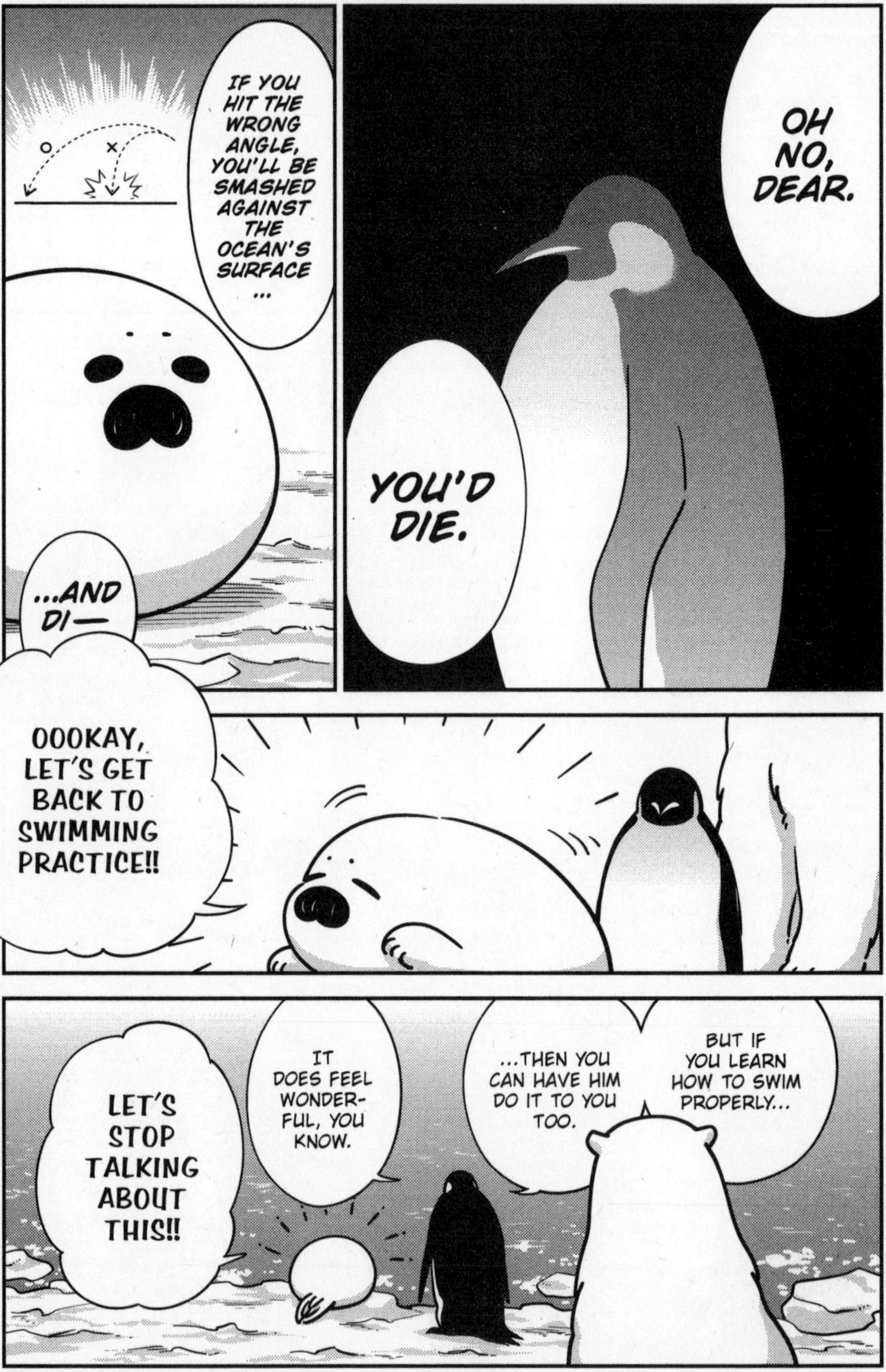
OH NO, DEAR.
YOU'D DIE.
IF YOU HIT THE WRONG ANGLE, YOU'LL BE SMASHED AGAINST THE OCEAN'S SURFACE ...
...AND DI—
OOOKAY, LET'S GET BACK TO SWIMMING PRACTICE!!
BUT IF YOU LEARN HOW TO SWIM PROPERLY...
...THEN YOU CAN HAVE HIM DO IT TO YOU TOO.
IT DOES FEEL WONDER-FUL, YOU KNOW.
LET'S STOP TALKING ABOUT THIS!!

SPLASH BUBBLE!!

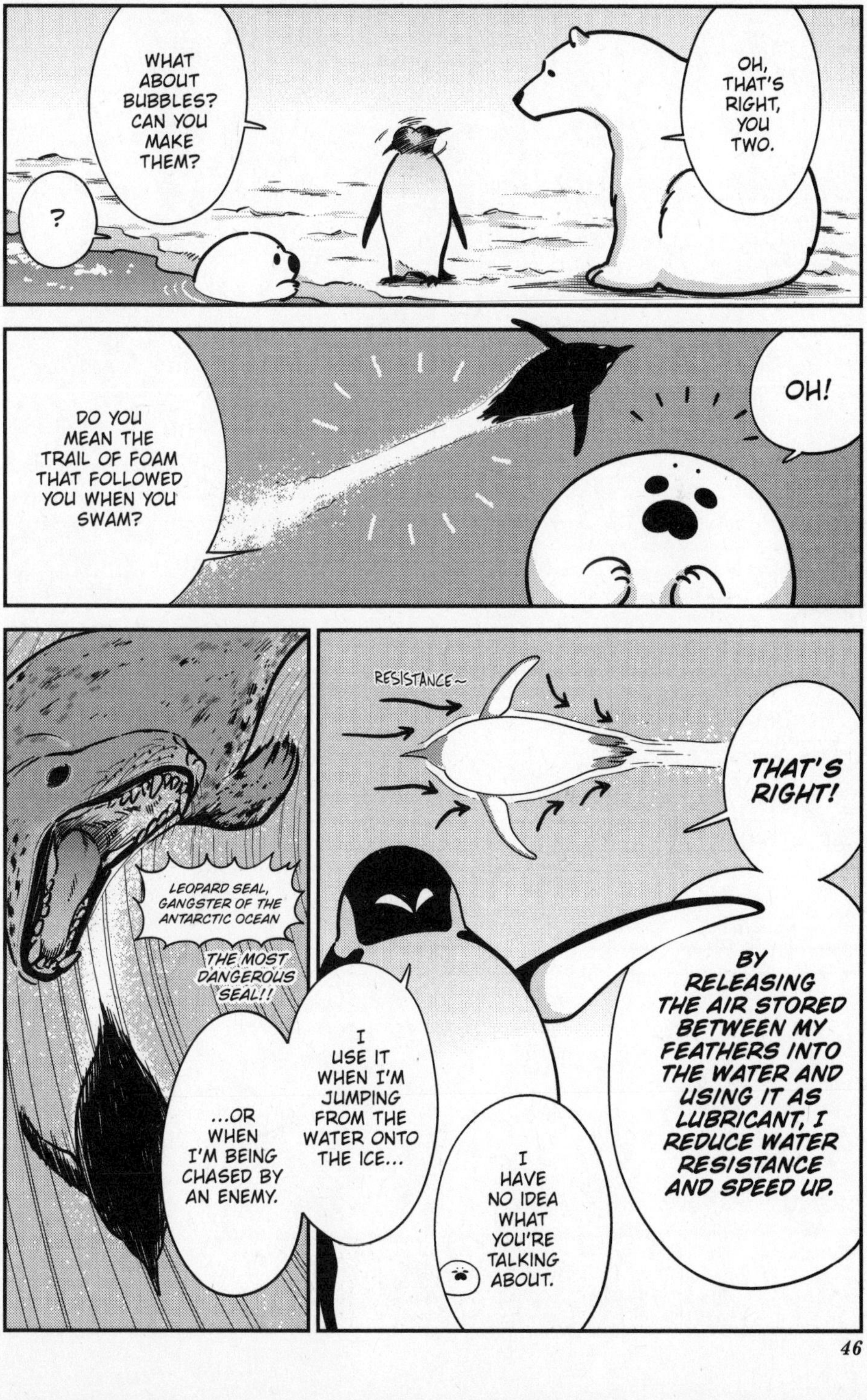

OH, THAT'S RIGHT, YOU TWO.
WHAT ABOUT BUBBLES? CAN YOU MAKE THEM?
?
OH!
DO YOU MEAN THE TRAIL OF FOAM THAT FOLLOWED YOU WHEN YOU SWAM?
THAT'S RIGHT!
RESISTANCE~
BY RELEASING THE AIR STORED BETWEEN MY FEATHERS INTO THE WATER AND USING IT AS LUBRICANT, I REDUCE WATER RESISTANCE AND SPEED UP.
I USE IT WHEN I'M JUMPING FROM THE WATER ONTO THE ICE...
I HAVE NO IDEA WHAT YOU'RE TALKING ABOUT.
LEOPARD SEAL, GANGSTER OF THE ANTARCTIC OCEAN
THE MOST DANGEROUS SEAL!!
...OR WHEN I'M BEING CHASED BY AN ENEMY.

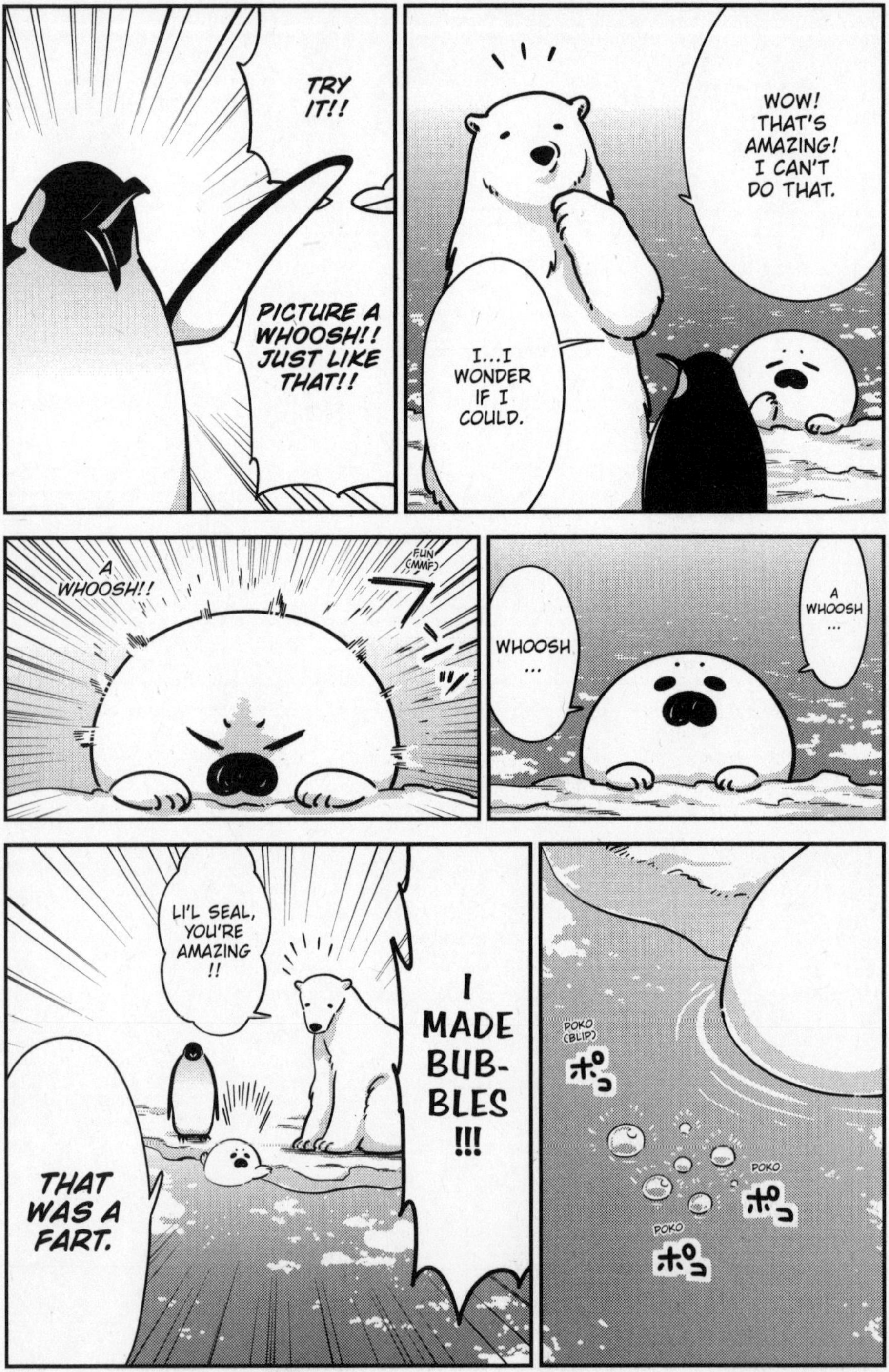
WOW! THAT'S AMAZING! I CAN'T DO THAT.
I...I WONDER IF I COULD.
TRY IT!!
PICTURE A WHOOSH!! JUST LIKE THAT!!
A WHOOSH ...
WHOOSH ...
A WHOOSH!!
FUN (MMF)
POKO (BLIP)
ポッ
POKO
ポッ
POKO
ポッ
LI'L SEAL, YOU'RE AMAZING !!
I MADE BUB-BLES !!!
THAT WAS A FART.

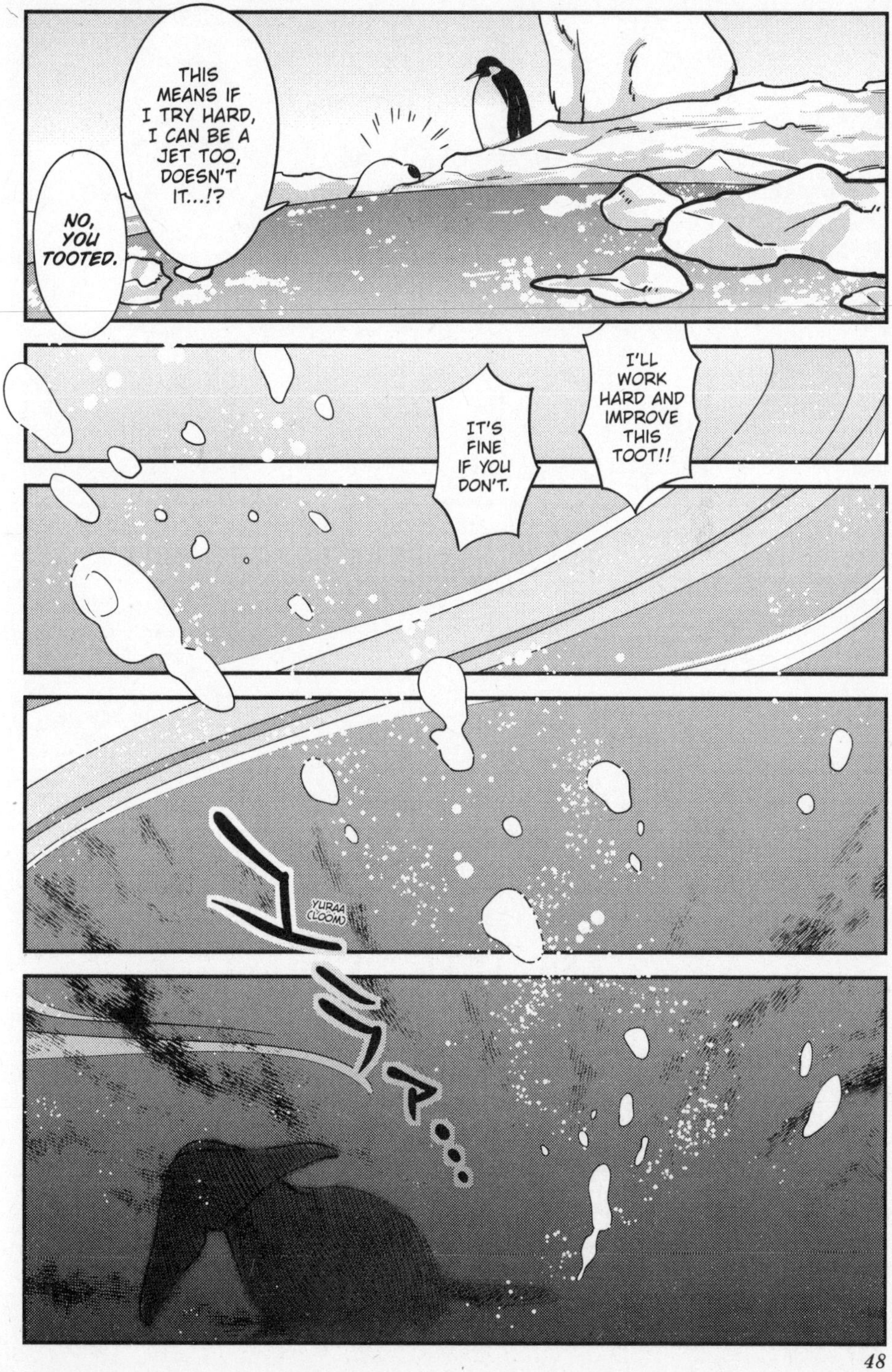
THIS MEANS IF I TRY HARD, I CAN BE A JET TOO, DOESN'T IT...!?
NO, YOU TOOTED.
I'LL WORK HARD AND IMPROVE THIS TOOT!!
IT'S FINE IF YOU DON'T.
YURAA (LOOM)

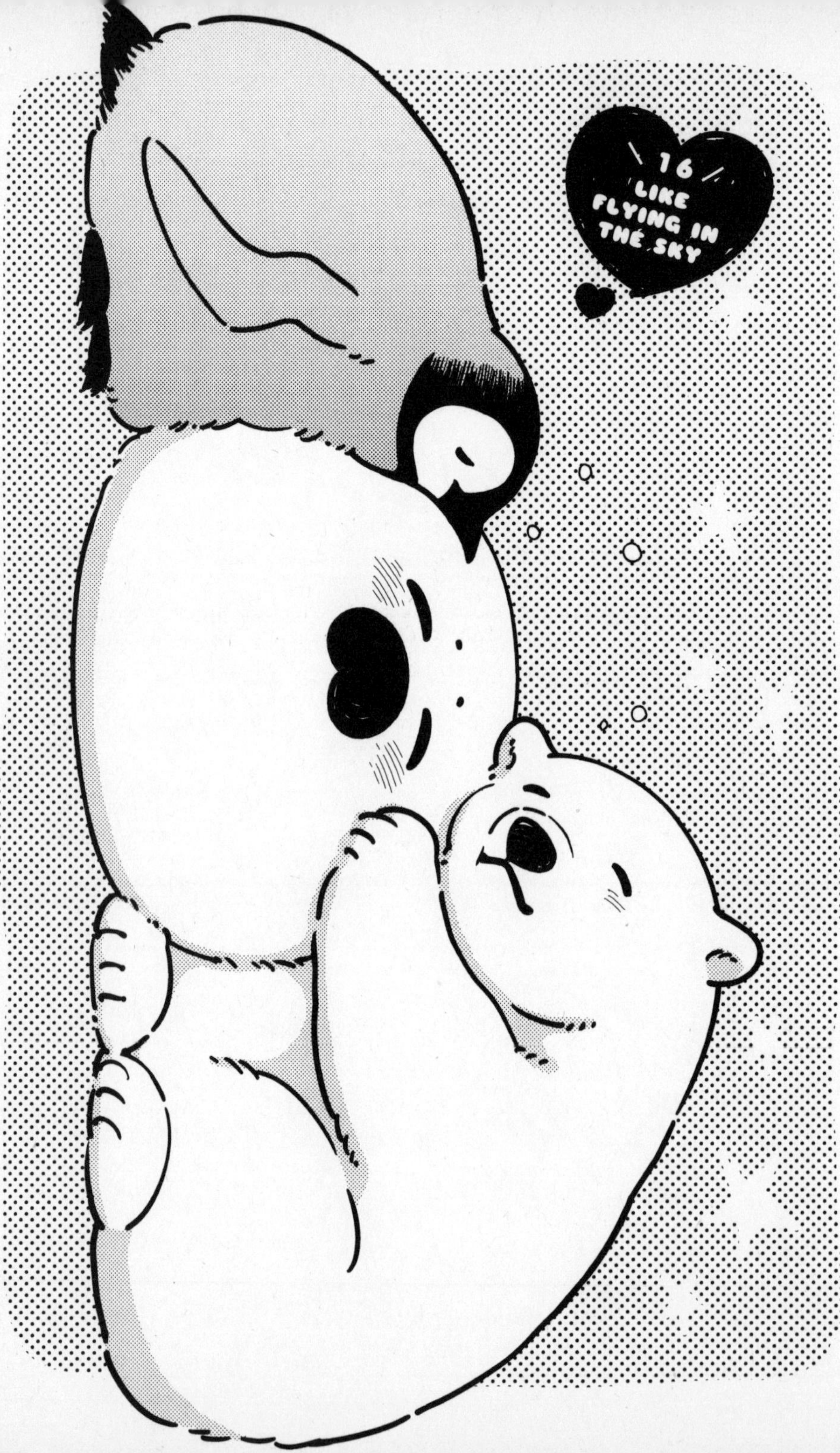
16
LIKE FLYING IN THE SKY

A DANGEROUS GUY

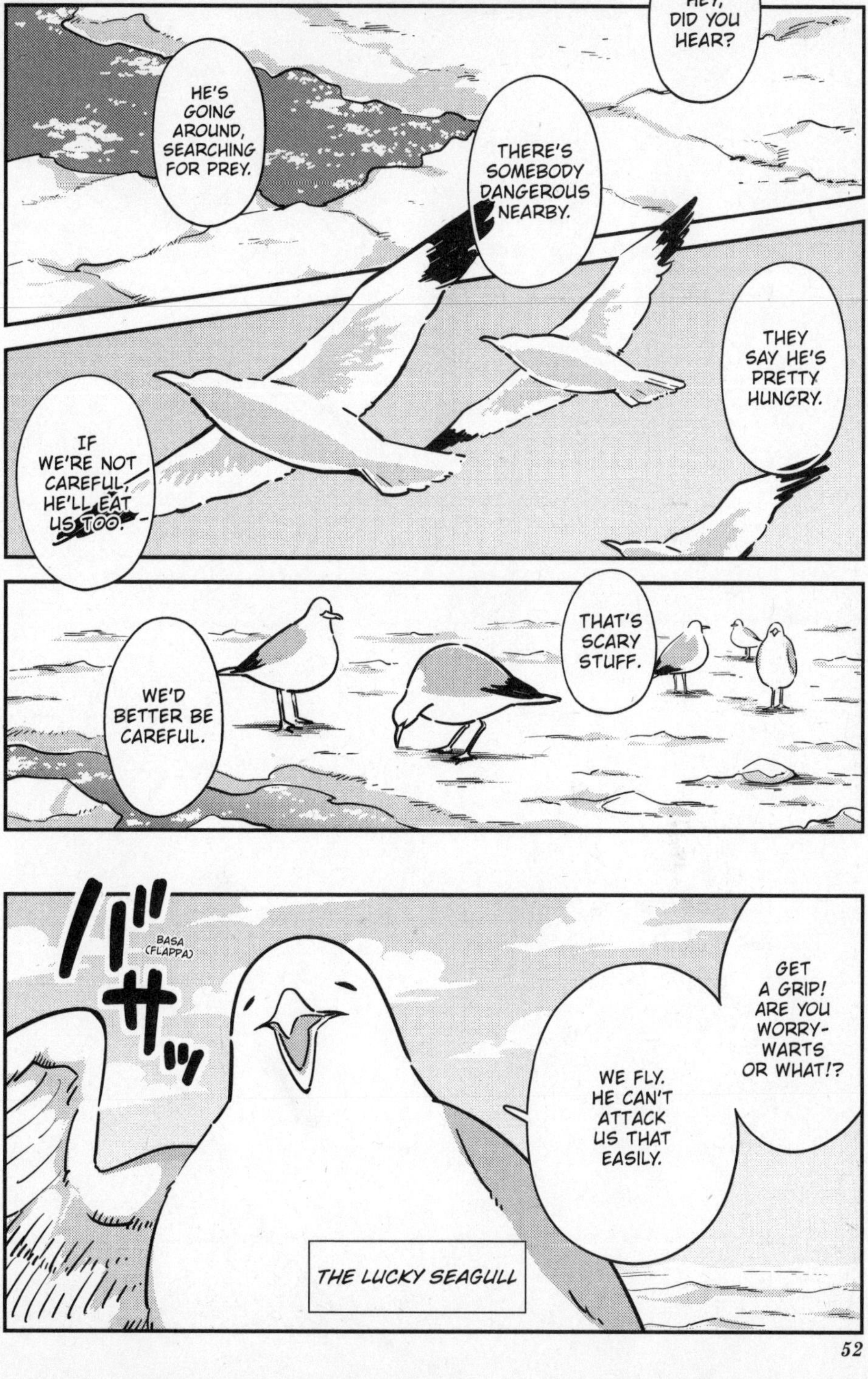
HEY, DID YOU HEAR?
THERE'S SOMEBODY DANGEROUS NEARBY.
HE'S GOING AROUND, SEARCHING FOR PREY.
THEY SAY HE'S PRETTY HUNGRY.
IF WE'RE NOT CAREFUL, HE'LL EAT US TOO.
THAT'S SCARY STUFF.
WE'D BETTER BE CAREFUL.
GET A GRIP! ARE YOU WORRY-WARTS OR WHAT!?
WE FLY. HE CAN'T ATTACK US THAT EASILY.
BASA (FLAPPA)
THE LUCKY SEAGULL

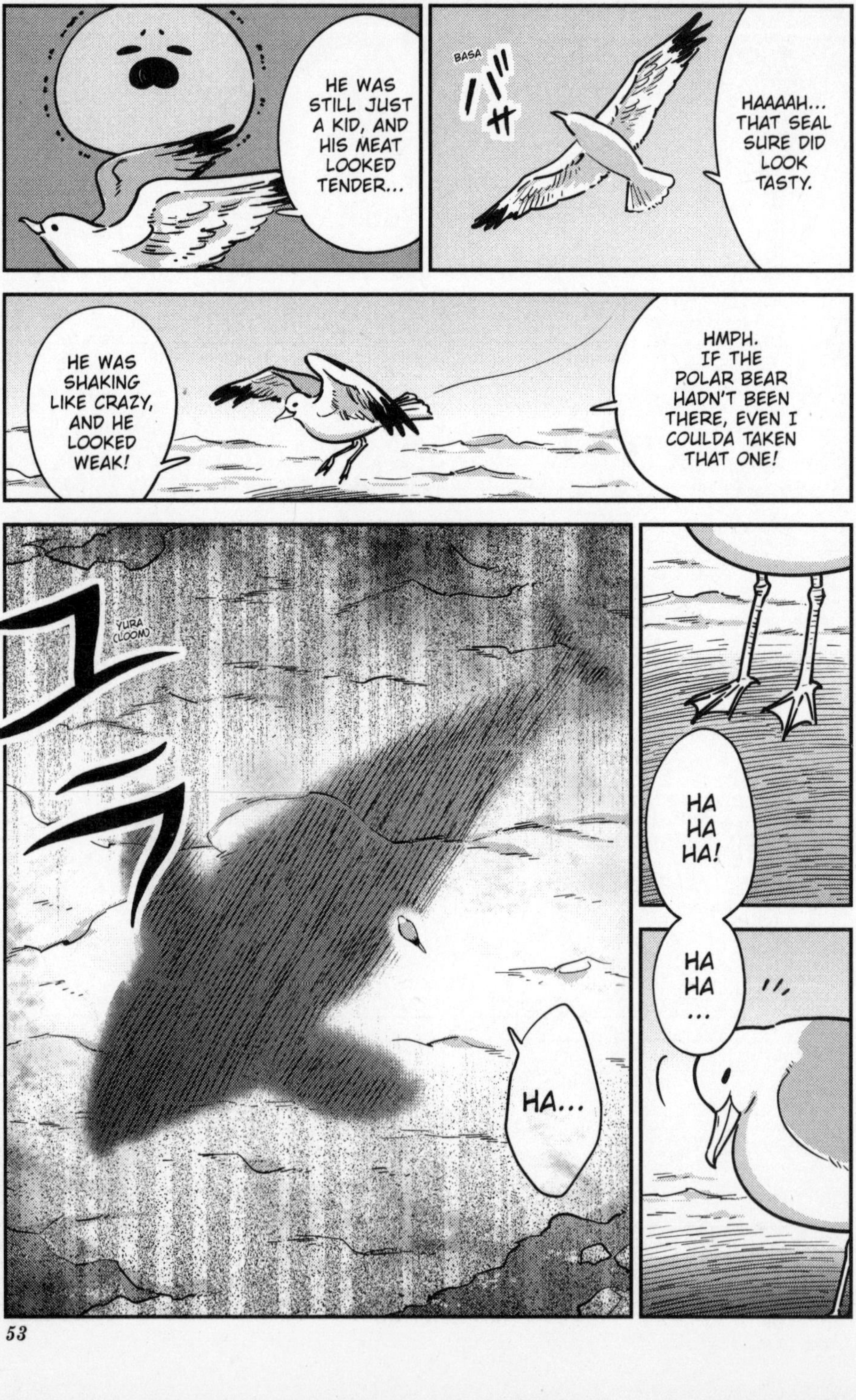
BASA
バサ
HAAAAH... THAT SEAL SURE DID LOOK TASTY.
HE WAS STILL JUST A KID, AND HIS MEAT LOOKED TENDER...
HMPH. IF THE POLAR BEAR HADN'T BEEN THERE, EVEN I COULDA TAKEN THAT ONE!
HE WAS SHAKING LIKE CRAZY, AND HE LOOKED WEAK!
HA HA HA!
HA HA ...
YURA (LOOM)
ユラ
HA...

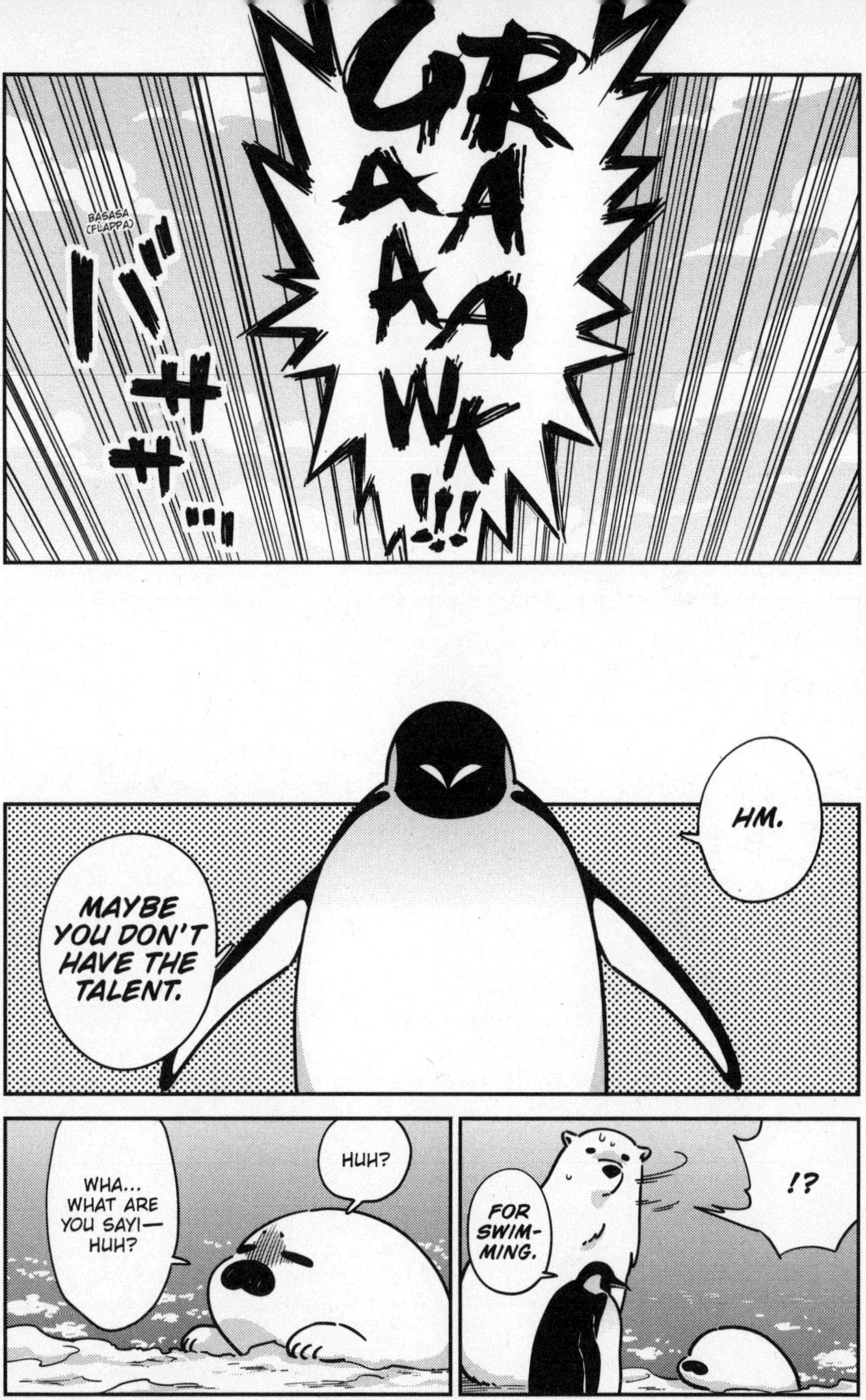
GRAAAAWK!!!
BASASA (FLAPPA)
HM.
MAYBE YOU DON'T HAVE THE TALENT.
!?
FOR SWIMMING.
HUH?
WHA... WHAT ARE YOU SAYI— HUH?

CATHY'S SPECIAL TRAINING

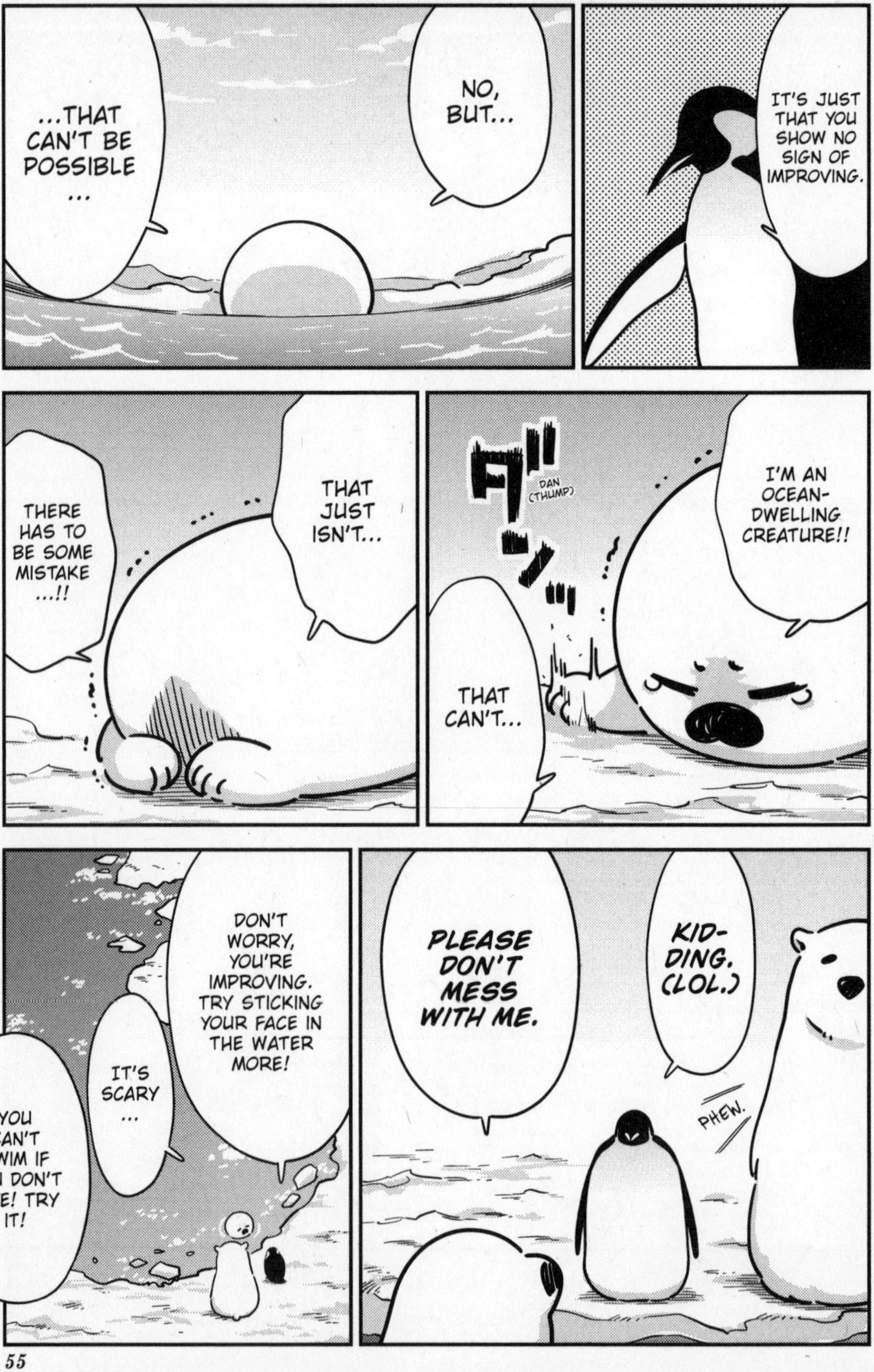

IT'S JUST THAT YOU SHOW NO SIGN OF IMPROVING.
NO, BUT...
...THAT CAN'T BE POSSIBLE ...
I'M AN OCEAN-DWELLING CREATURE!!
DAN (THUMP)
THAT CAN'T...
THAT JUST ISN'T...
THERE HAS TO BE SOME MISTAKE ...!!
KID-DING. (LOL.)
PLEASE DON'T MESS WITH ME.
PHEW.
DON'T WORRY, YOU'RE IMPROVING. TRY STICKING YOUR FACE IN THE WATER MORE!
IT'S SCARY ...
YOU CAN'T SWIM IF YOU DON'T DIVE! TRY IT!

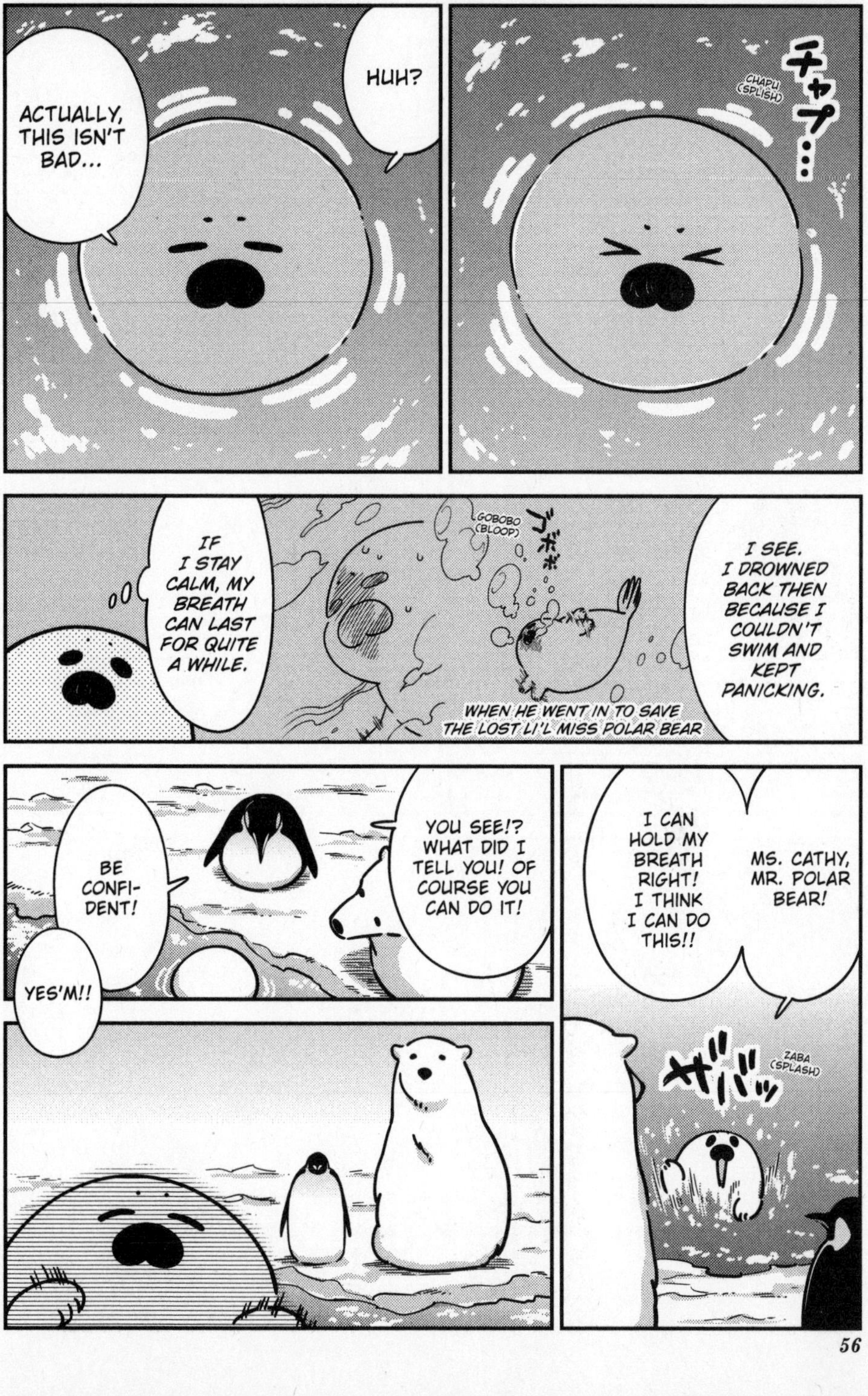
チャプ…
CHAPU (SPLISH)
HUH?
ACTUALLY, THIS ISN'T BAD...
I SEE. I DROWNED BACK THEN BECAUSE I COULDN'T SWIM AND KEPT PANICKING.
ゴボボ
GOBOBO (BLOOP)
WHEN HE WENT IN TO SAVE THE LOST LI'L MISS POLAR BEAR
IF I STAY CALM, MY BREATH CAN LAST FOR QUITE A WHILE.
MS. CATHY, MR. POLAR BEAR!
I CAN HOLD MY BREATH RIGHT! I THINK I CAN DO THIS!!
ザバッ
ZABA (SPLASH)
YOU SEE!? WHAT DID I TELL YOU! OF COURSE YOU CAN DO IT!
BE CONFI-DENT!
YES'M!!

THE POWER OF LOVE

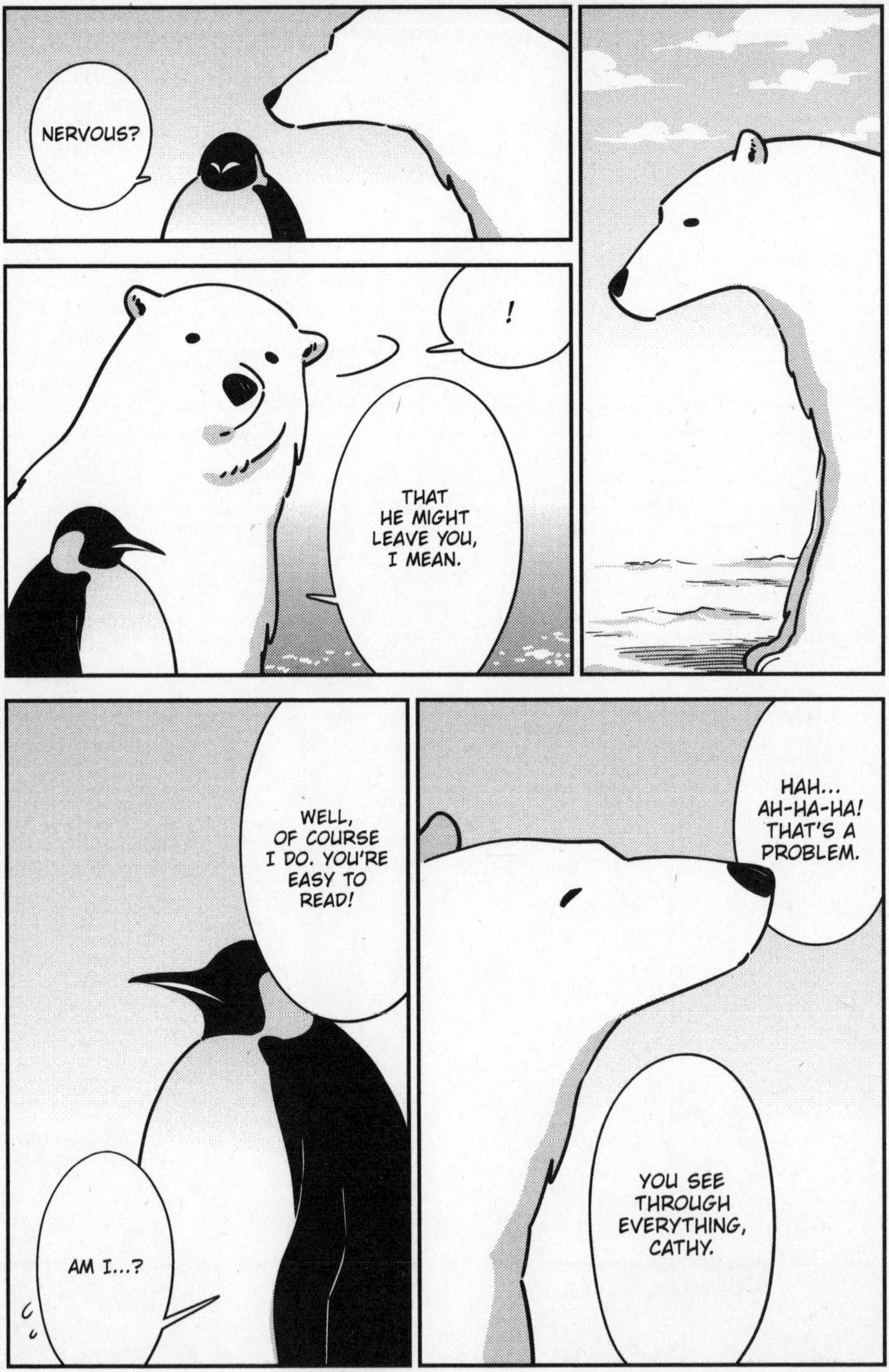

NERVOUS?
!
THAT HE MIGHT LEAVE YOU, I MEAN.
HAH... AH-HA-HA! THAT'S A PROBLEM.
YOU SEE THROUGH EVERYTHING, CATHY.
WELL, OF COURSE I DO. YOU'RE EASY TO READ!
AM I...?

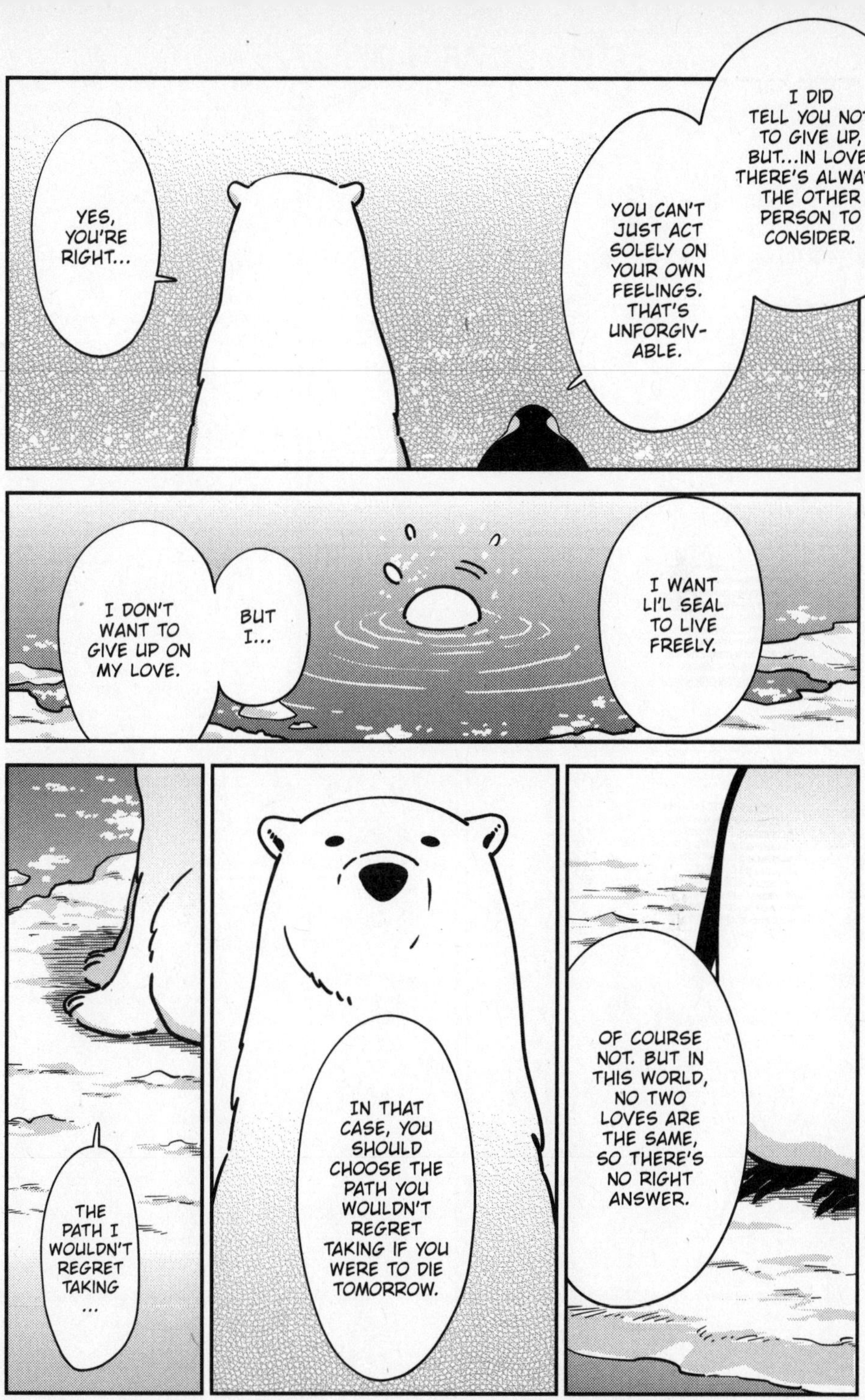
I DID TELL YOU NOT TO GIVE UP, BUT...IN LOVE, THERE'S ALWAYS THE OTHER PERSON TO CONSIDER.
YOU CAN'T JUST ACT SOLELY ON YOUR OWN FEELINGS. THAT'S UNFORGIV-ABLE.
YES, YOU'RE RIGHT...
I WANT LI'L SEAL TO LIVE FREELY.
BUT I...
I DON'T WANT TO GIVE UP ON MY LOVE.
OF COURSE NOT. BUT IN THIS WORLD, NO TWO LOVES ARE THE SAME, SO THERE'S NO RIGHT ANSWER.
IN THAT CASE, YOU SHOULD CHOOSE THE PATH YOU WOULDN'T REGRET TAKING IF YOU WERE TO DIE TOMORROW.
THE PATH I WOULDN'T REGRET TAKING ...

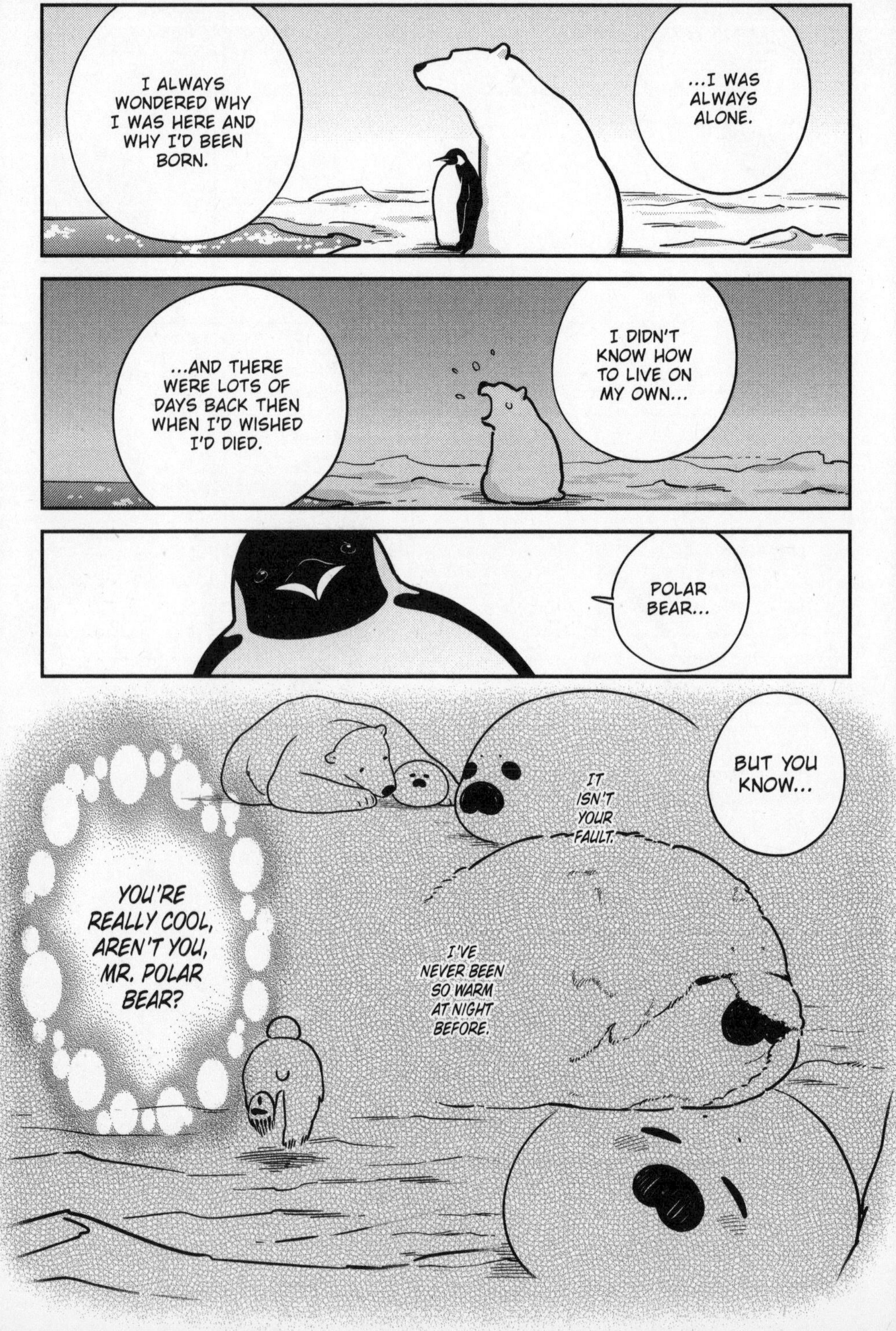
...I WAS ALWAYS ALONE.
I ALWAYS WONDERED WHY I WAS HERE AND WHY I'D BEEN BORN.
I DIDN'T KNOW HOW TO LIVE ON MY OWN...
...AND THERE WERE LOTS OF DAYS BACK THEN WHEN I'D WISHED I'D DIED.
POLAR BEAR...
BUT YOU KNOW...
IT ISN'T YOUR FAULT.
I'VE NEVER BEEN SO WARM AT NIGHT BEFORE.
YOU'RE REALLY COOL, AREN'T YOU, MR. POLAR BEAR?

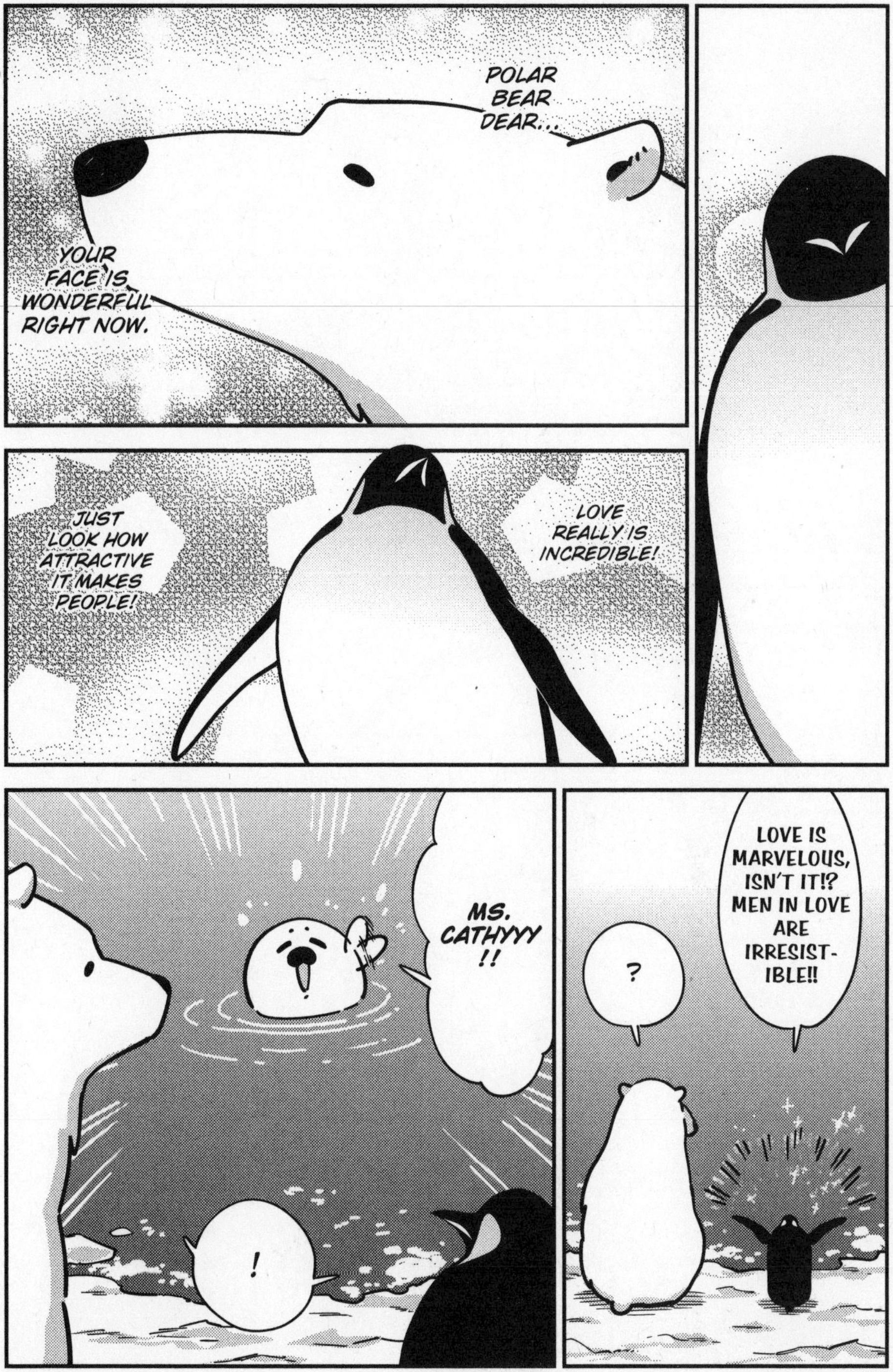
POLAR BEAR DEAR...
YOUR FACE IS WONDERFUL RIGHT NOW.
LOVE REALLY IS INCREDIBLE!
JUST LOOK HOW ATTRACTIVE IT MAKES PEOPLE!
LOVE IS MARVELOUS, ISN'T IT!? MEN IN LOVE ARE IRRESIST-IBLE!!
?
MS. CATHYYY!!
!

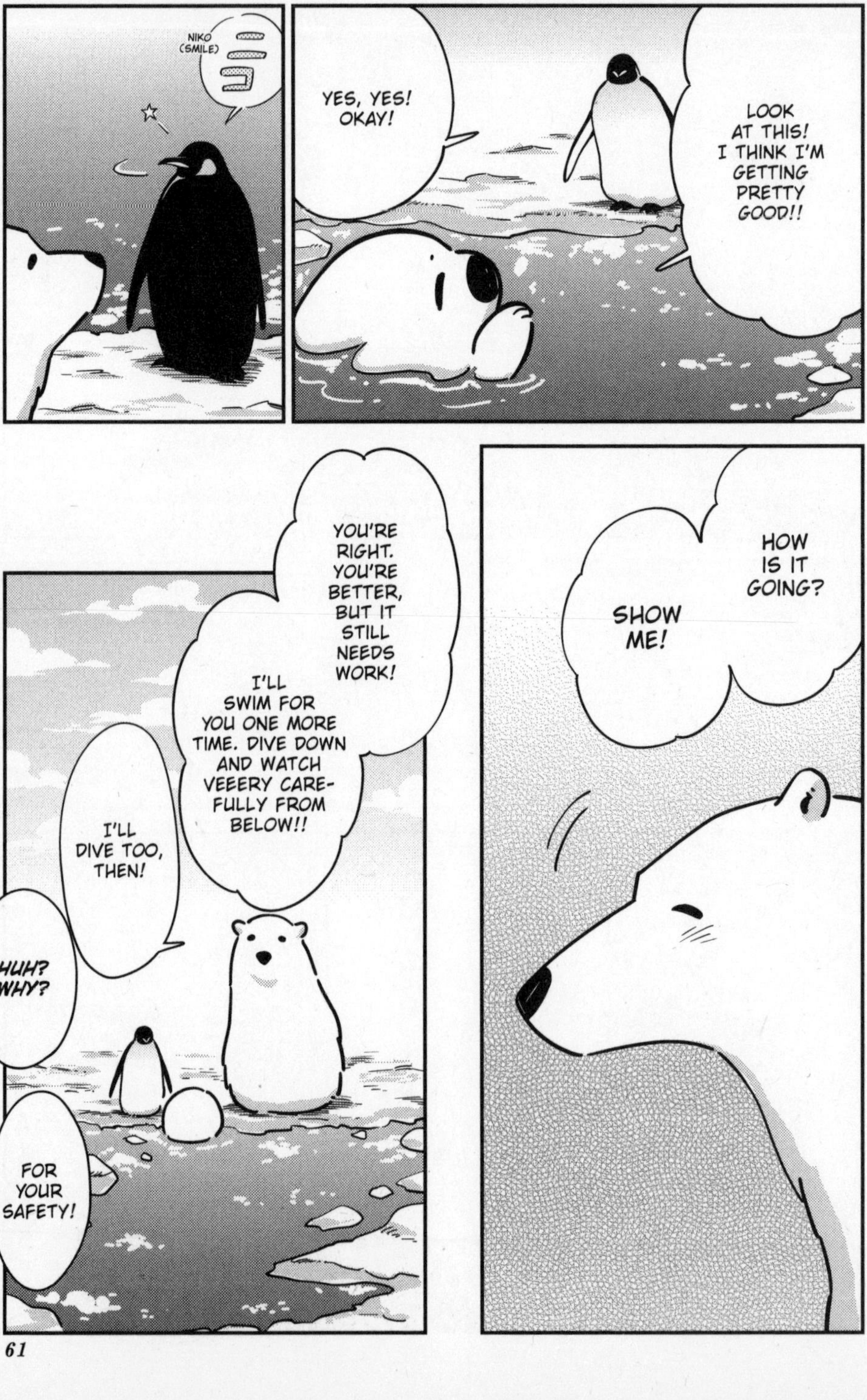
LOOK AT THIS! I THINK I'M GETTING PRETTY GOOD!!
YES, YES! OKAY!
NIKO (SMILE)
HOW IS IT GOING?
SHOW ME!
YOU'RE RIGHT. YOU'RE BETTER, BUT IT STILL NEEDS WORK!
I'LL SWIM FOR YOU ONE MORE TIME. DIVE DOWN AND WATCH VEEERY CARE-FULLY FROM BELOW!!
I'LL DIVE TOO, THEN!
HUH? WHY?
FOR YOUR SAFETY!

FLYING THROUGH THE SEA

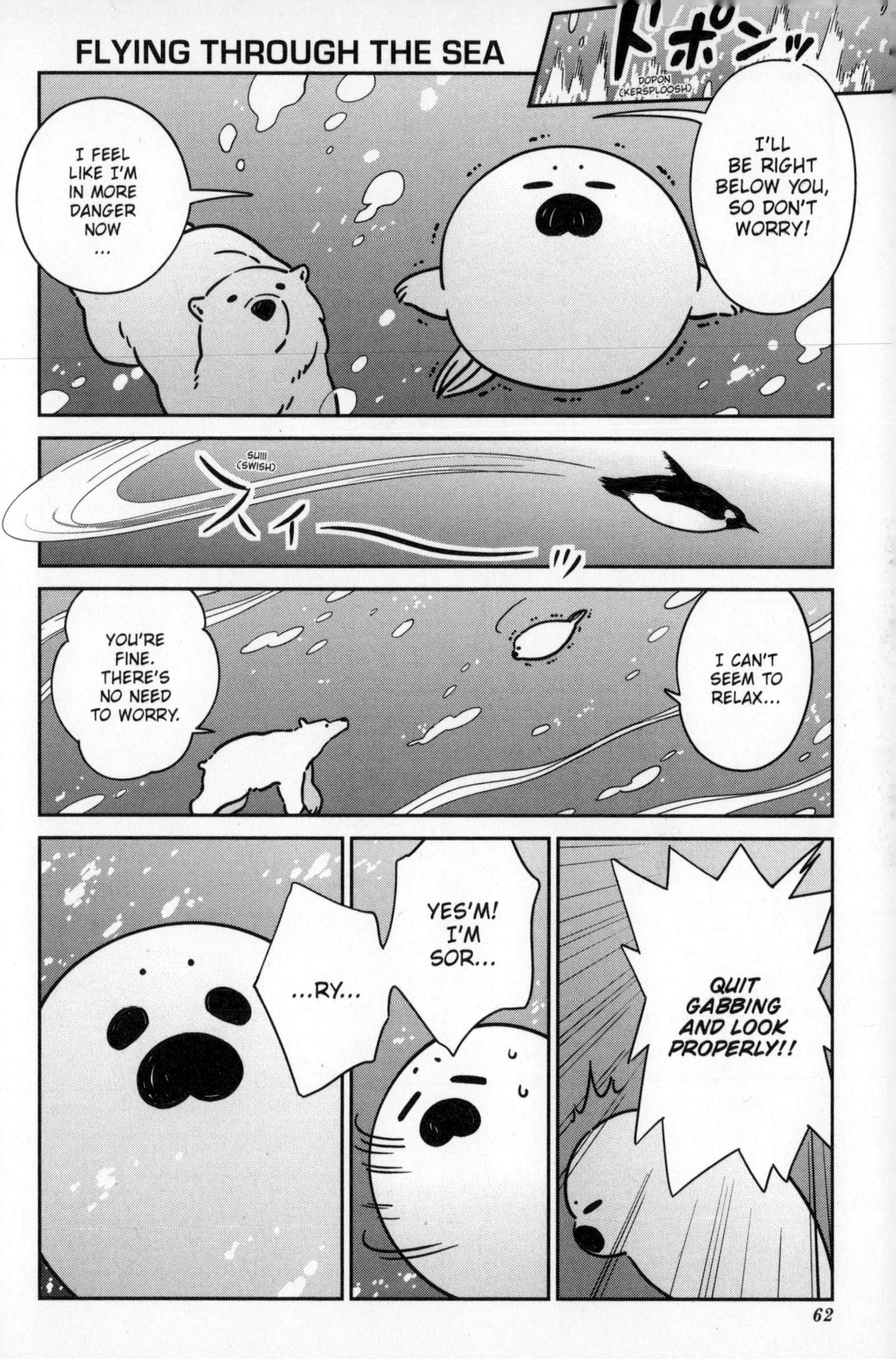
ドポンッ
DOPON (KERSPLOOSH)
I'LL BE RIGHT BELOW YOU, SO DON'T WORRY!
I FEEL LIKE I'M IN MORE DANGER NOW ...
スイ―ッ
SUIII (SWISH)
I CAN'T SEEM TO RELAX...
YOU'RE FINE. THERE'S NO NEED TO WORRY.
QUIT GABBING AND LOOK PROPERLY!!
YES'M! I'M SOR...
...RY...

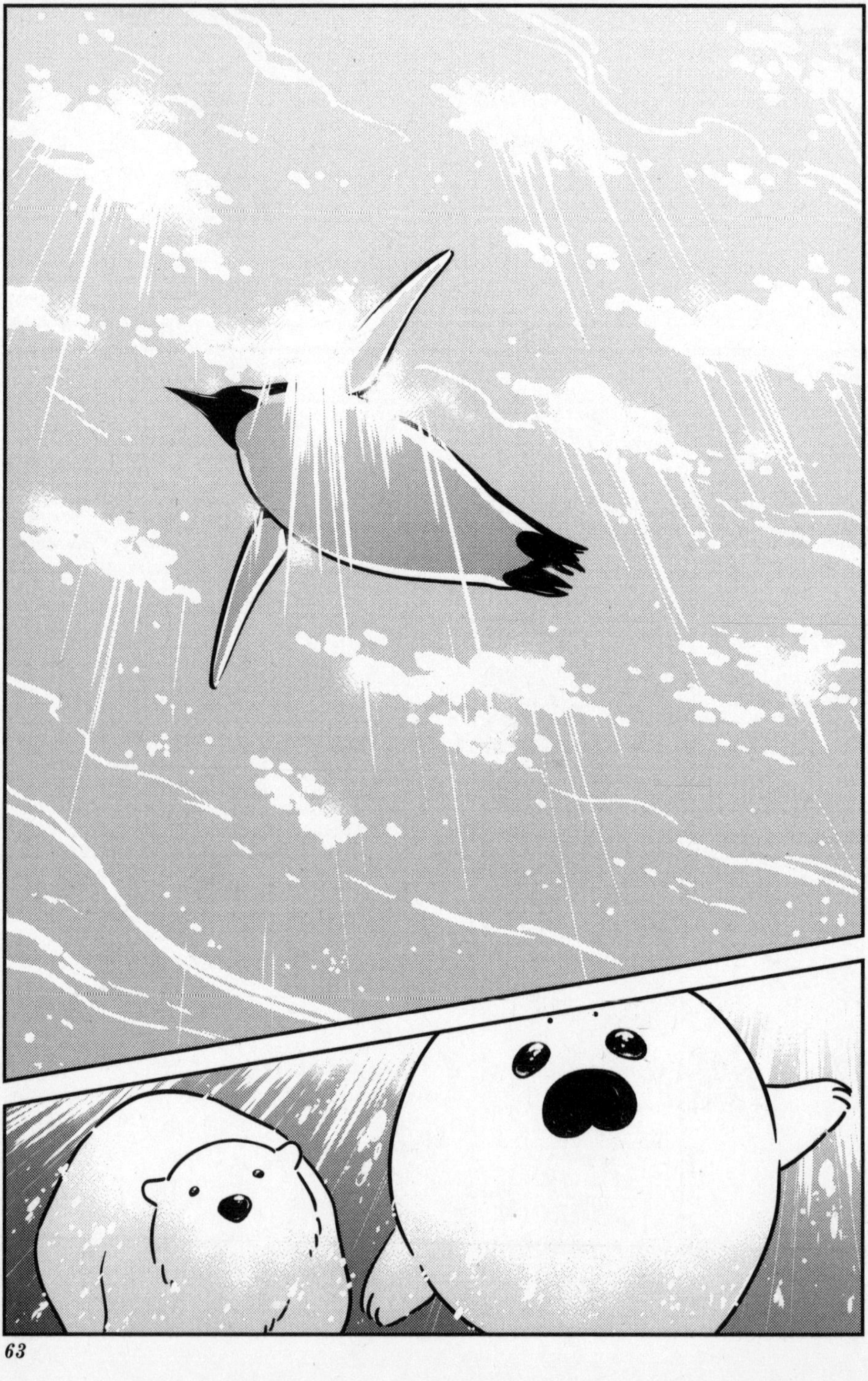

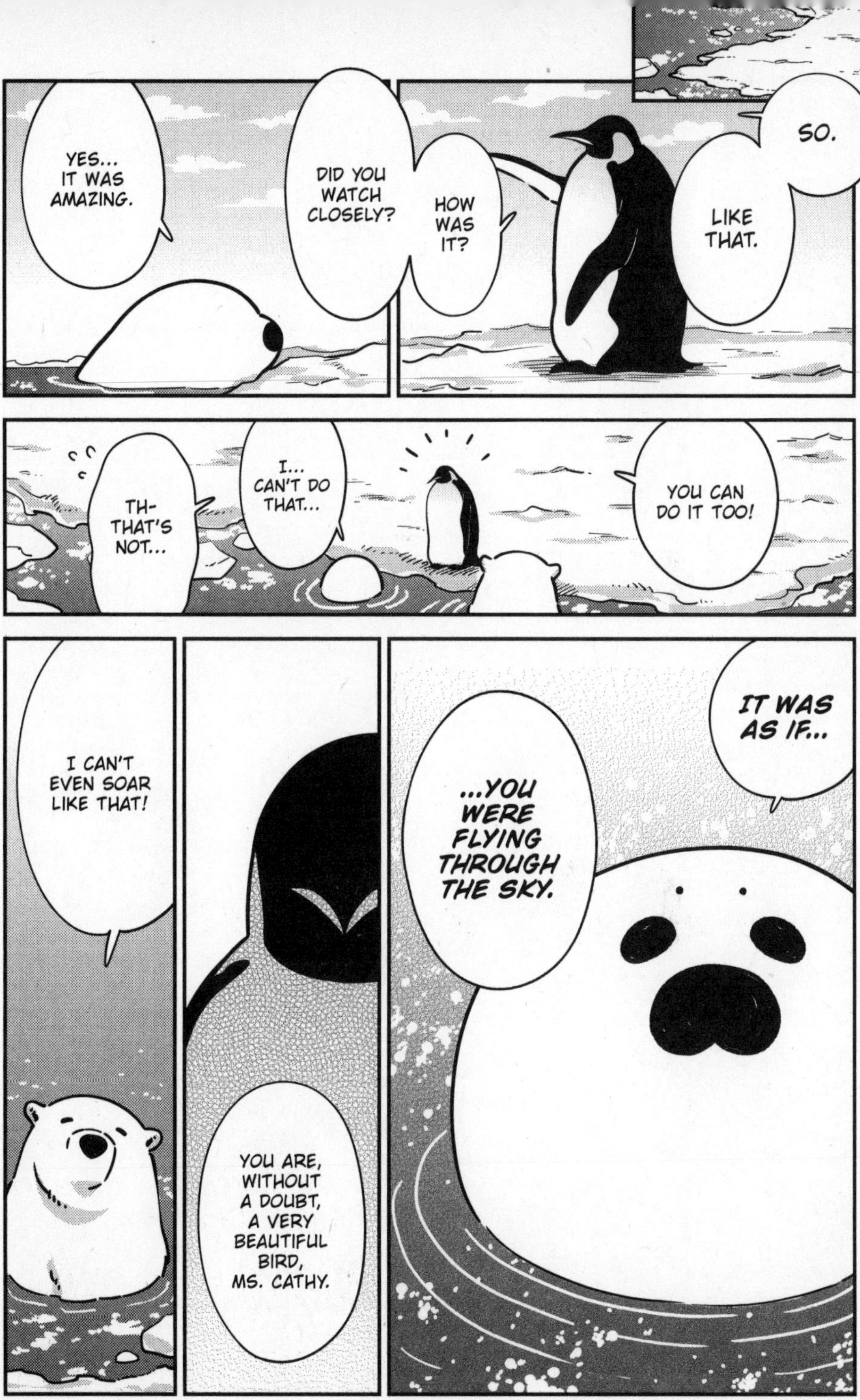
SO.
LIKE THAT.
DID YOU WATCH CLOSELY?
HOW WAS IT?
YES... IT WAS AMAZING.
YOU CAN DO IT TOO!
I... CAN'T DO THAT...
TH- THAT'S NOT...
IT WAS AS IF...
...YOU WERE FLYING THROUGH THE SKY.
YOU ARE, WITHOUT A DOUBT, A VERY BEAUTIFUL BIRD, MS. CATHY.
I CAN'T EVEN SOAR LIKE THAT!

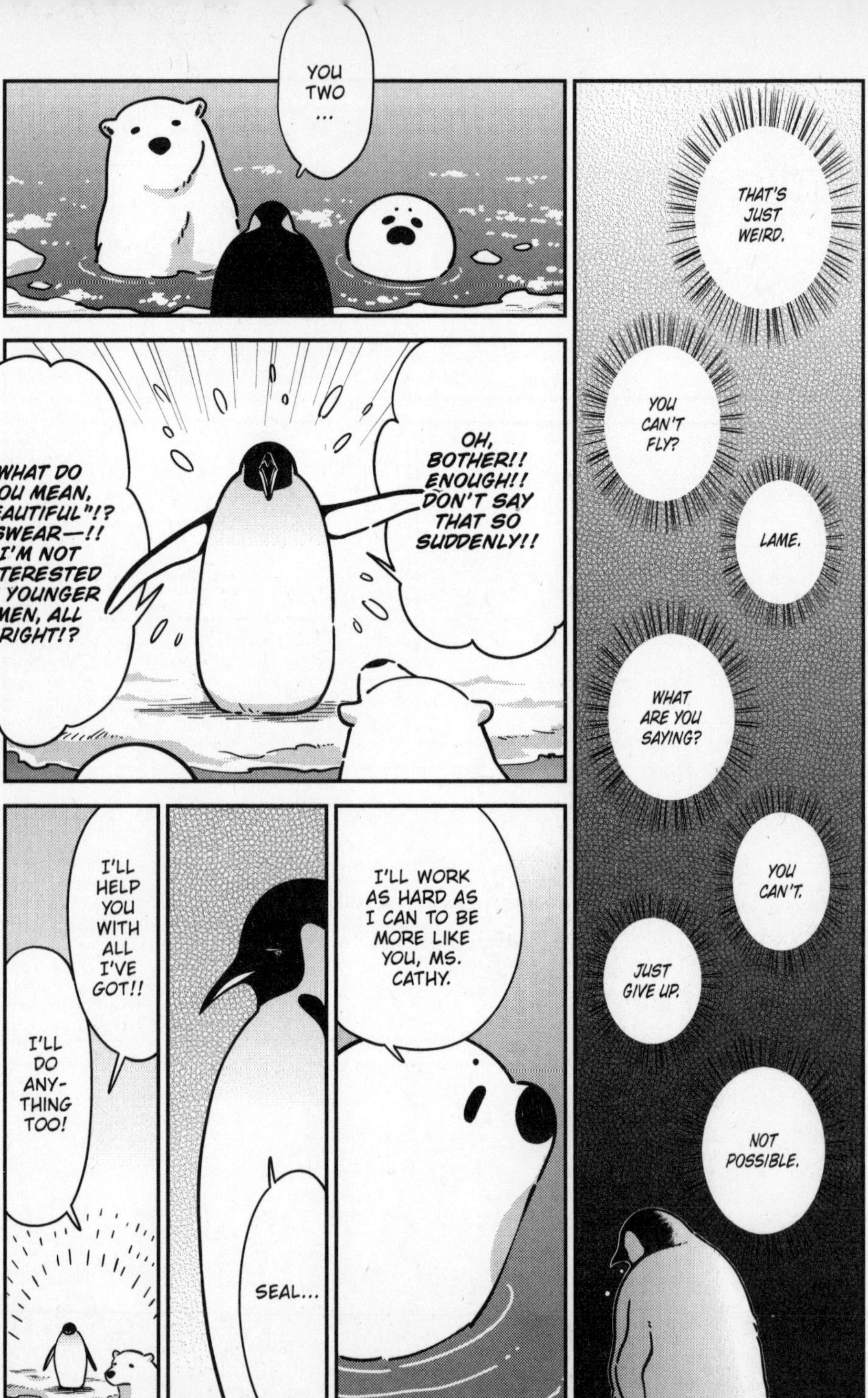
THAT'S JUST WEIRD.
YOU CAN'T FLY?
LAME.
WHAT ARE YOU SAYING?
YOU CAN'T.
JUST GIVE UP.
NOT POSSIBLE.
YOU TWO...
OH, BOTHER!! ENOUGH!! DON'T SAY THAT SO SUDDENLY!!
WHAT DO YOU MEAN, "BEAUTIFUL"!? I SWEAR—!! I'M NOT INTERESTED IN YOUNGER MEN, ALL RIGHT!?
I'LL WORK AS HARD AS I CAN TO BE MORE LIKE YOU, MS. CATHY.
SEAL...
I'LL HELP YOU WITH ALL I'VE GOT!!
I'LL DO ANY-THING TOO!

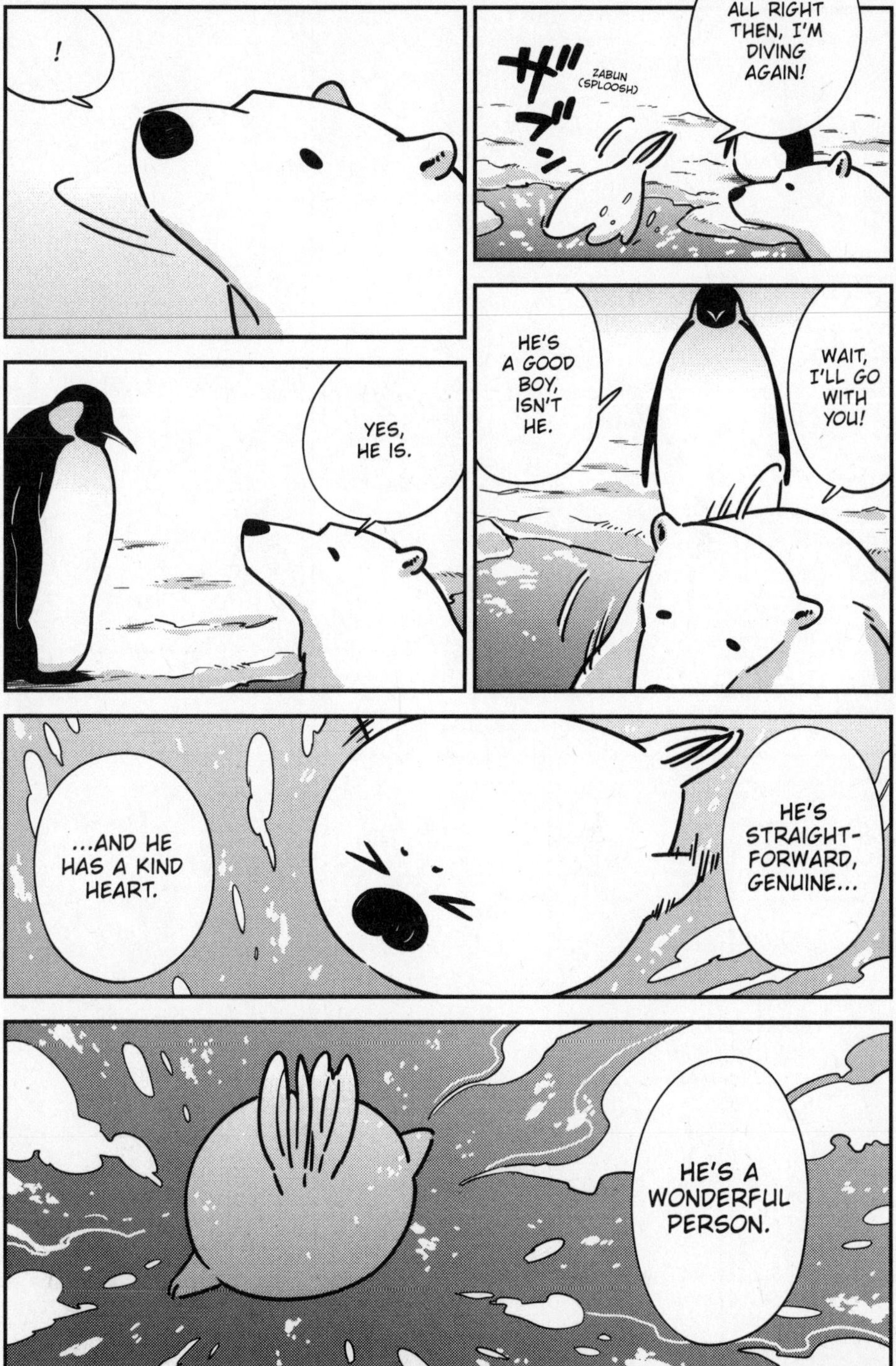
ALL RIGHT THEN, I'M DIVING AGAIN!
ザブン
ZABUN (SPLOOSH)
!
WAIT, I'LL GO WITH YOU!
HE'S A GOOD BOY, ISN'T HE.
YES, HE IS.
HE'S STRAIGHT-FORWARD, GENUINE...
...AND HE HAS A KIND HEART.
HE'S A WONDERFUL PERSON.

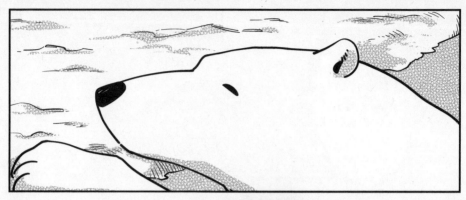

...MATCH PER-FECTLY.

YOU TWO...

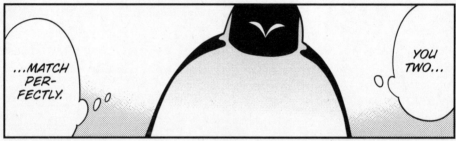

I UNDER-STAND...

I CAN SEE WHY YOU'D FALL FOR HIM.

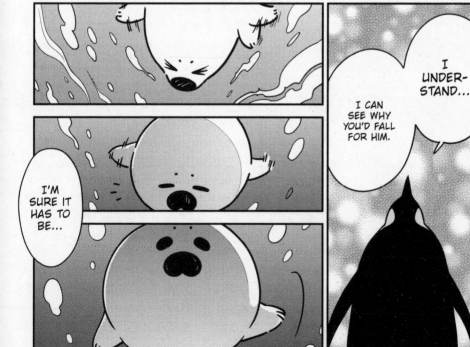

I'M SURE IT HAS TO BE...

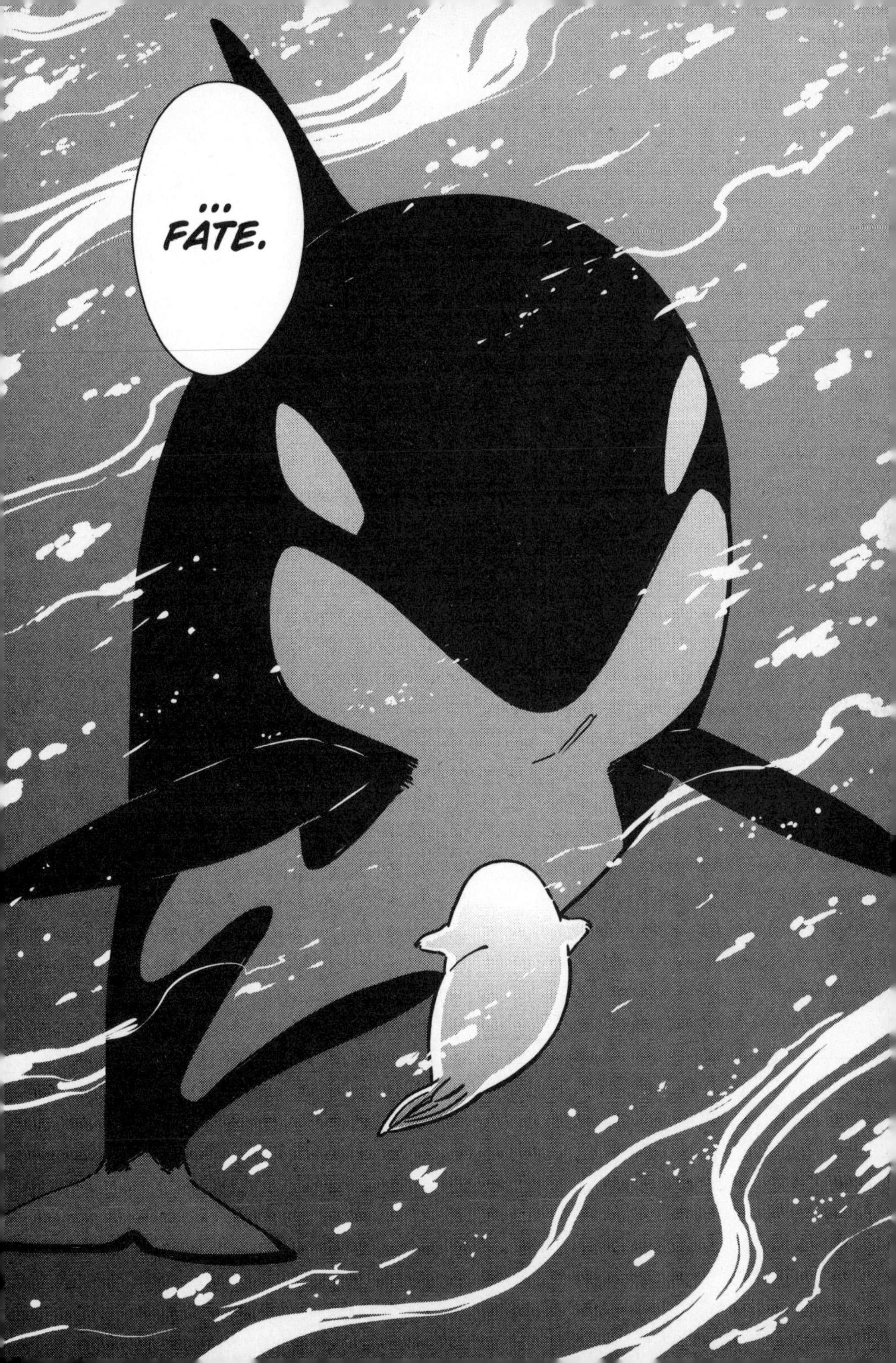
...FÄTE.

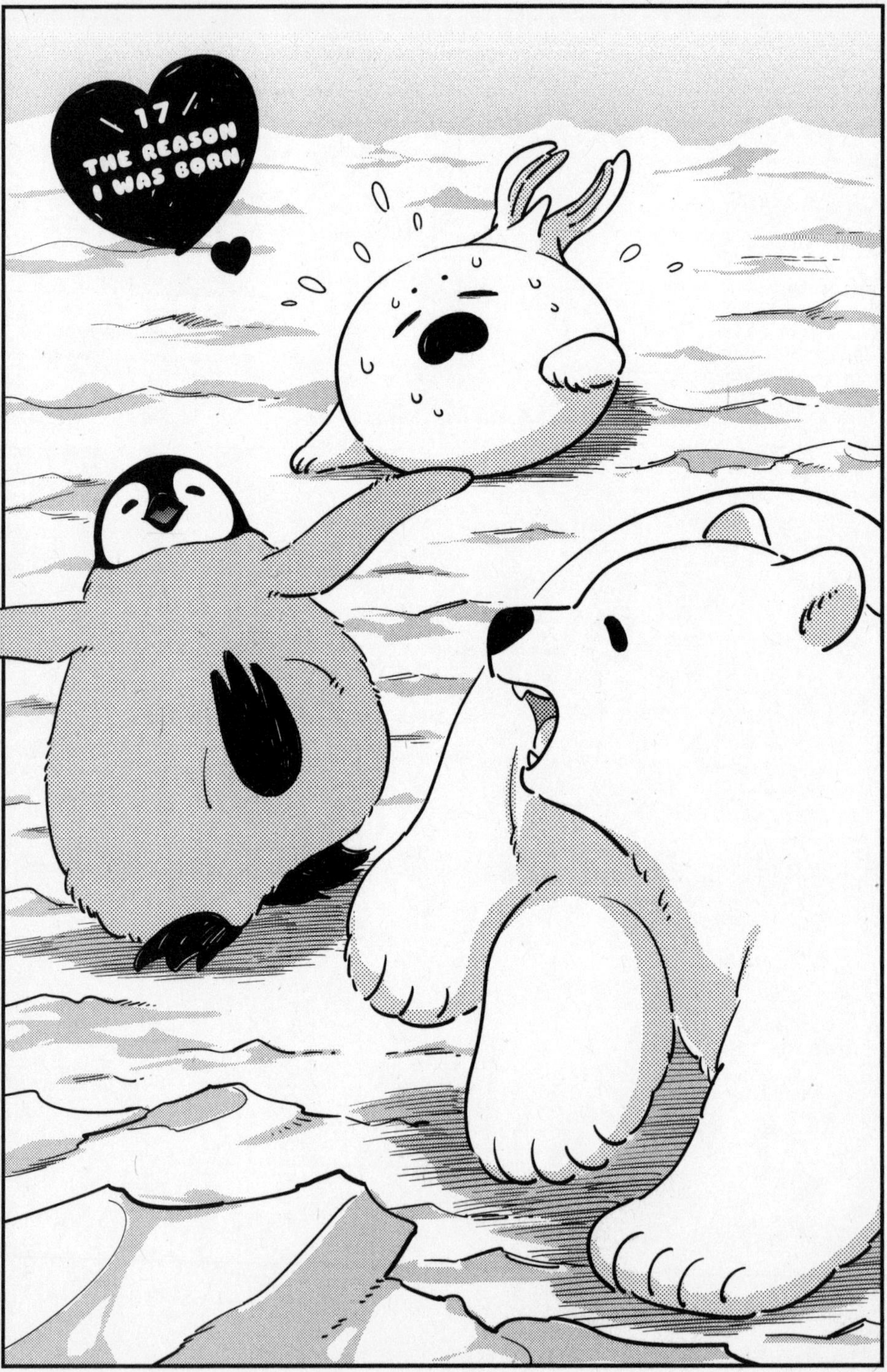
17
THE REASON I WAS BORN

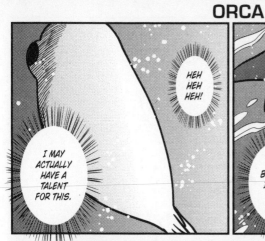

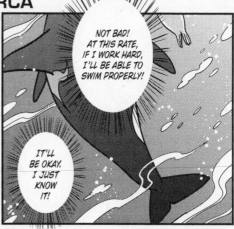

NOT BAD! AT THIS RATE, IF I WORK HARD, I'LL BE ABLE TO SWIM PROPERLY!
IT'LL BE OKAY. I JUST KNOW IT!
HEH HEH HEH!
I MAY ACTUALLY HAVE A TALENT FOR THIS.
ズオオ
ZUOOO (WHOOOO)

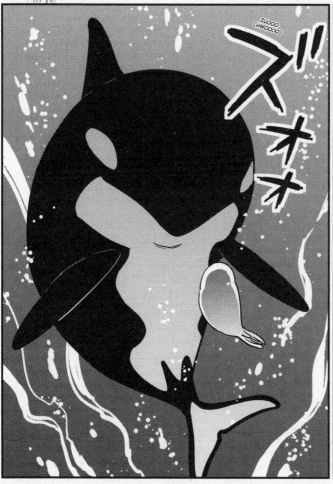

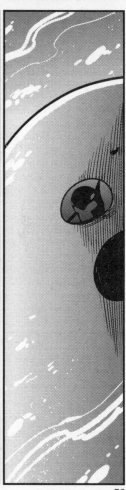

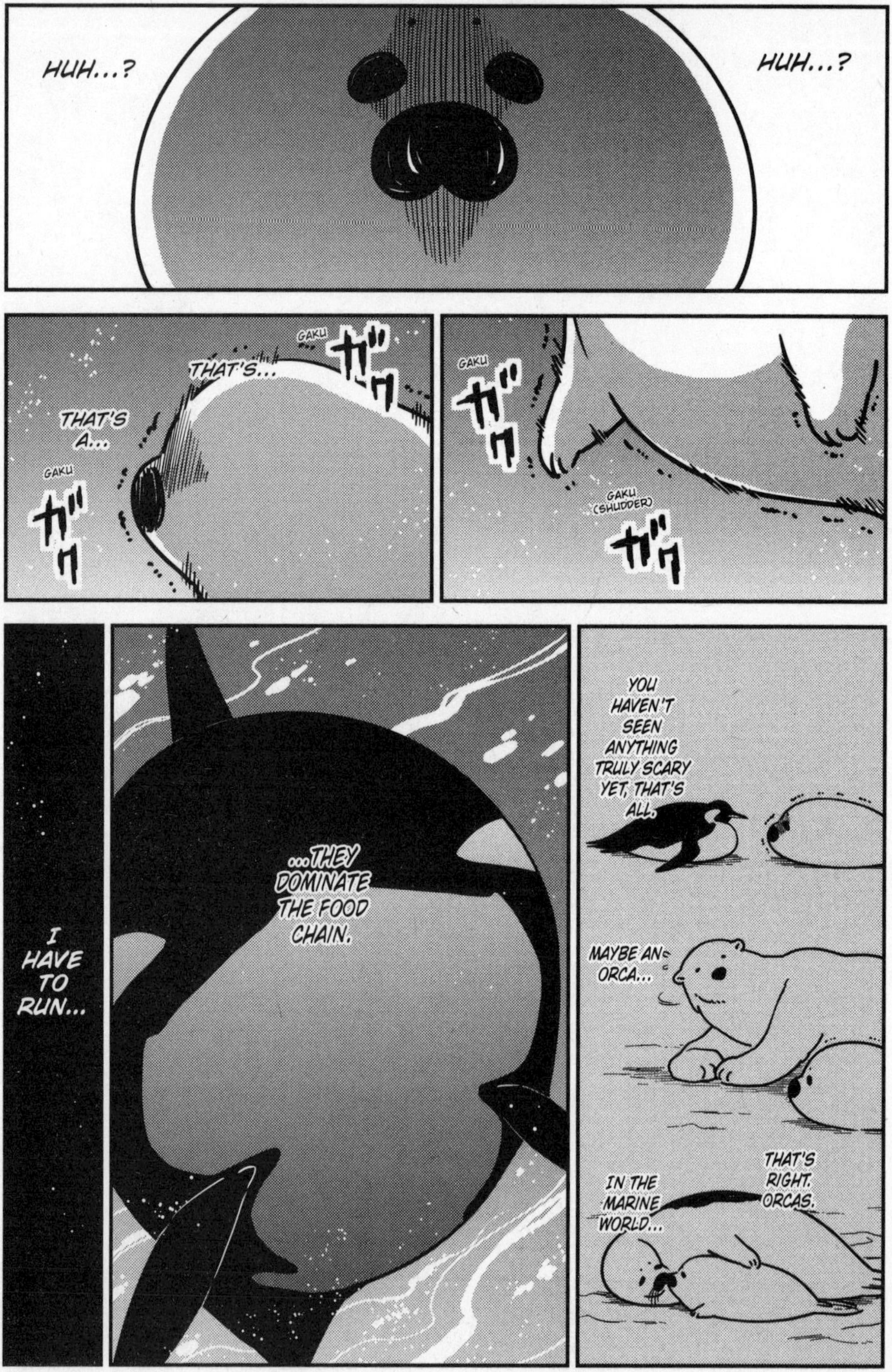
HUH...?
HUH...?
GAKU
ガク
GAKU (SHUDDER)
ガク
GAKU
ガク
THAT'S...
THAT'S A...
GAKU
ガク
YOU HAVEN'T SEEN ANYTHING TRULY SCARY YET, THAT'S ALL.
MAYBE AN ORCA...
THAT'S RIGHT. ORCAS.
IN THE MARINE WORLD...
...THEY DOMINATE THE FOOD CHAIN.
I HAVE TO RUN...

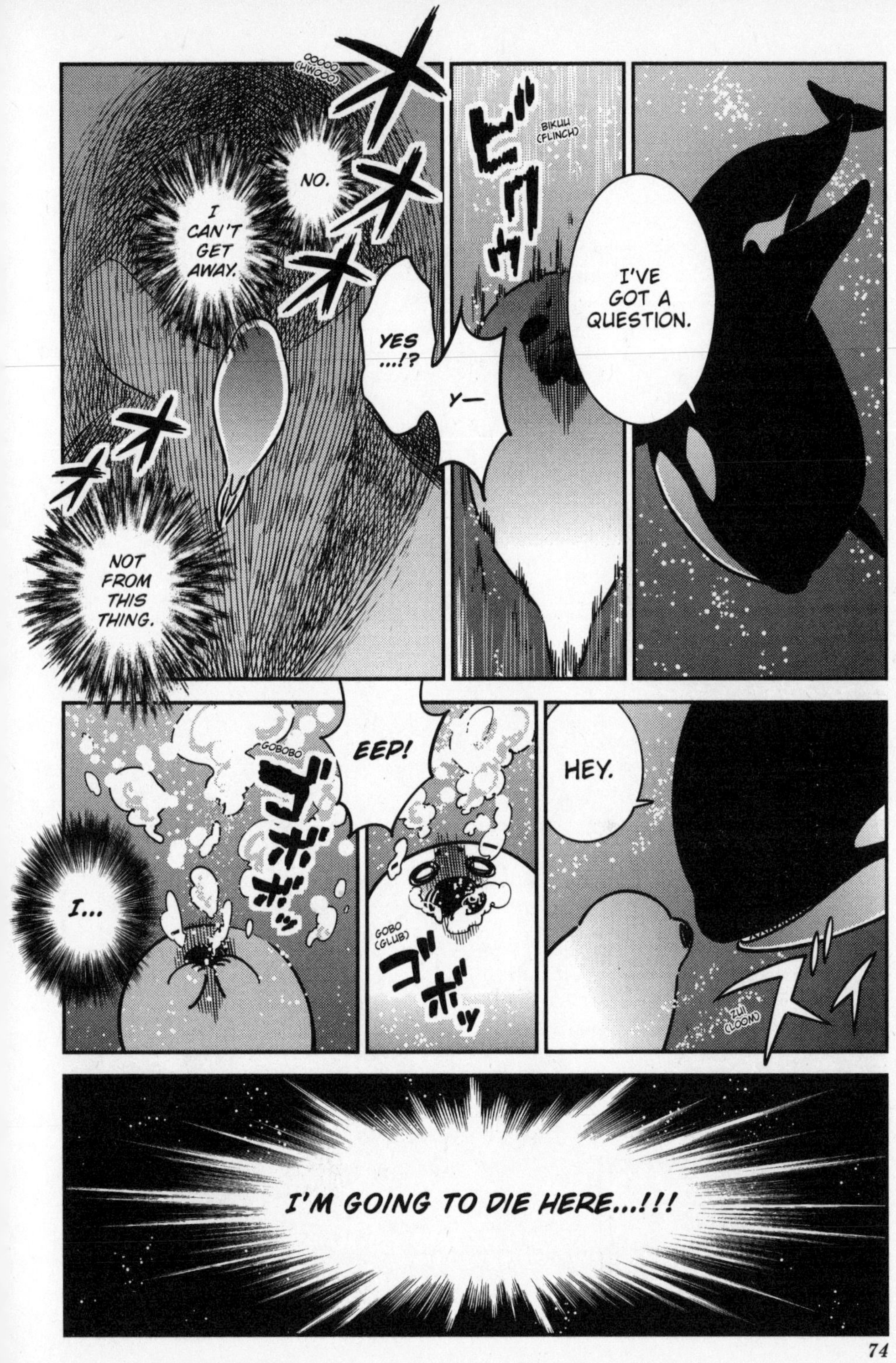

I'VE GOT A QUESTION.
BIKUU (FLINCH)
YES ...!?
Y—
OOOOO (HWOOO)
NO.
I CAN'T GET AWAY.
NOT FROM THIS THING.
HEY.
ZUI (LOOM)
EEP!
GOBO (GLUB)
GOBOBO
I...
I'M GOING TO DIE HERE...!!!

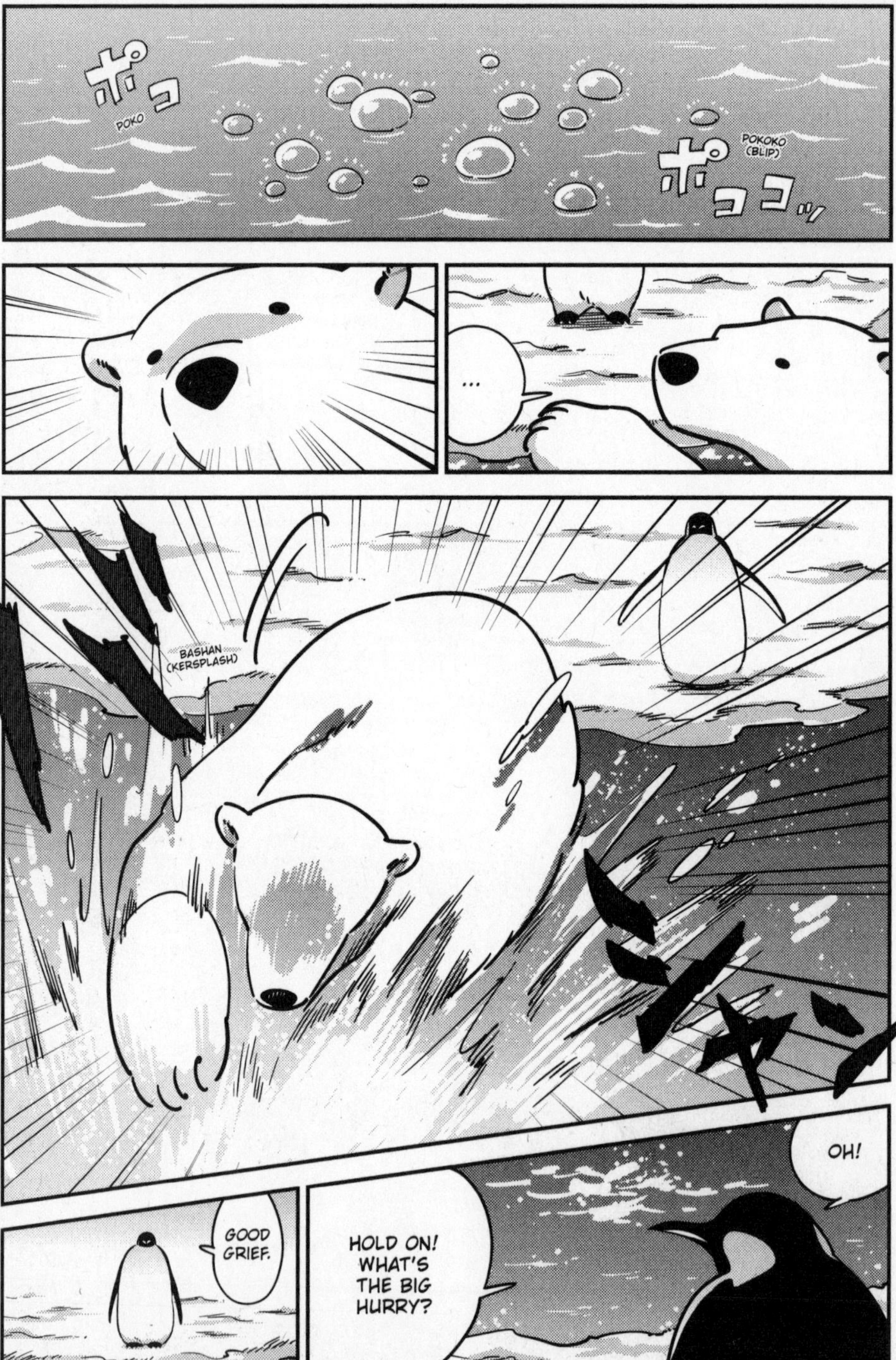
POKOKO (BLIP)
ポココッ
ポコ
POKO
...
BASHAN (KERSPLASH)
OH!
HOLD ON! WHAT'S THE BIG HURRY?
GOOD GRIEF.

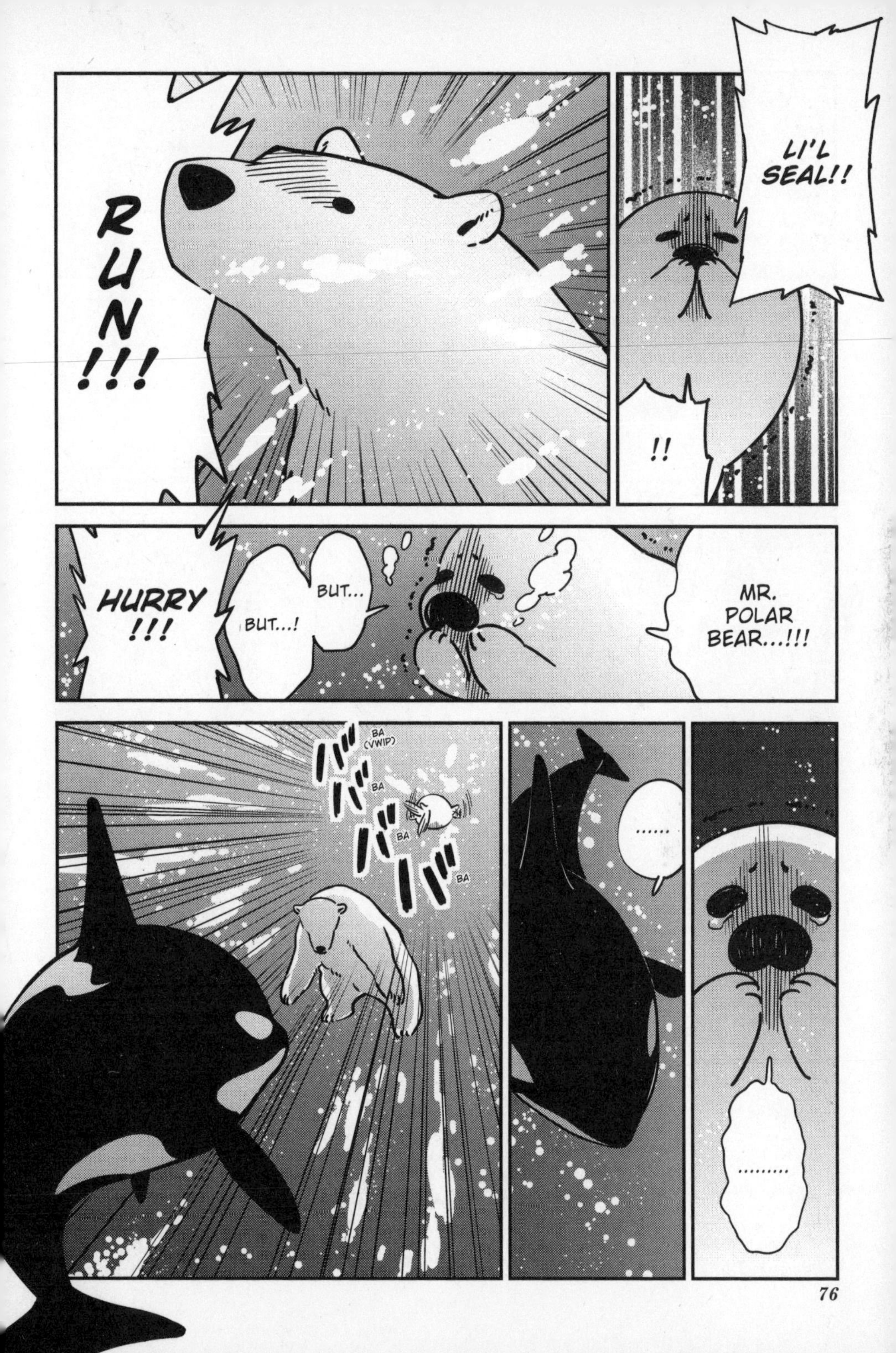

LI'L SEAL!!
!!
RUN!!!
MR. POLAR BEAR...!!!
BUT...
BUT...!
HURRY!!!
....
......
BA (VWIP)
BA
BA
BA

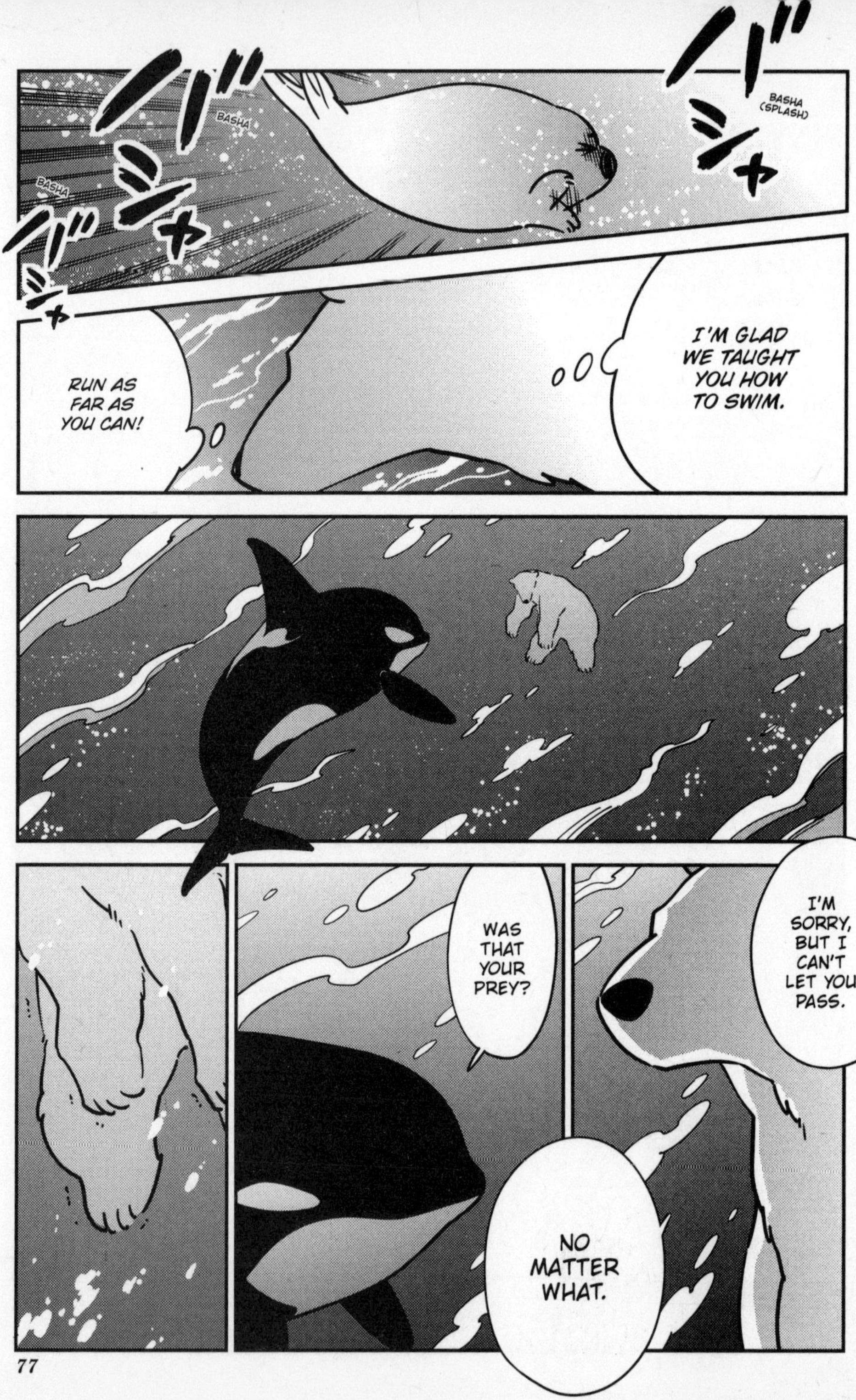
バシャ
BASHA (SPLASH)
バシャ
BASHA
バシャ
BASHA
I'M GLAD WE TAUGHT YOU HOW TO SWIM.
RUN AS FAR AS YOU CAN!
I'M SORRY, BUT I CAN'T LET YOU PASS.
WAS THAT YOUR PREY?
NO MATTER WHAT.

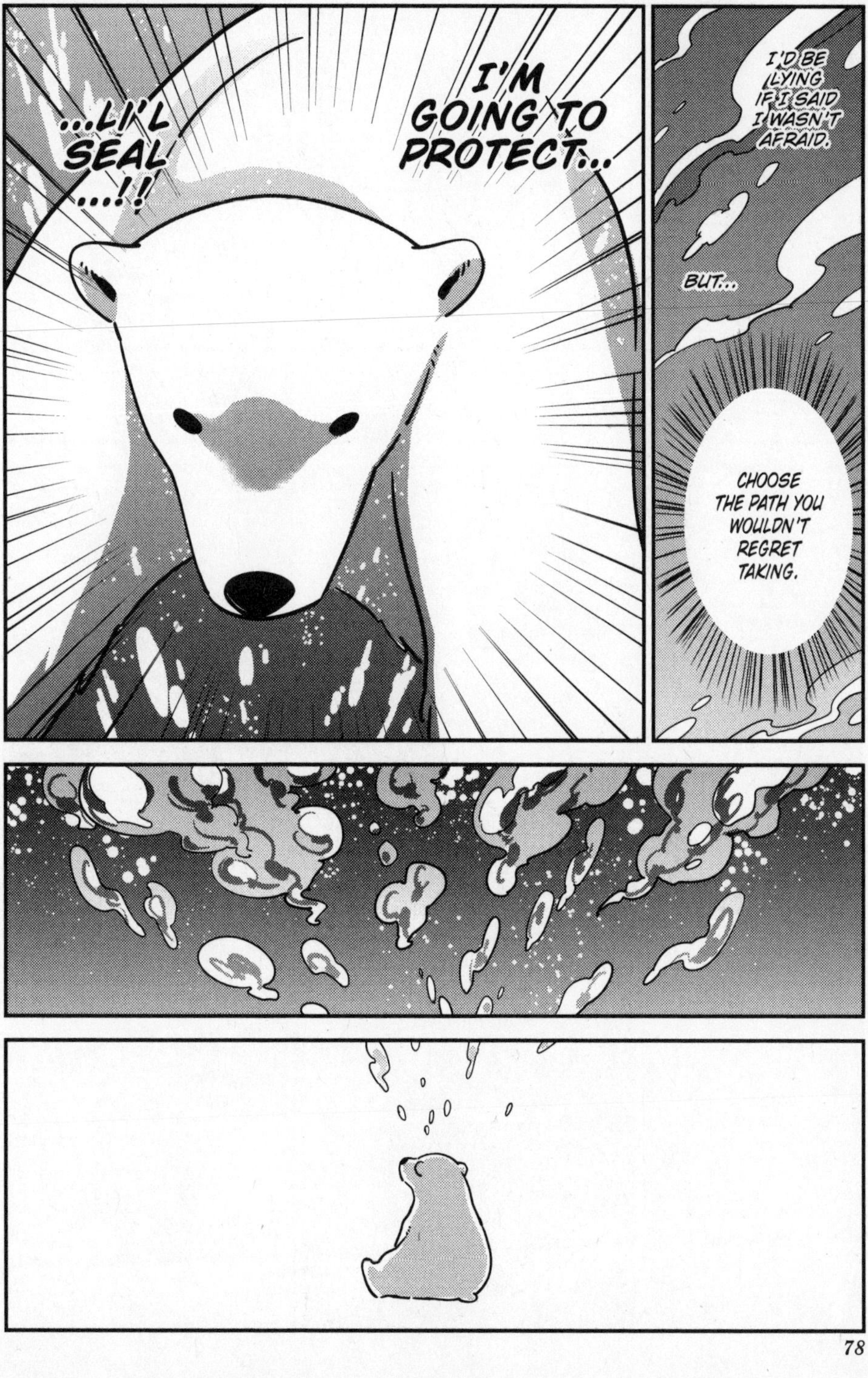
I'D BE LYING IF I SAID I WASN'T AFRAID.
BUT...
CHOOSE THE PATH YOU WOULDN'T REGRET TAKING.
I'M GOING TO PROTECT...
...LI'L SEAL ...!!

REASON

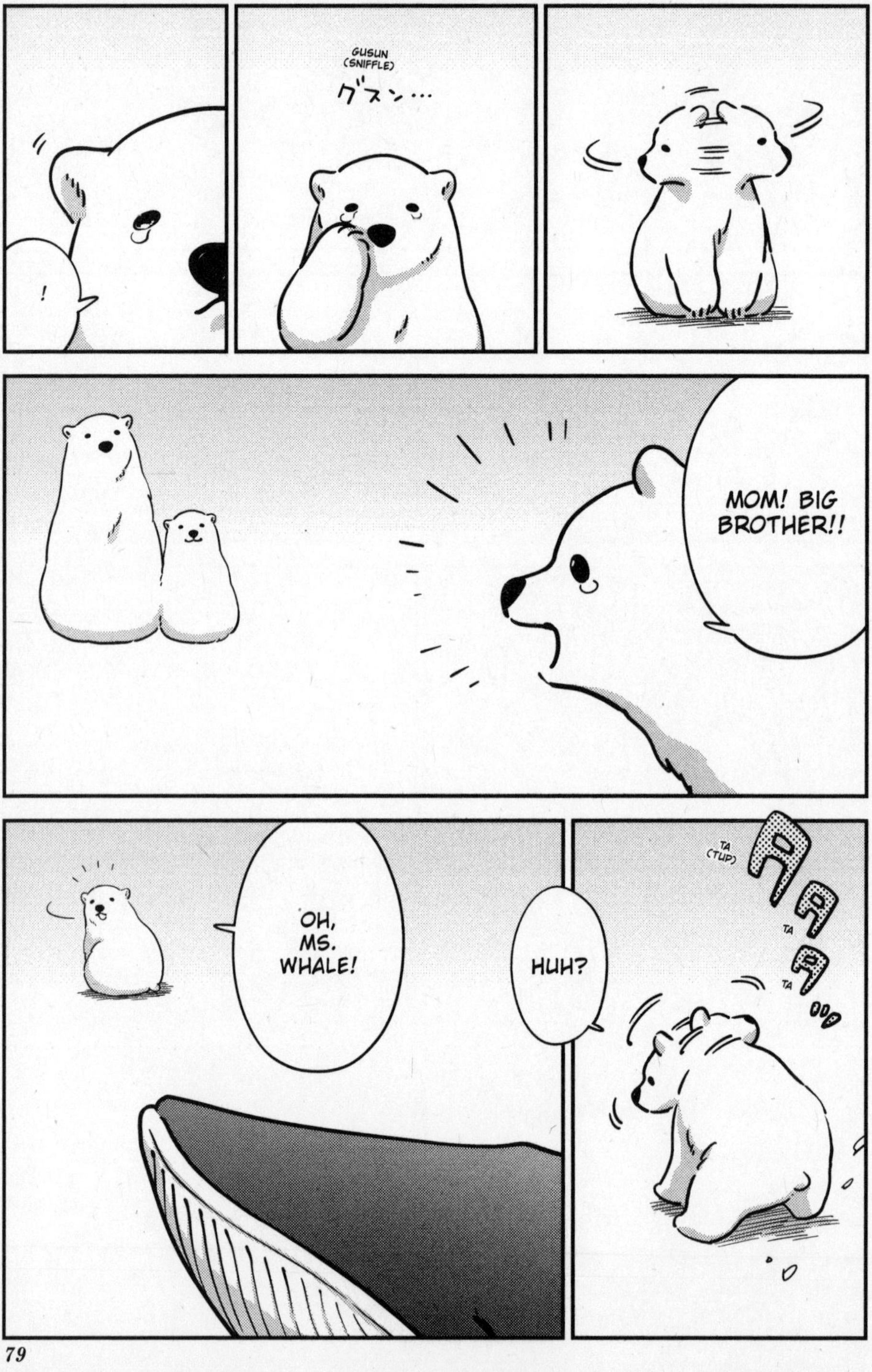
GUSUN
(SNIFFLE)
グスン…
!
MOM! BIG BROTHER!!
TA
(TUP)
TA
TA
HUH?
OH, MS. WHALE!

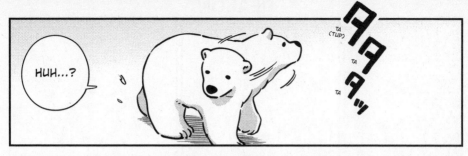

HUH...?

TA TA TA TA (TUP)

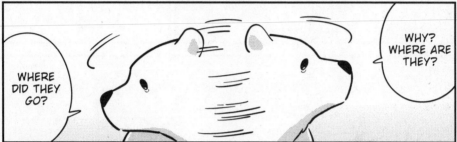

WHY? WHERE ARE THEY?

WHERE DID THEY GO?

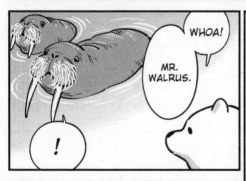

WHOA!

MR. WALRUS.

!

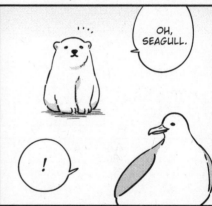

OH, SEAGULL.

!

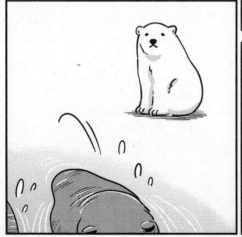

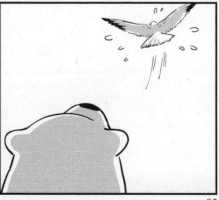

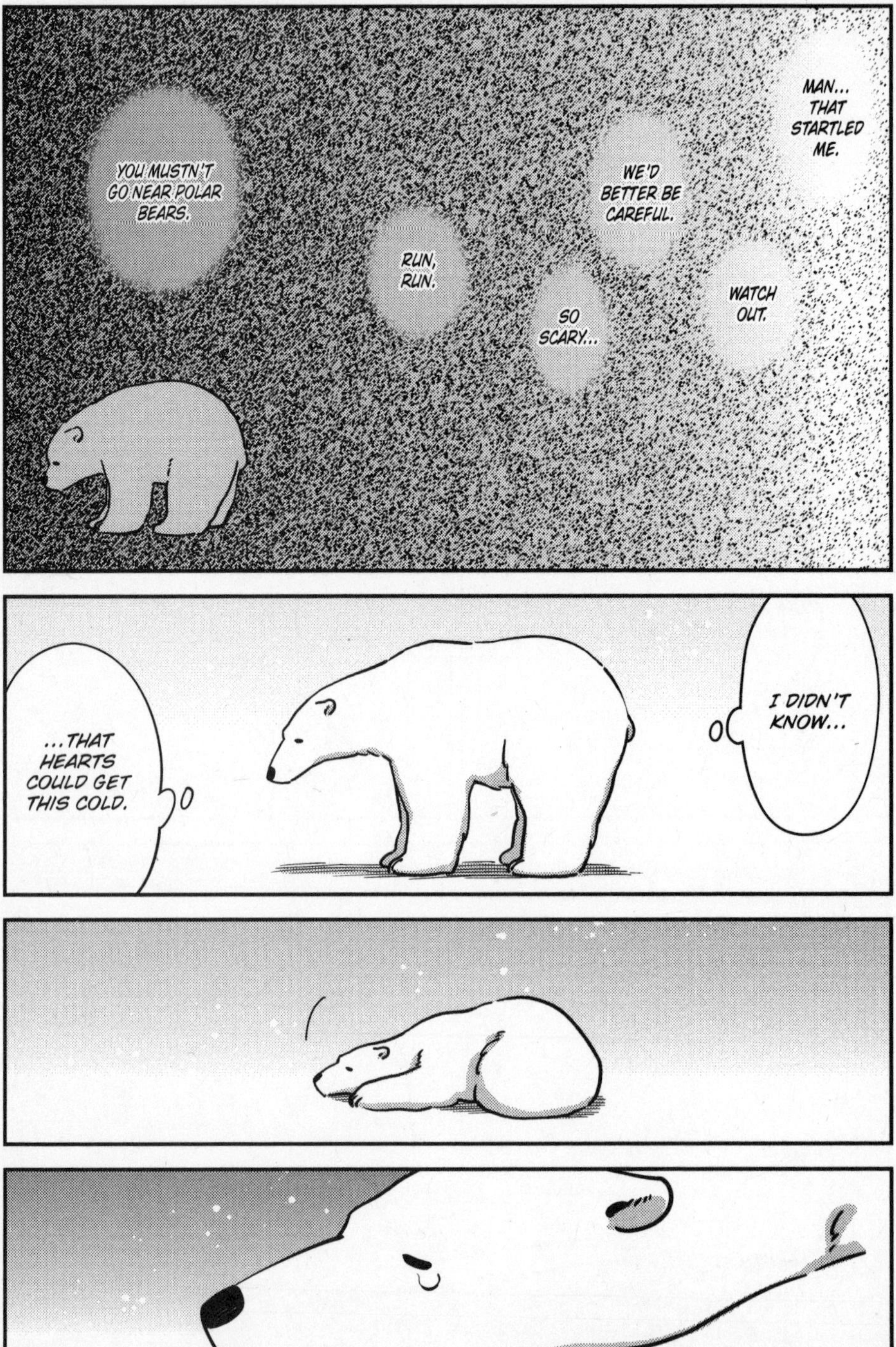
MAN... THAT STARTLED ME.
WATCH OUT.
WE'D BETTER BE CAREFUL.
SO SCARY...
RUN, RUN.
YOU MUSTN'T GO NEAR POLAR BEARS.
I DIDN'T KNOW...
...THAT HEARTS COULD GET THIS COLD.

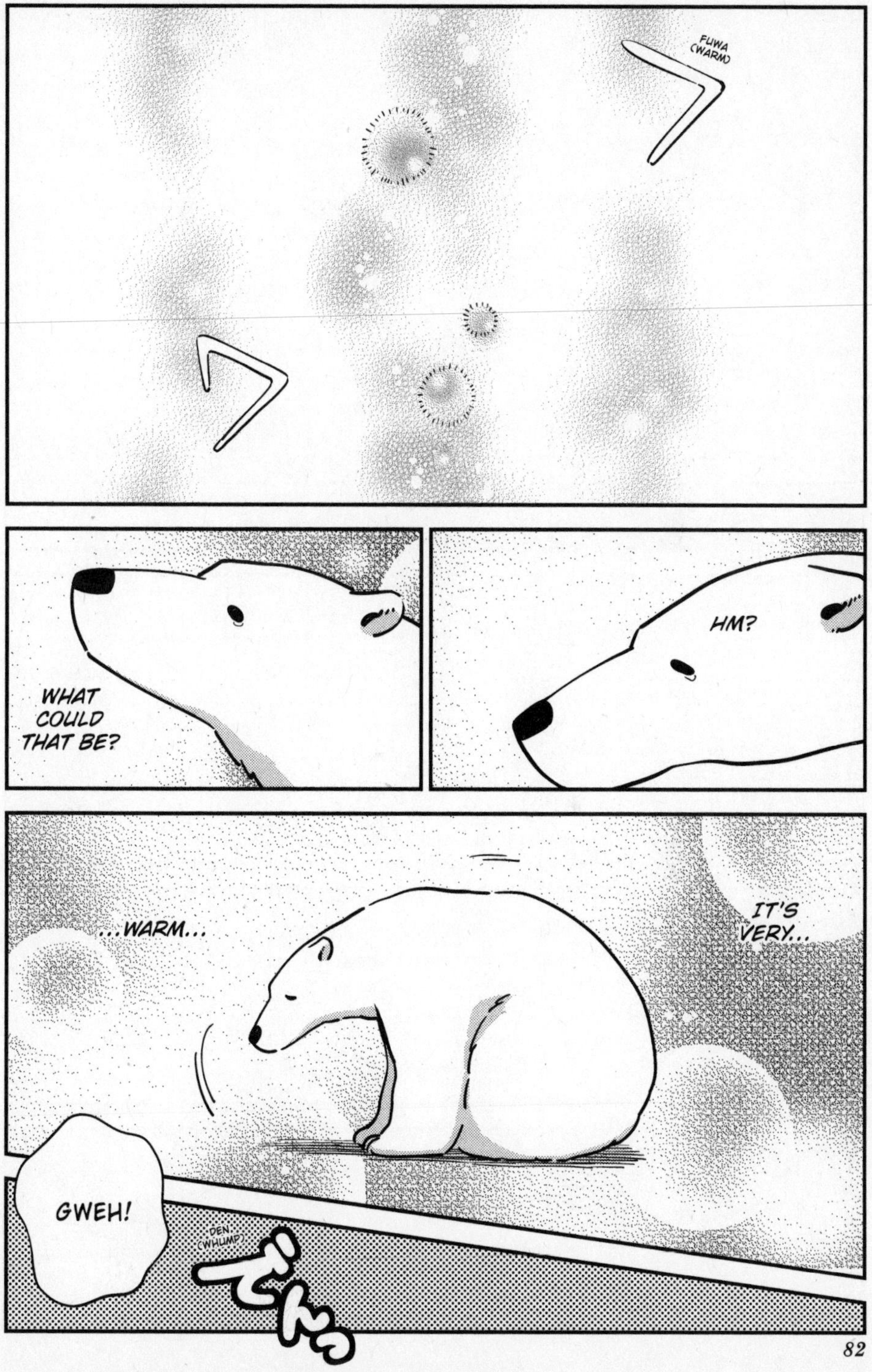
FUWA (WARM)
HM?
WHAT COULD THAT BE?
IT'S VERY...
...WARM...
GWEH!
DEN (WHUMP)
でんっ

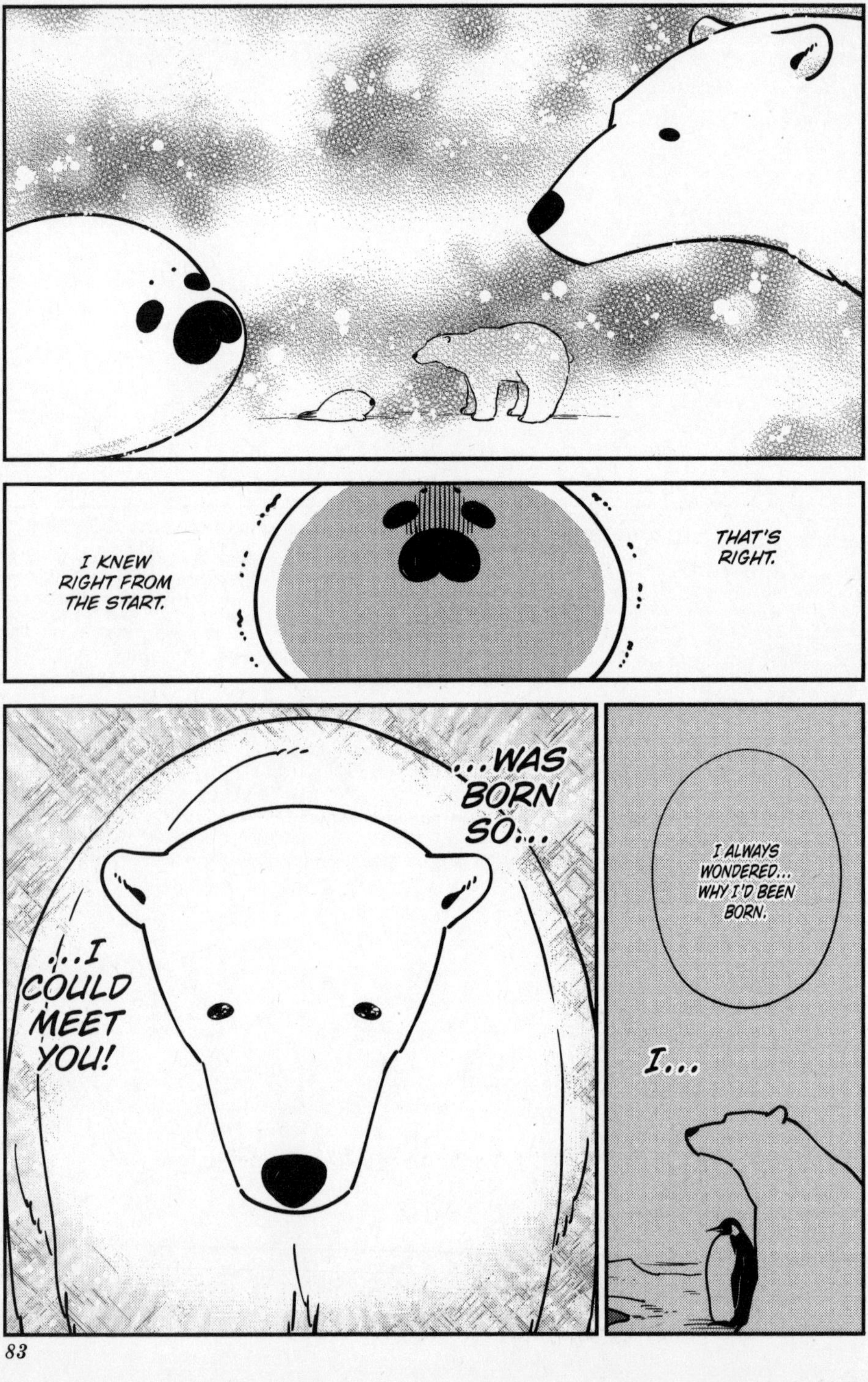
THAT'S RIGHT.
I KNEW RIGHT FROM THE START.
I ALWAYS WONDERED... WHY I'D BEEN BORN.
I...
...WAS BORN SO...
...I COULD MEET YOU!

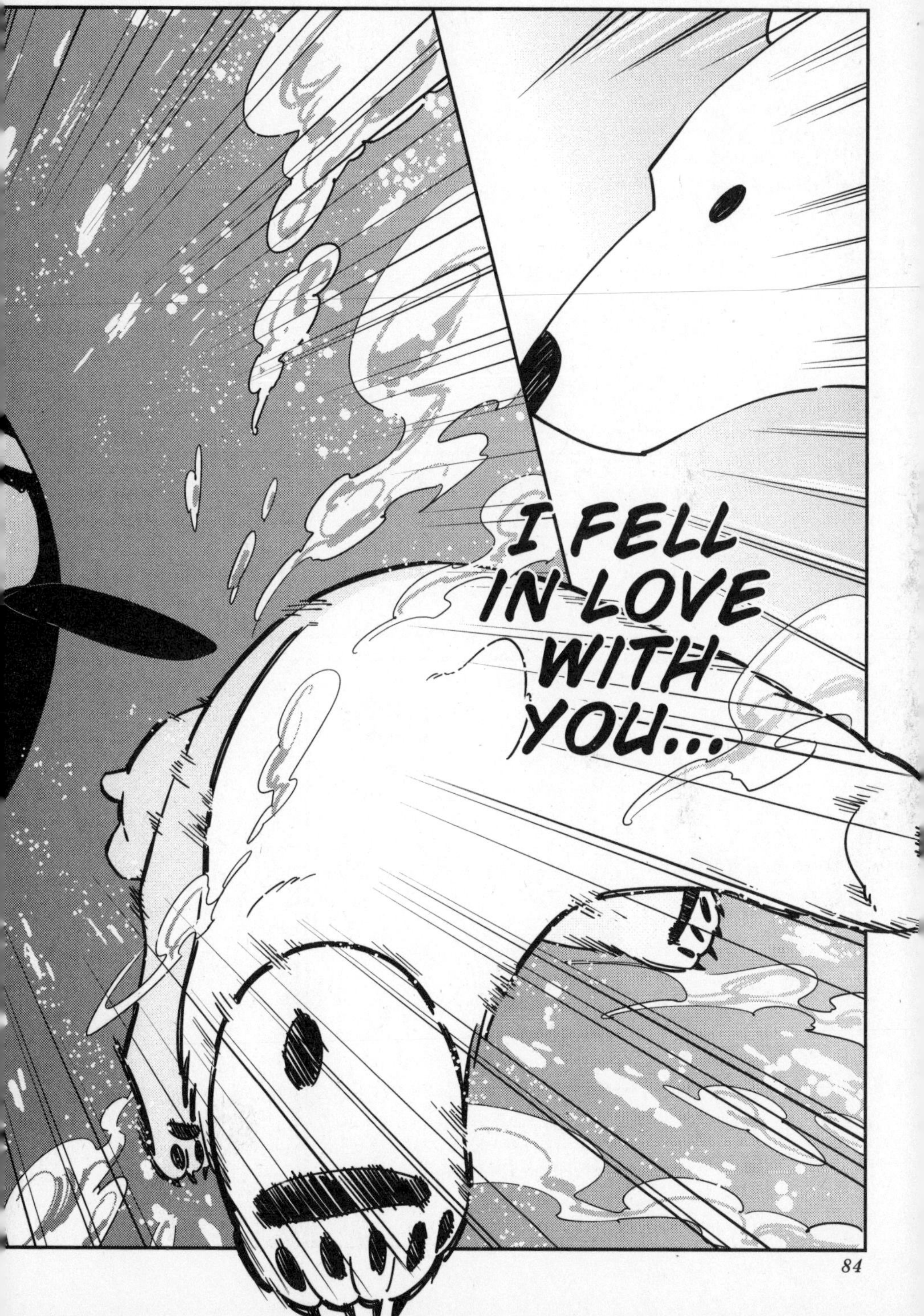
I FELL IN LOVE WITH YOU...

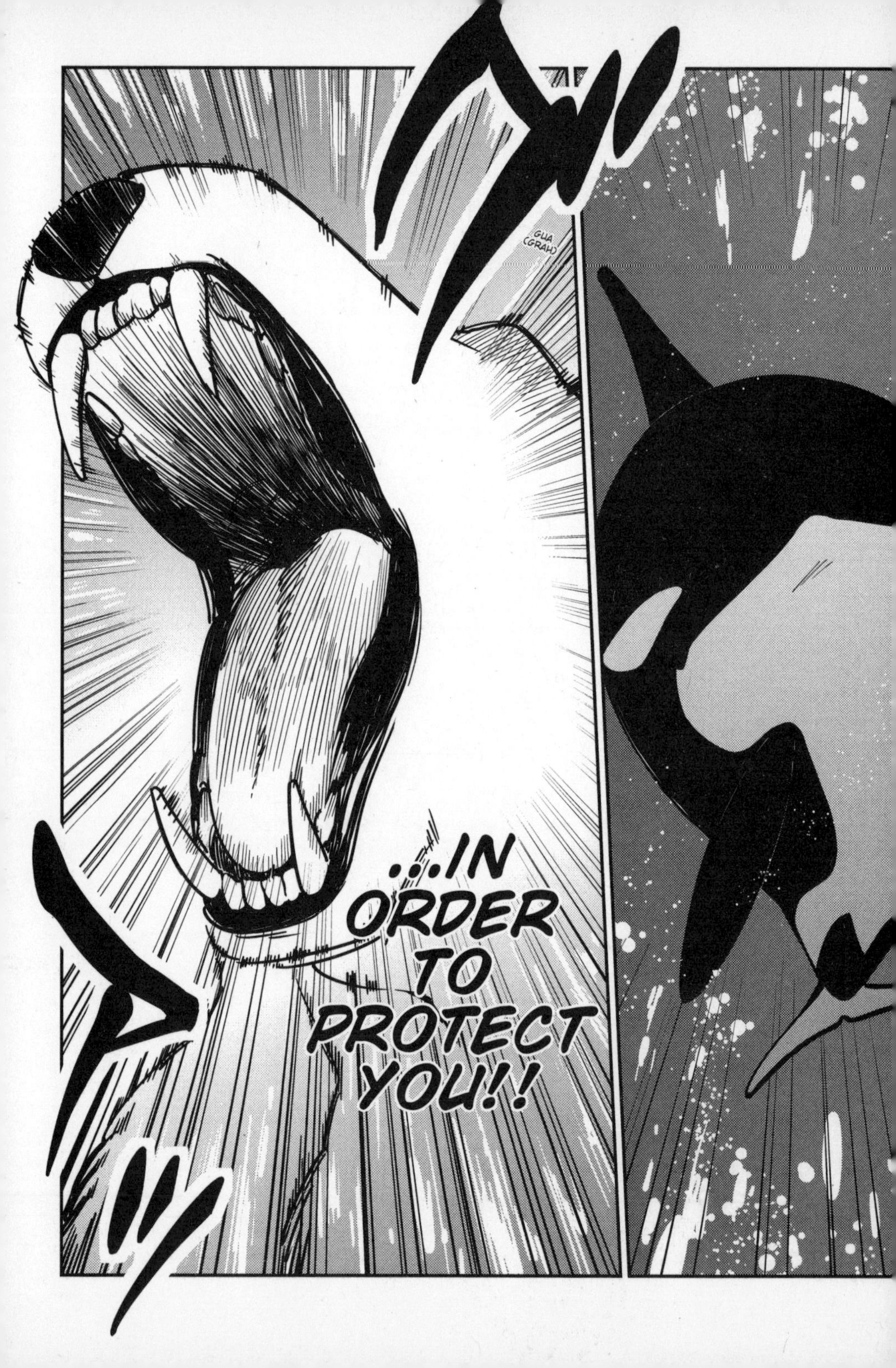
GUA (GRAH)
...IN ORDER TO PROTECT YOU!!

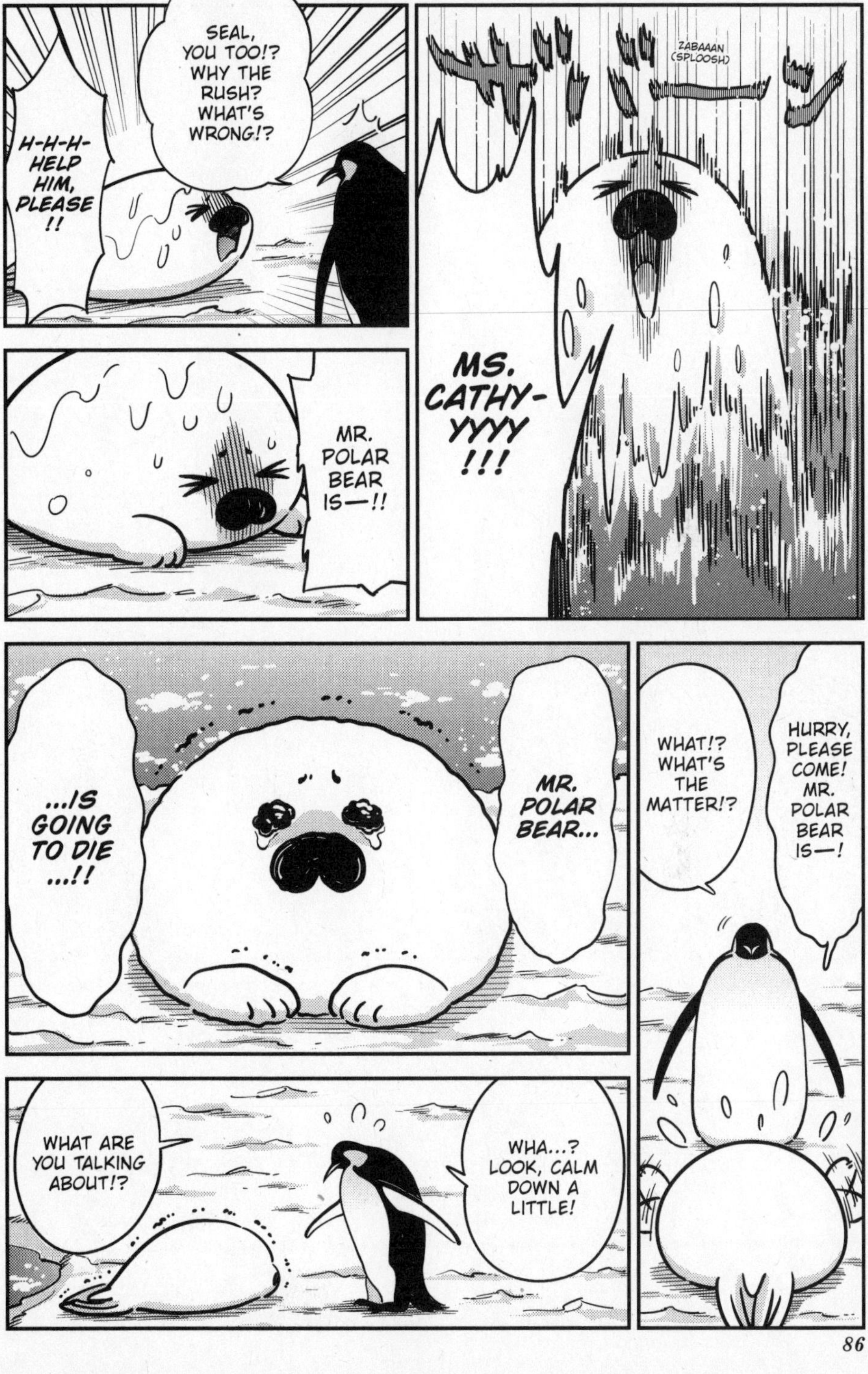
ZABAAAN (SPLOOSH)
MS. CATHY-YYYY!!!
SEAL, YOU TOO!? WHY THE RUSH? WHAT'S WRONG!?
H-H-H-HELP HIM, PLEASE!!
MR. POLAR BEAR IS—!!
HURRY, PLEASE COME! MR. POLAR BEAR IS—!
WHAT!? WHAT'S THE MATTER!?
MR. POLAR BEAR...
...IS GOING TO DIE...!!
WHA...? LOOK, CALM DOWN A LITTLE!
WHAT ARE YOU TALKING ABOUT!?

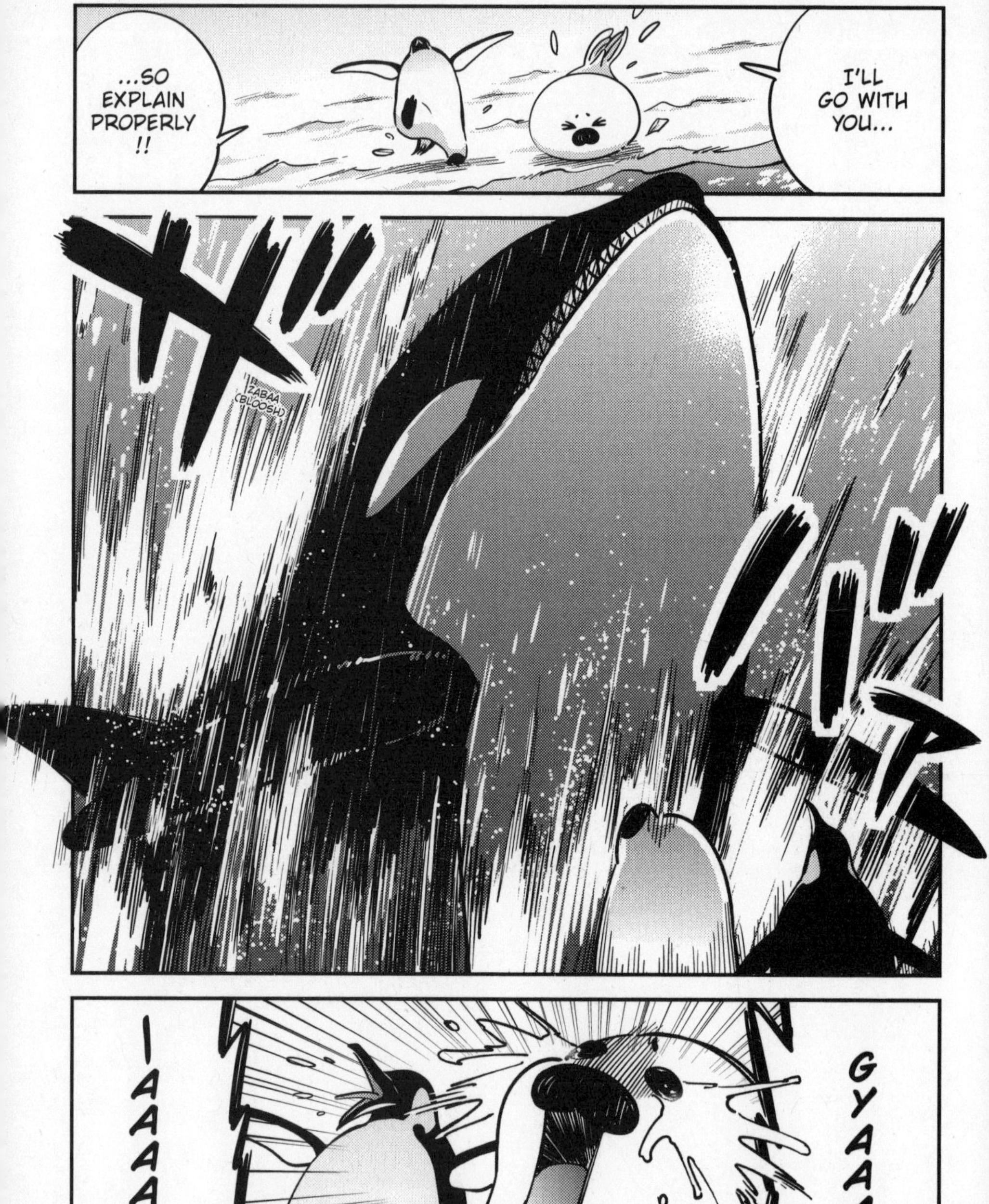
I'LL GO WITH YOU...
...SO EXPLAIN PROPERLY !!
ZABAA (BLOOSH)
GYAAAAAI
IAAAAAAH!!!!

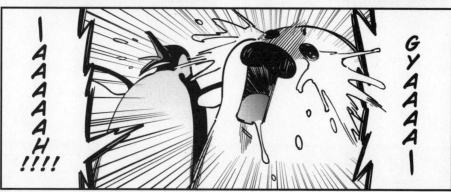

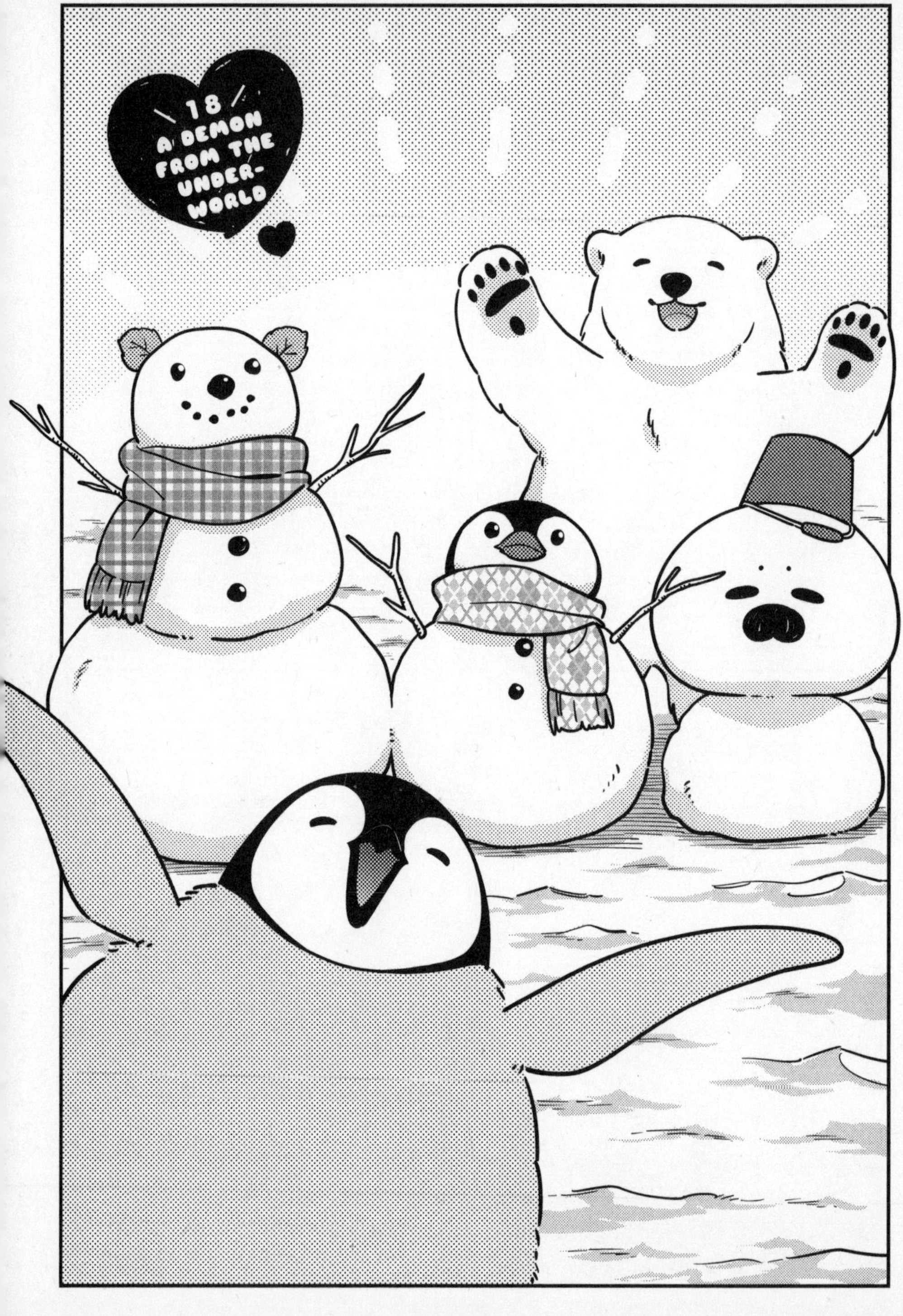
18
A DEMON FROM THE UNDER-WORLD

A DEMON FROM THE UNDERWORLD

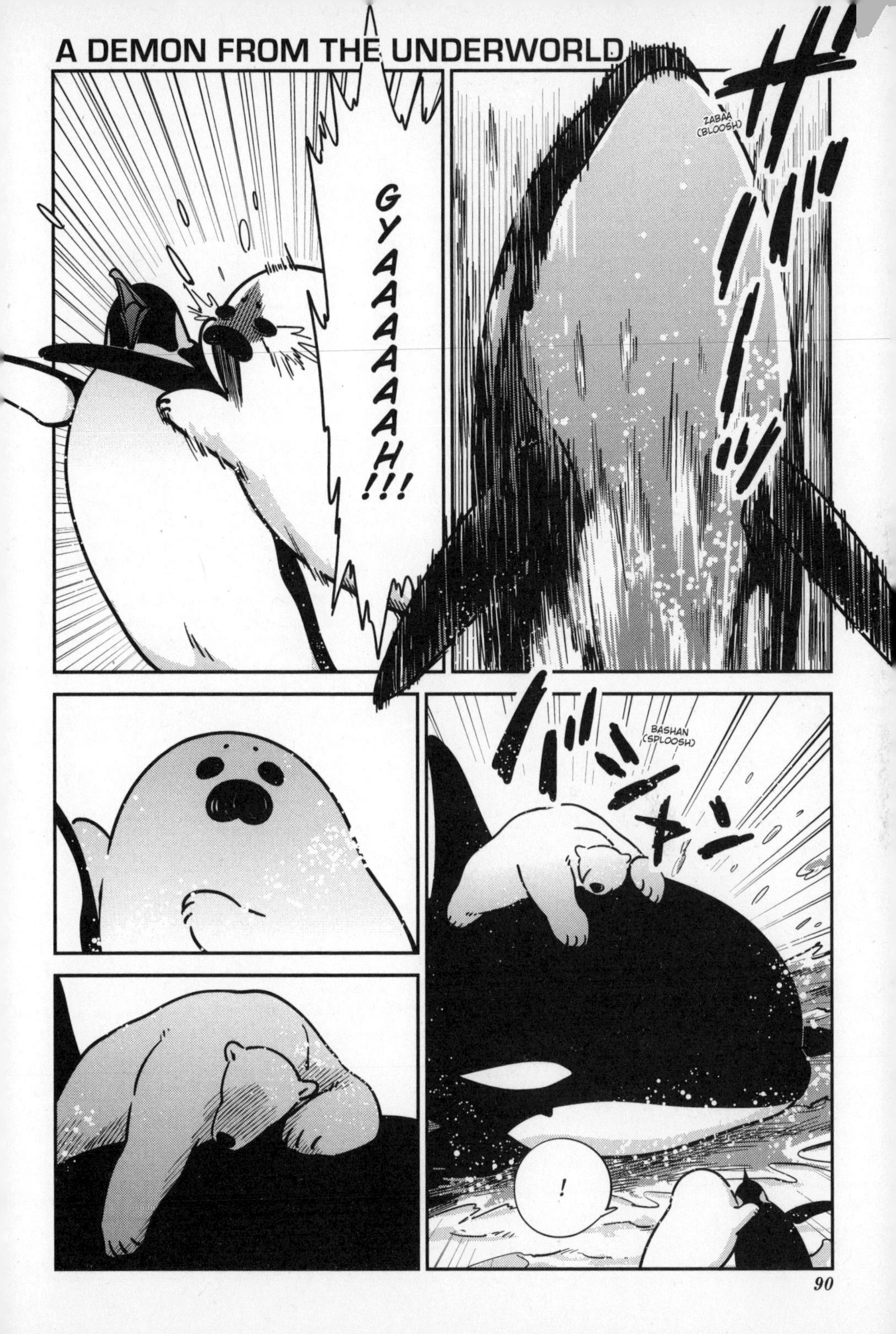
ZABAA (BLOOSH)
GYAAAAAAH!!!
BASHAN (SPLOOSH)
!

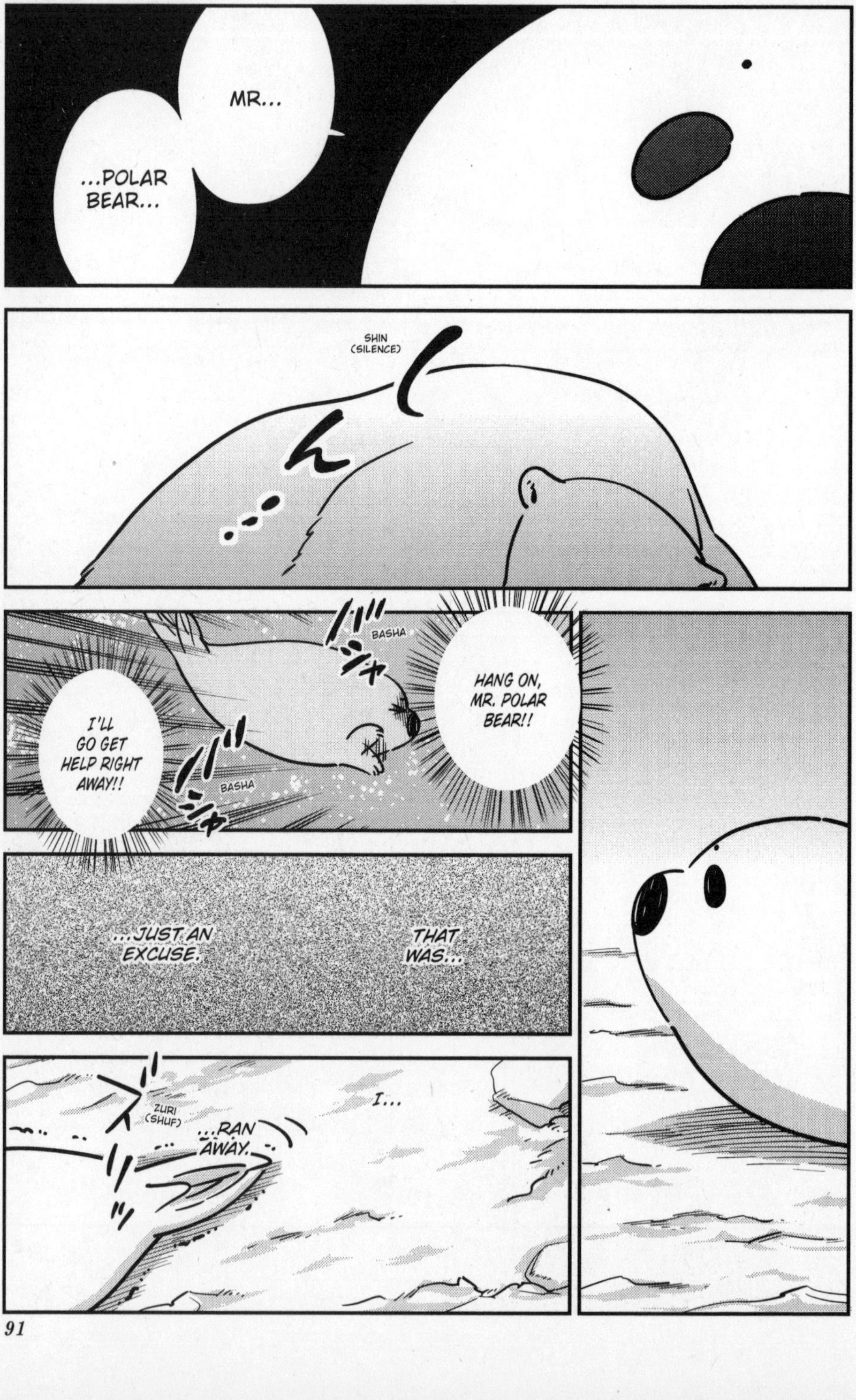

MR...
...POLAR BEAR...
SHIN (SILENCE)
HANG ON, MR. POLAR BEAR!!
BASHA
BASHA
I'LL GO GET HELP RIGHT AWAY!!
THAT WAS...
...JUST AN EXCUSE.
I...
ZURI (SHUF)
...RAN AWAY.

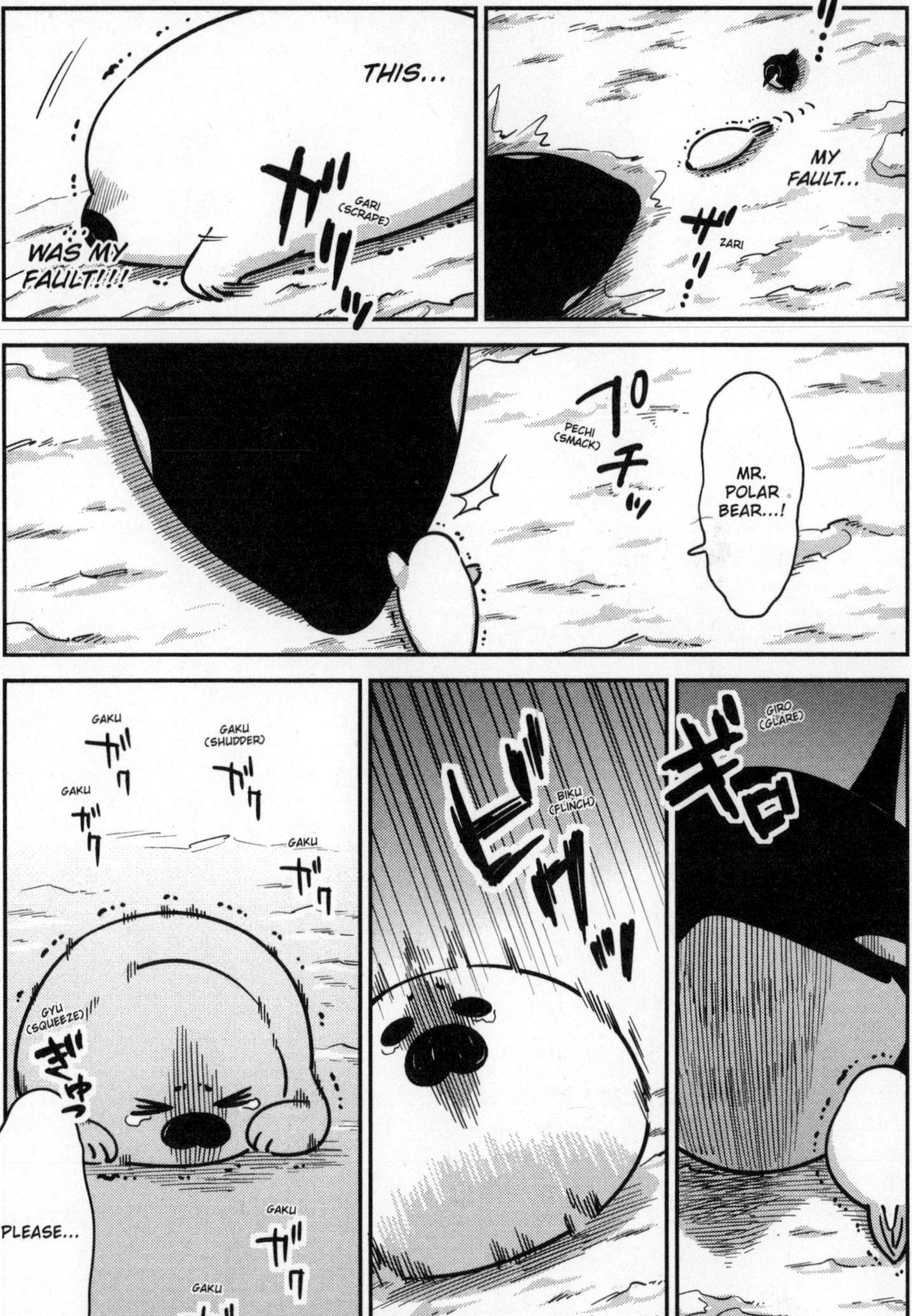
ZARI (SHUF)
MY FAULT...
ZARI
THIS...
GARI (SCRAPE)
WAS MY FAULT!!!!
PECHI (SMACK)
MR. POLAR BEAR...!
GIRO (GLARE)
BIKU (FLINCH)
GAKU
GAKU (SHUDDER)
GAKU
GAKU
GYU (SQUEEZE)
PLEASE...
GAKU
GAKU

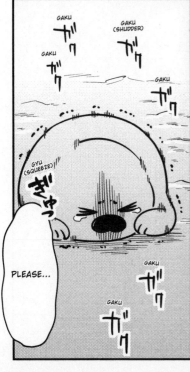

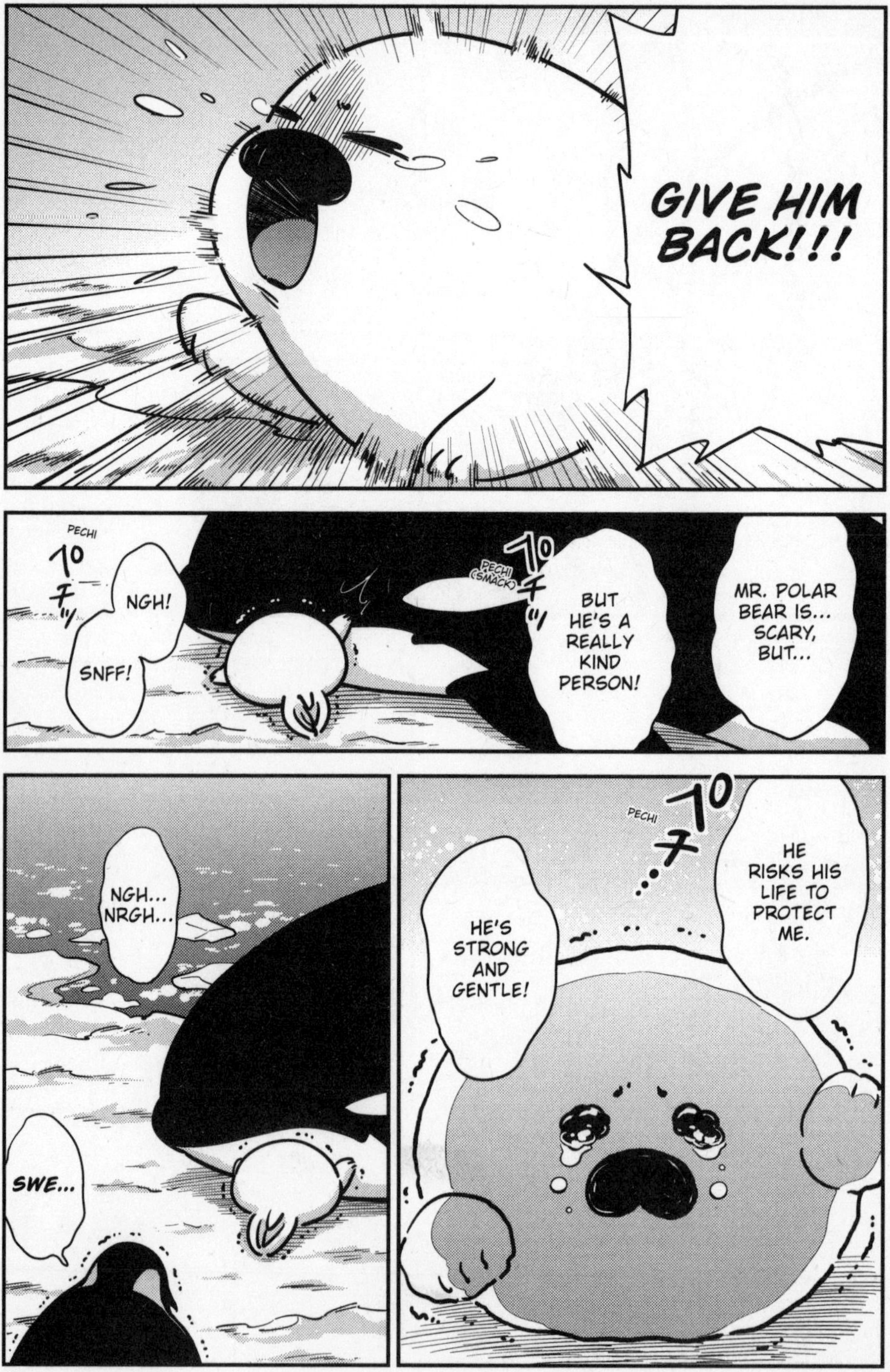
GIVE HIM BACK!!!
MR. POLAR BEAR IS... SCARY, BUT...
ペチッ
PECHI (SMACK)
BUT HE'S A REALLY KIND PERSON!
ペチッ
PECHI
NGH!
SNFF!
ペチ
PECHI
HE RISKS HIS LIFE TO PROTECT ME.
HE'S STRONG AND GENTLE!
NGH... NRGH...
SWE...

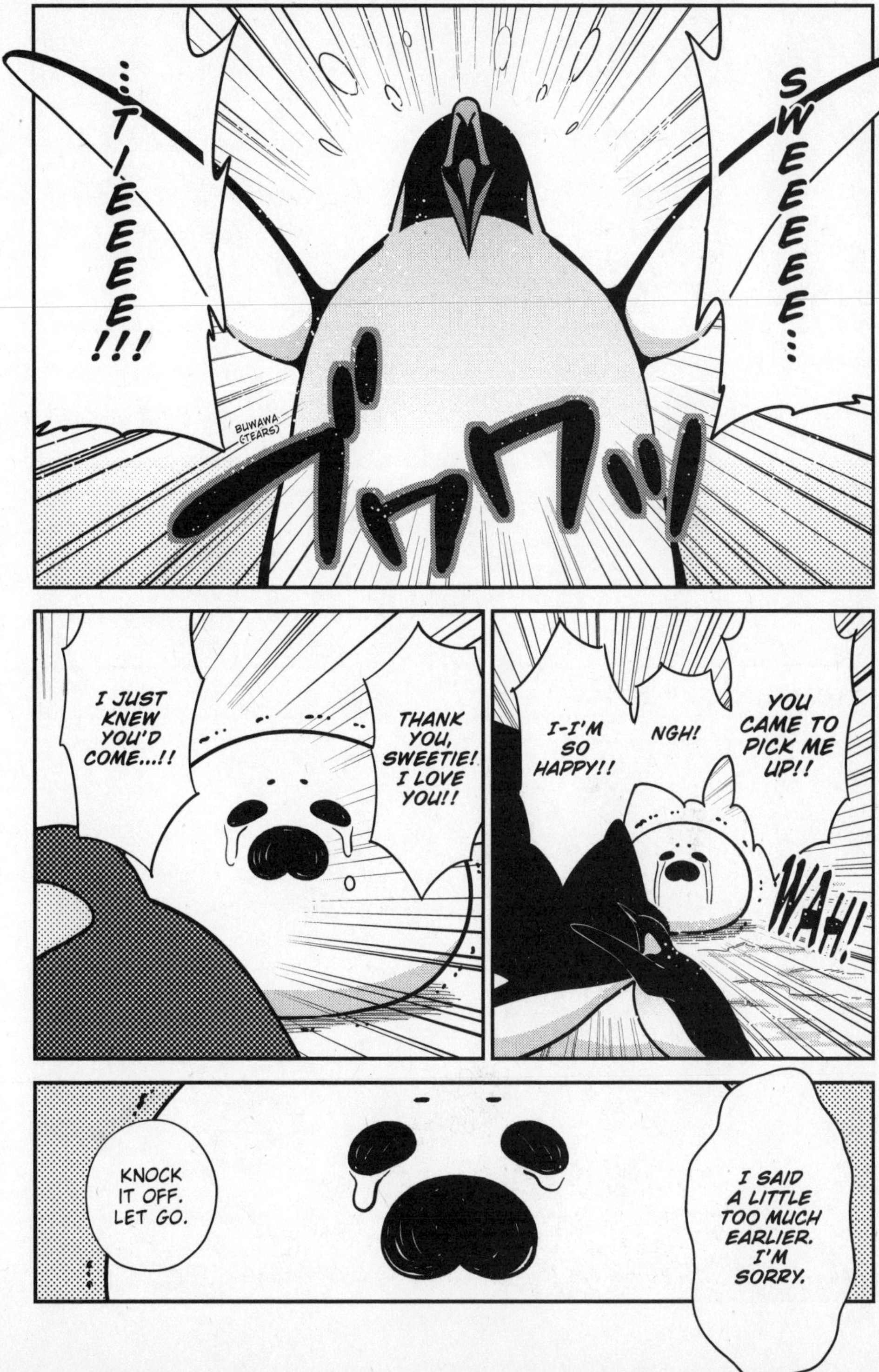
SWEEEEEE...
...T-I-EEEE!!!
ブワワッ
BUWAWA (TEARS)
YOU CAME TO PICK ME UP!!
NGH!
I-I'M SO HAPPY!!
WAH!
THANK YOU, SWEETIE! I LOVE YOU!!
I JUST KNEW YOU'D COME...!!
I SAID A LITTLE TOO MUCH EARLIER. I'M SORRY.
KNOCK IT OFF. LET GO.

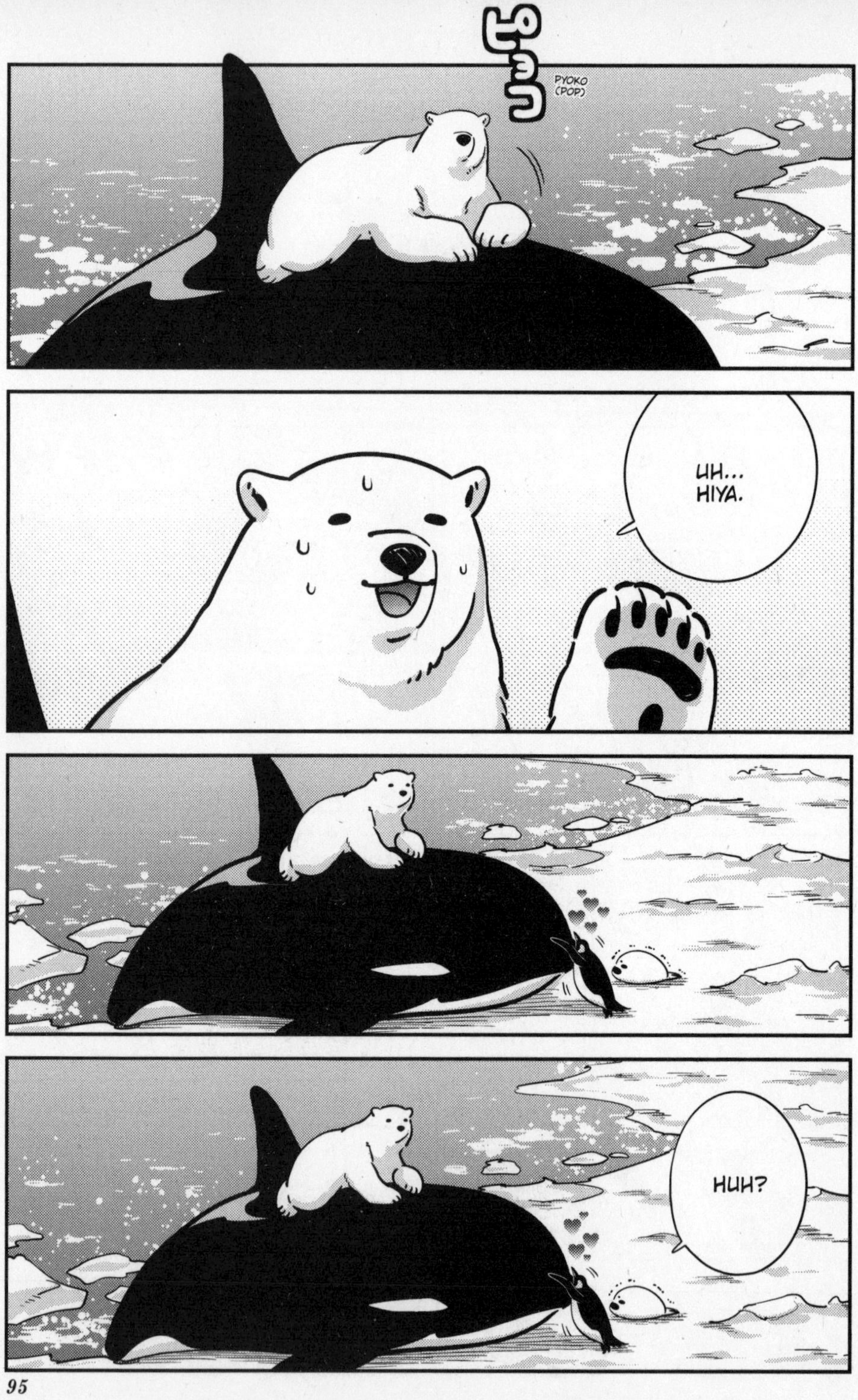
PYOKO
(POP)
UH... HIYA.
HUH?

THE TRUTH

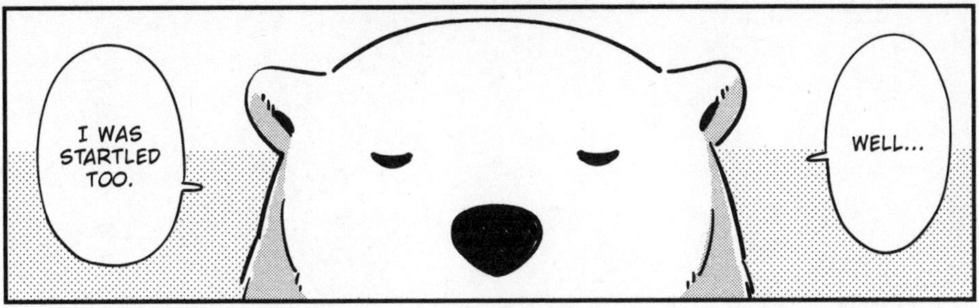
WELL...
I WAS STARTLED TOO.

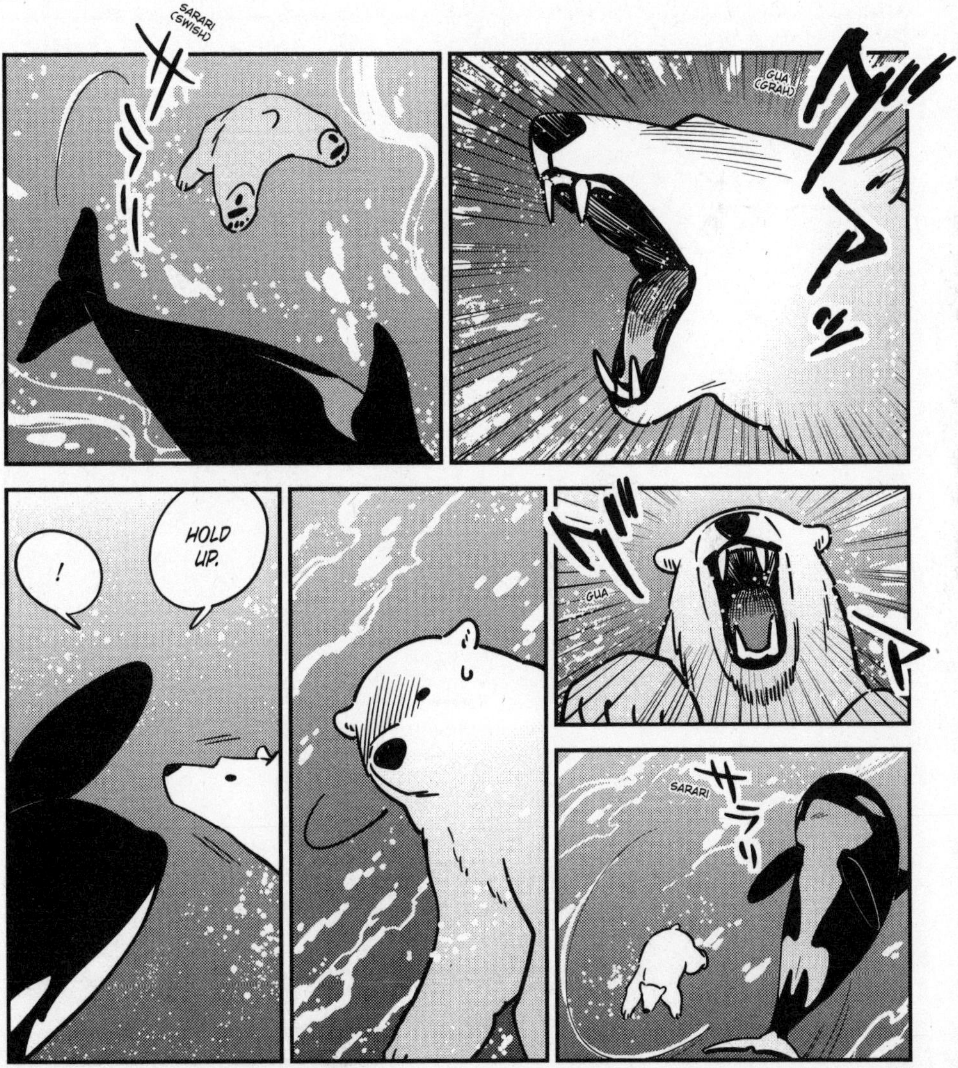
GUA (GRAH)
SARARI (SWISH)
GUA
SARARI
HOLD UP.
!

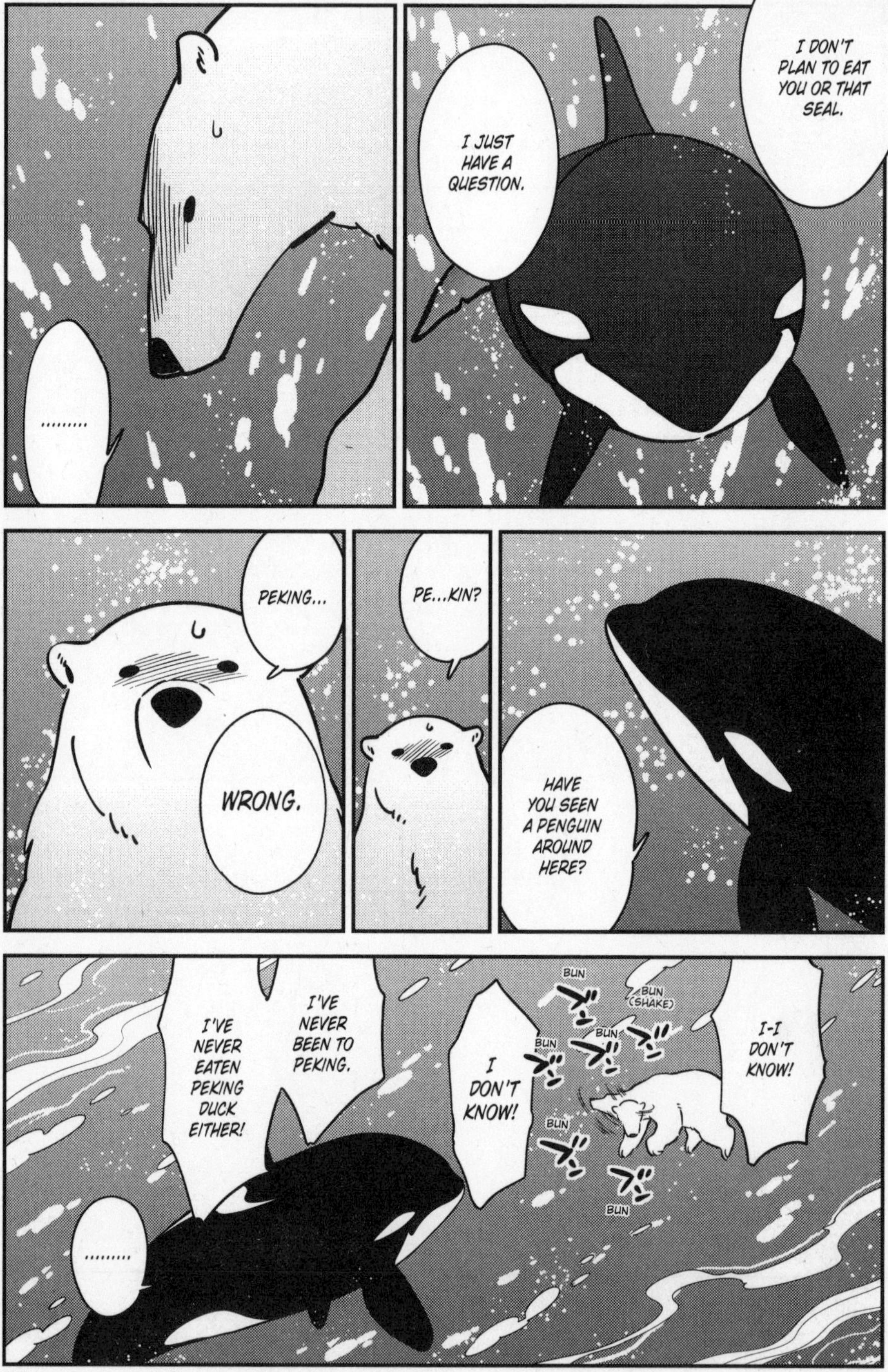
I DON'T PLAN TO EAT YOU OR THAT SEAL.
I JUST HAVE A QUESTION.
....
HAVE YOU SEEN A PENGUIN AROUND HERE?
PE...KIN?
PEKING...
WRONG.
I-I DON'T KNOW!
BUN
BUN (SHAKE)
BUN
BUN
BUN
BUN
I DON'T KNOW!
I'VE NEVER BEEN TO PEKING.
I'VE NEVER EATEN PEKING DUCK EITHER!
....

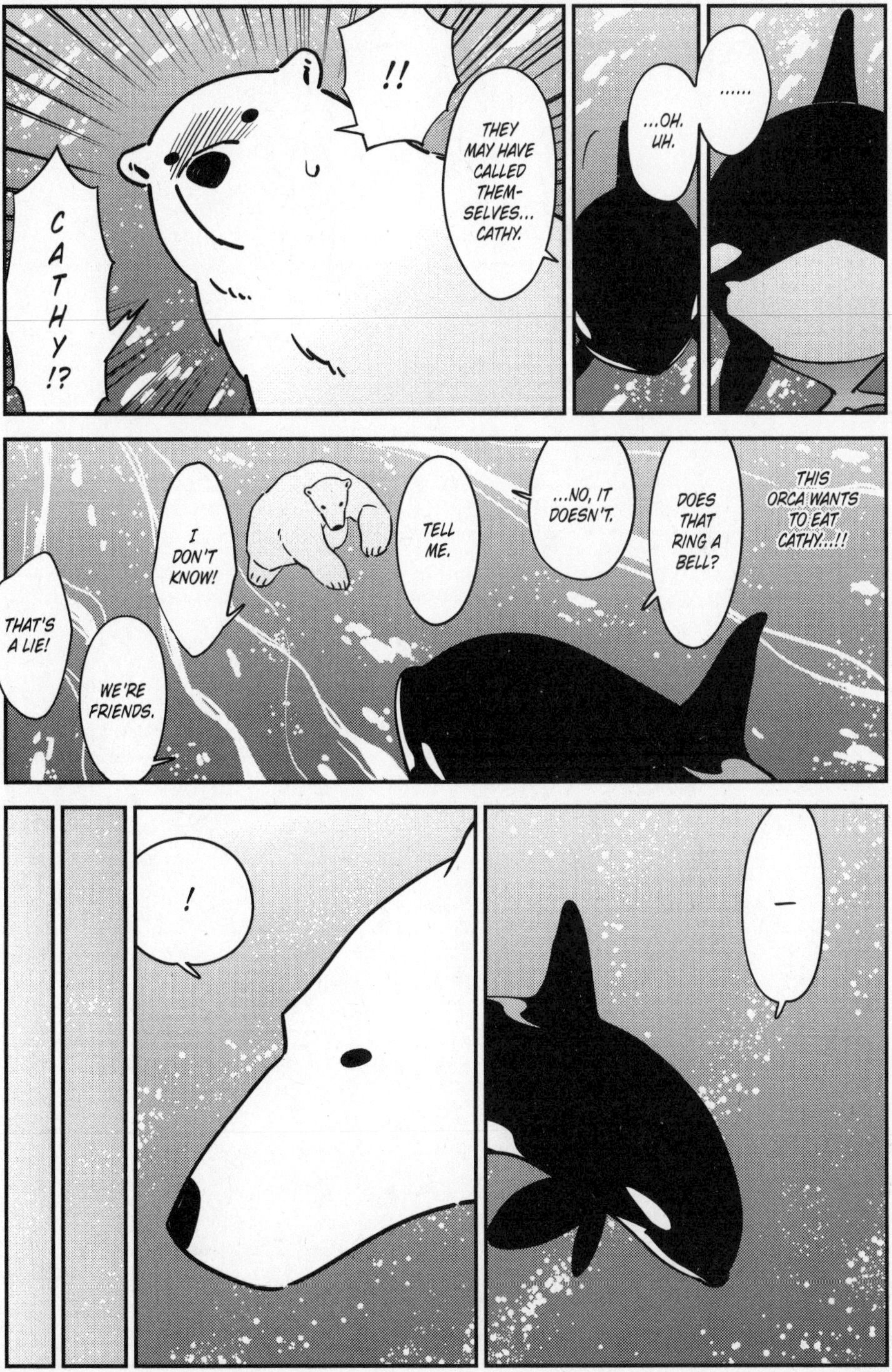
......
...OH. UH.
THEY MAY HAVE CALLED THEMSELVES... CATHY.
!!
CATHY!?
THIS ORCA WANTS TO EAT CATHY...!!
DOES THAT RING A BELL?
...NO, IT DOESN'T.
TELL ME.
I DON'T KNOW!
WE'RE FRIENDS.
THAT'S A LIE!
—
!

CATHY'S SWEETIE

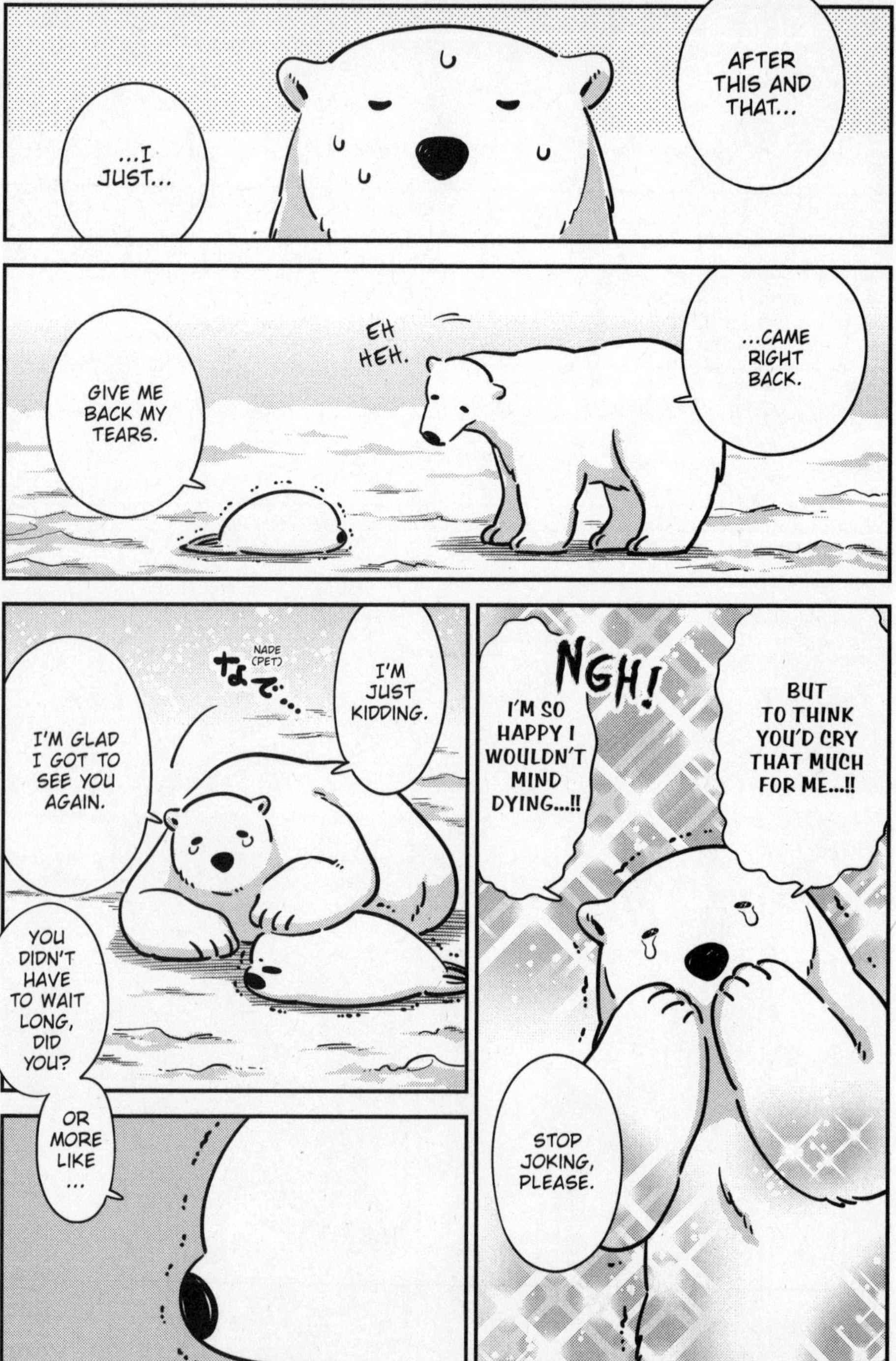

AFTER THIS AND THAT...
...I JUST...
...CAME RIGHT BACK.
EH HEH.
GIVE ME BACK MY TEARS.
BUT TO THINK YOU'D CRY THAT MUCH FOR ME...!!
NGH!
I'M SO HAPPY I WOULDN'T MIND DYING...!!
STOP JOKING, PLEASE.
I'M JUST KIDDING.
なで…
NADE (PET)
I'M GLAD I GOT TO SEE YOU AGAIN.
YOU DIDN'T HAVE TO WAIT LONG, DID YOU?
OR MORE LIKE ...

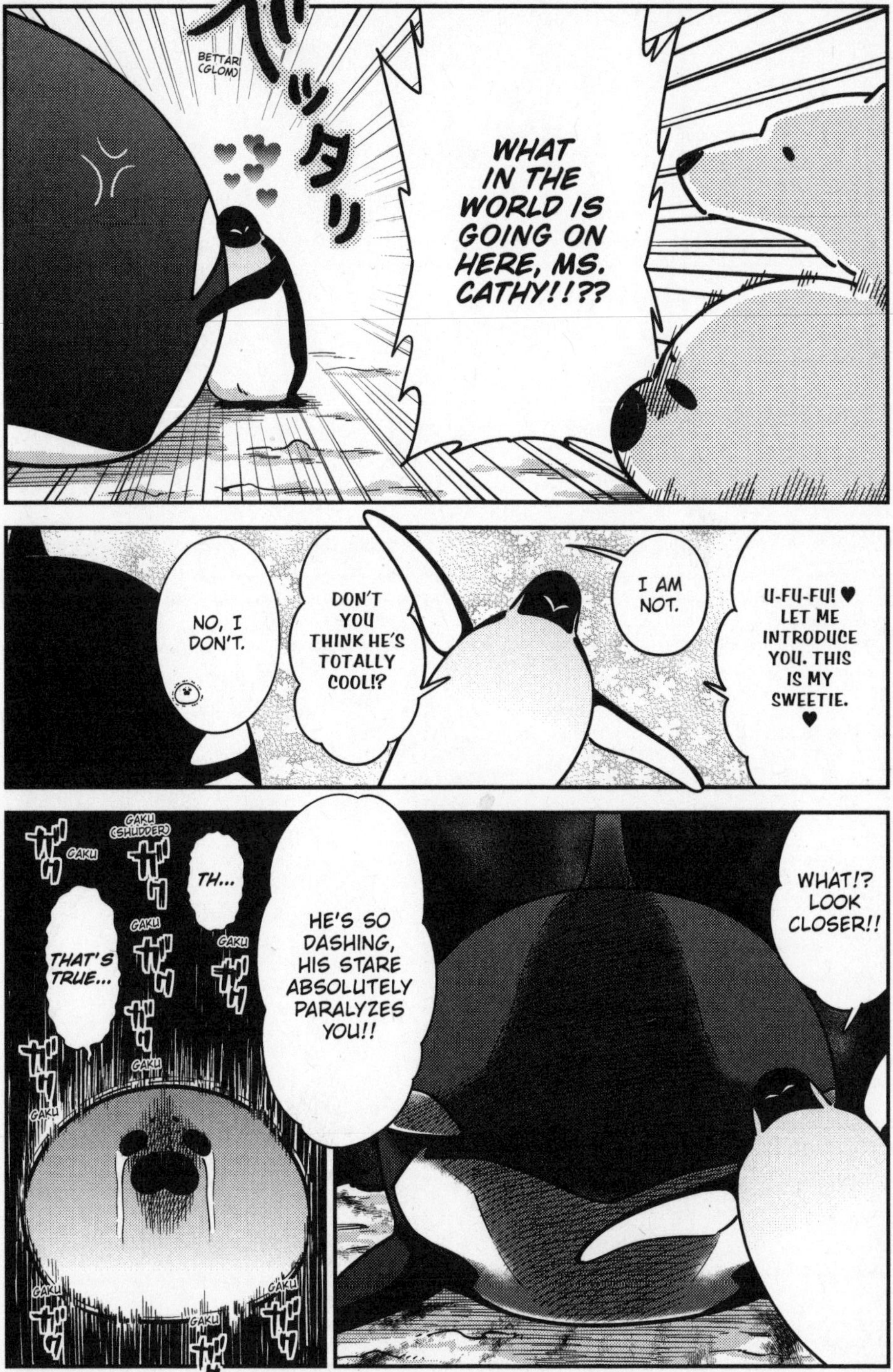
WHAT IN THE WORLD IS GOING ON HERE, MS. CATHY!!??
ベッタリ
BETTARI (GLOM)
U-FU-FU! ♥ LET ME INTRODUCE YOU. THIS IS MY SWEETIE. ♥
I AM NOT.
DON'T YOU THINK HE'S TOTALLY COOL!?
NO, I DON'T.
WHAT!? LOOK CLOSER!!
HE'S SO DASHING, HIS STARE ABSOLUTELY PARALYZES YOU!!
TH...
THAT'S TRUE...
GAKU (SHUDDER)
GAKU

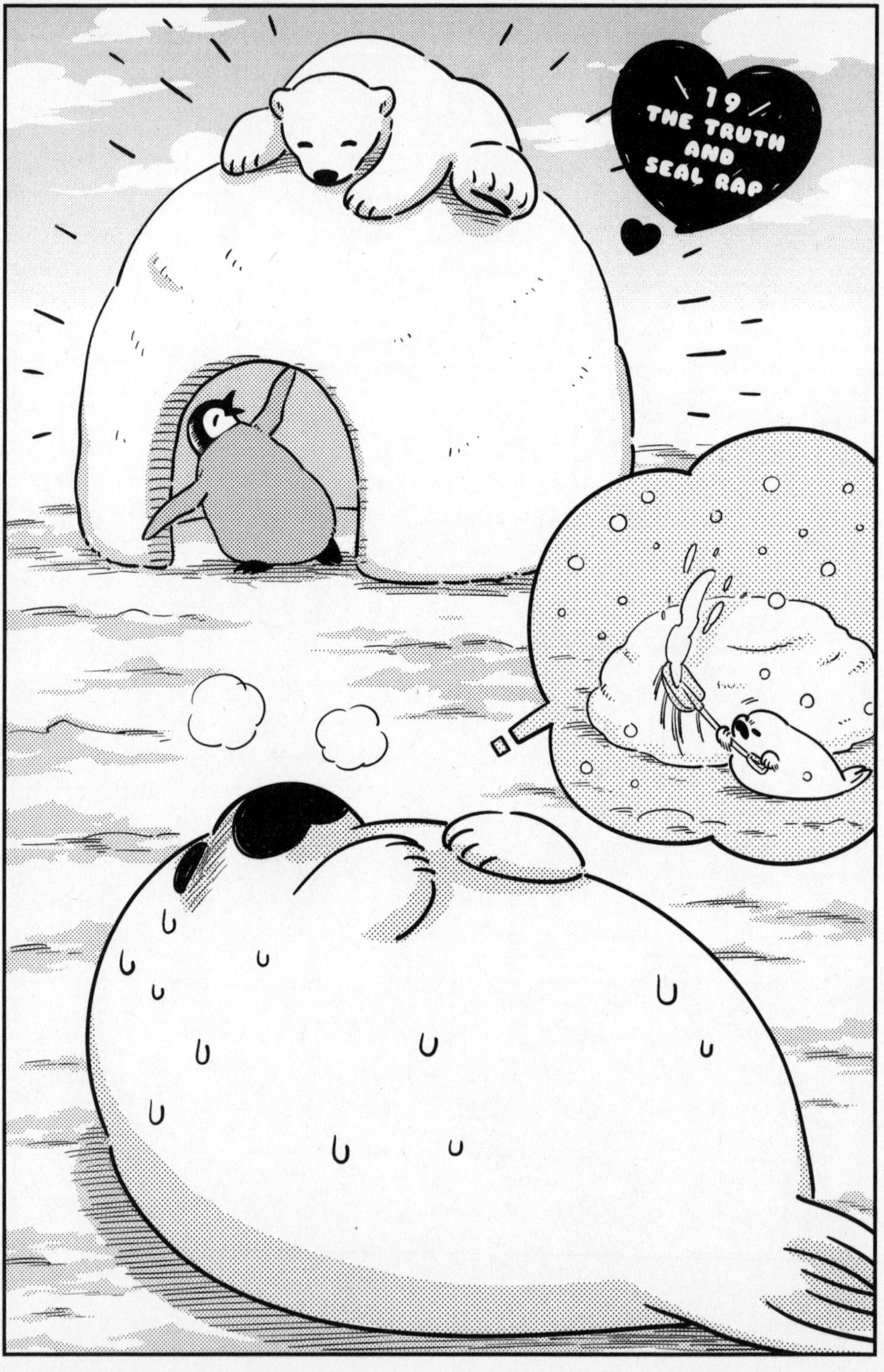
19
THE TRUTH AND SEAL RAP

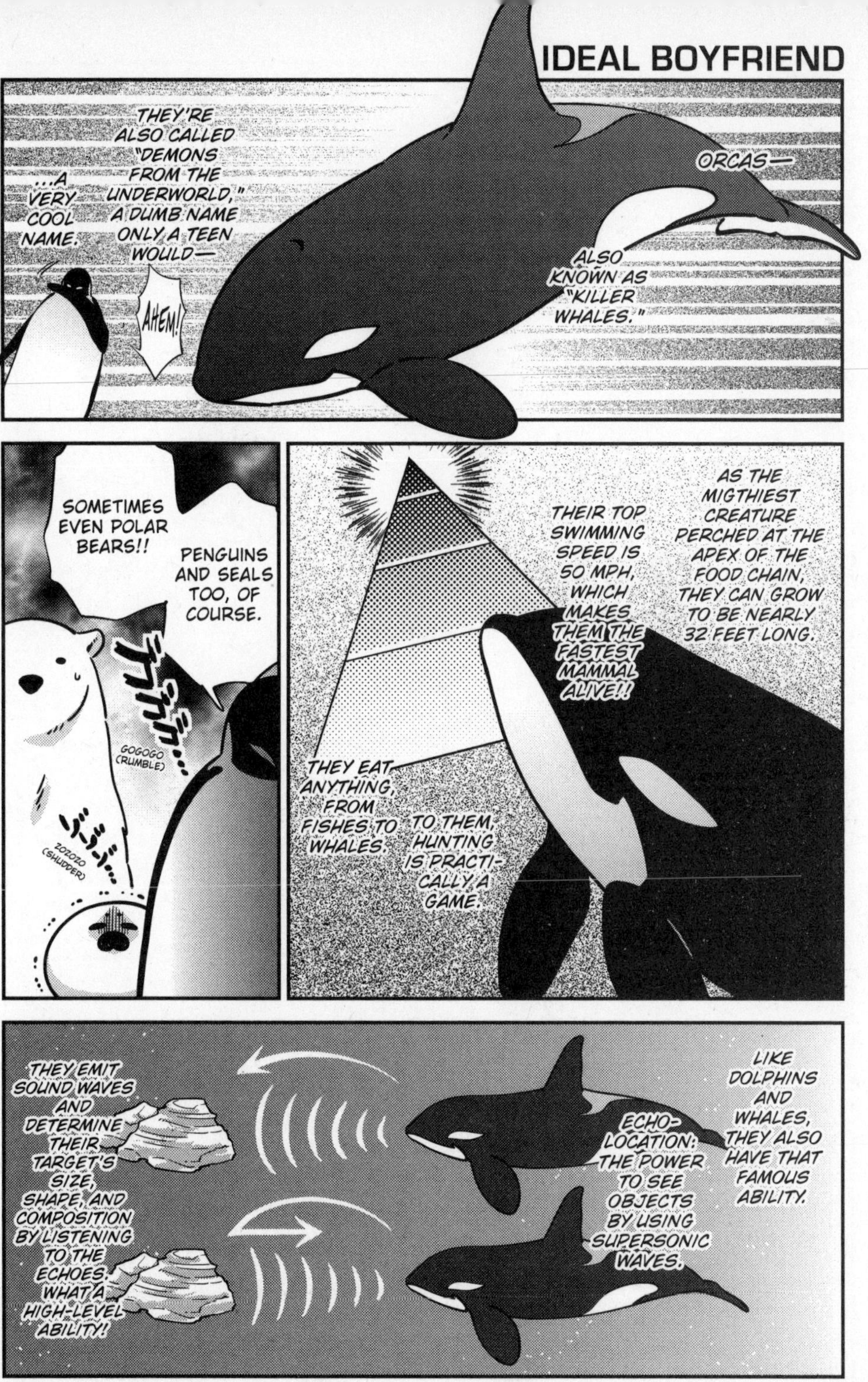
ORCAS—
ALSO KNOWN AS "KILLER WHALES."
THEY'RE ALSO CALLED "DEMONS FROM THE UNDERWORLD," A DUMB NAME ONLY A TEEN WOULD—
AHEM!
...A VERY COOL NAME.
AS THE MIGTHIEST CREATURE PERCHED AT THE APEX OF THE FOOD CHAIN, THEY CAN GROW TO BE NEARLY 32 FEET LONG.
THEIR TOP SWIMMING SPEED IS 50 MPH, WHICH MAKES THEM THE FASTEST MAMMAL ALIVE!!
THEY EAT ANYTHING, FROM FISHES TO WHALES.
TO THEM, HUNTING IS PRACTICALLY A GAME.
PENGUINS AND SEALS TOO, OF COURSE.
SOMETIMES EVEN POLAR BEARS!!
ゴゴゴ…
GOGOGO (RUMBLE)
ゾゾゾ…
ZOZOZO (SHUDDER)
LIKE DOLPHINS AND WHALES, THEY ALSO HAVE THAT FAMOUS ABILITY.
ECHO-LOCATION: THE POWER TO SEE OBJECTS BY USING SUPERSONIC WAVES.
THEY EMIT SOUND WAVES AND DETERMINE THEIR TARGET'S SIZE, SHAPE, AND COMPOSITION BY LISTENING TO THE ECHOES. WHAT A HIGH-LEVEL ABILITY!

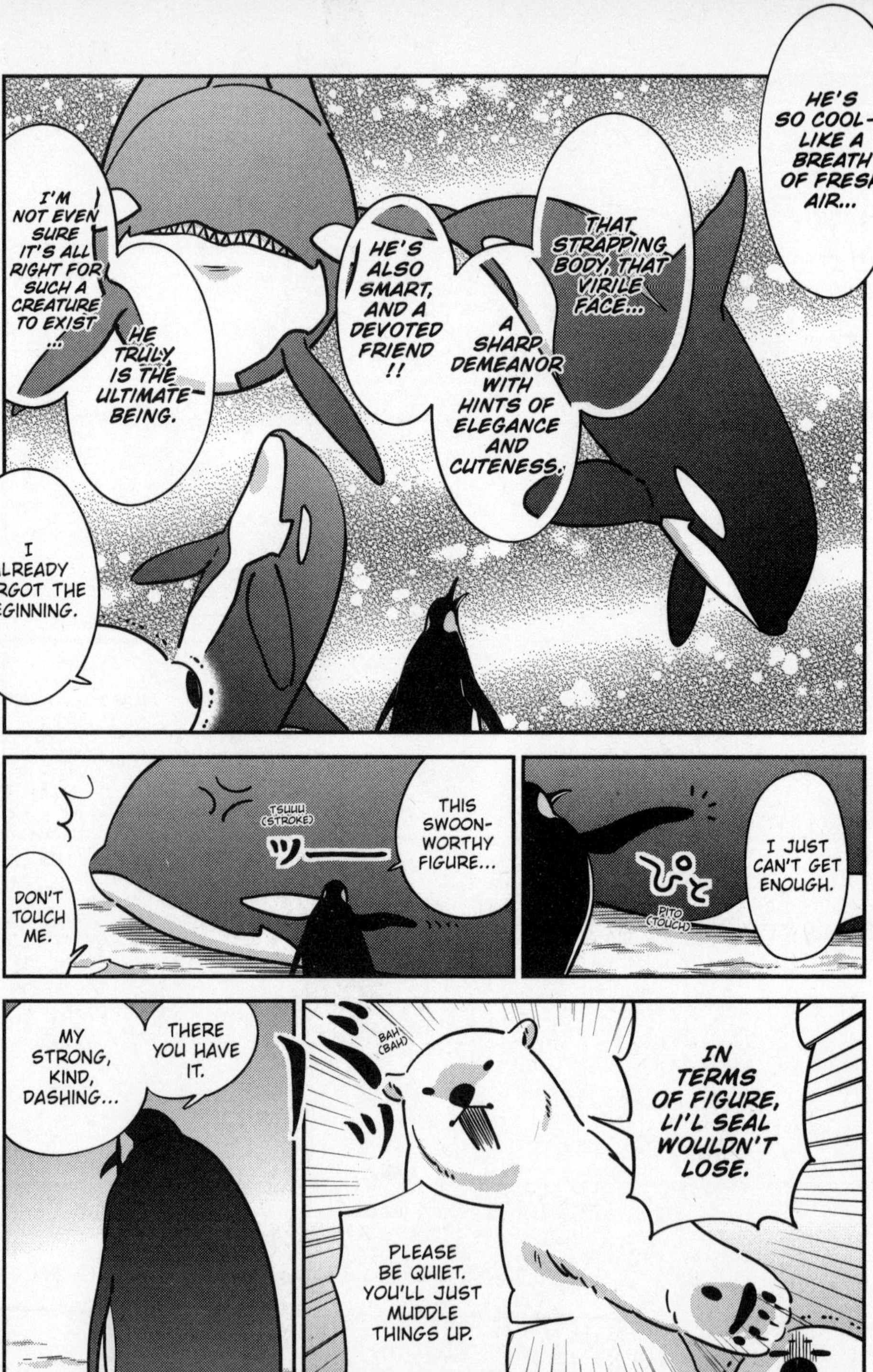
HE'S SO COOL— LIKE A BREATH OF FRESH AIR...
THAT STRAPPING BODY, THAT VIRILE FACE...
A SHARP DEMEANOR WITH HINTS OF ELEGANCE AND CUTENESS.
HE'S ALSO SMART, AND A DEVOTED FRIEND!!
I'M NOT EVEN SURE IT'S ALL RIGHT FOR SUCH A CREATURE TO EXIST...
HE TRULY IS THE ULTIMATE BEING.
I ALREADY FORGOT THE BEGINNING.
I JUST CAN'T GET ENOUGH.
PITO (TOUCH)
THIS SWOON-WORTHY FIGURE...
TSUUU (STROKE)
DON'T TOUCH ME.
IN TERMS OF FIGURE, LI'L SEAL WOULDN'T LOSE.
BAH (BAH)
PLEASE BE QUIET. YOU'LL JUST MUDDLE THINGS UP.
THERE YOU HAVE IT.
MY STRONG, KIND, DASHING...

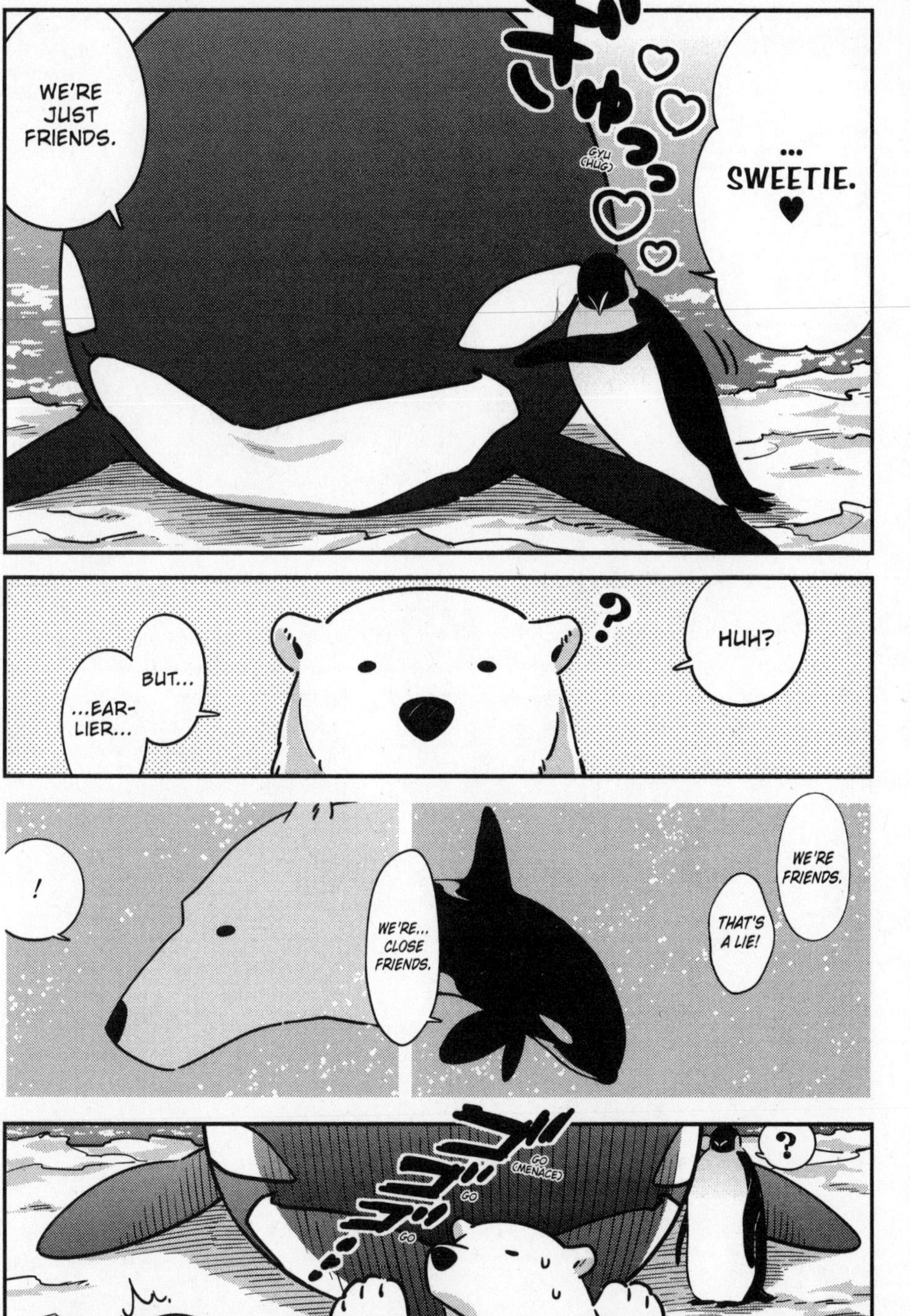
...SWEETIE. ♥
ぎゅっ
GYU (HUG)
WE'RE JUST FRIENDS.
HUH?
?
BUT... ...EAR-LIER...
WE'RE FRIENDS.
THAT'S A LIE!
WE'RE... CLOSE FRIENDS.
!
?
GO (MENACE)
GO
GO

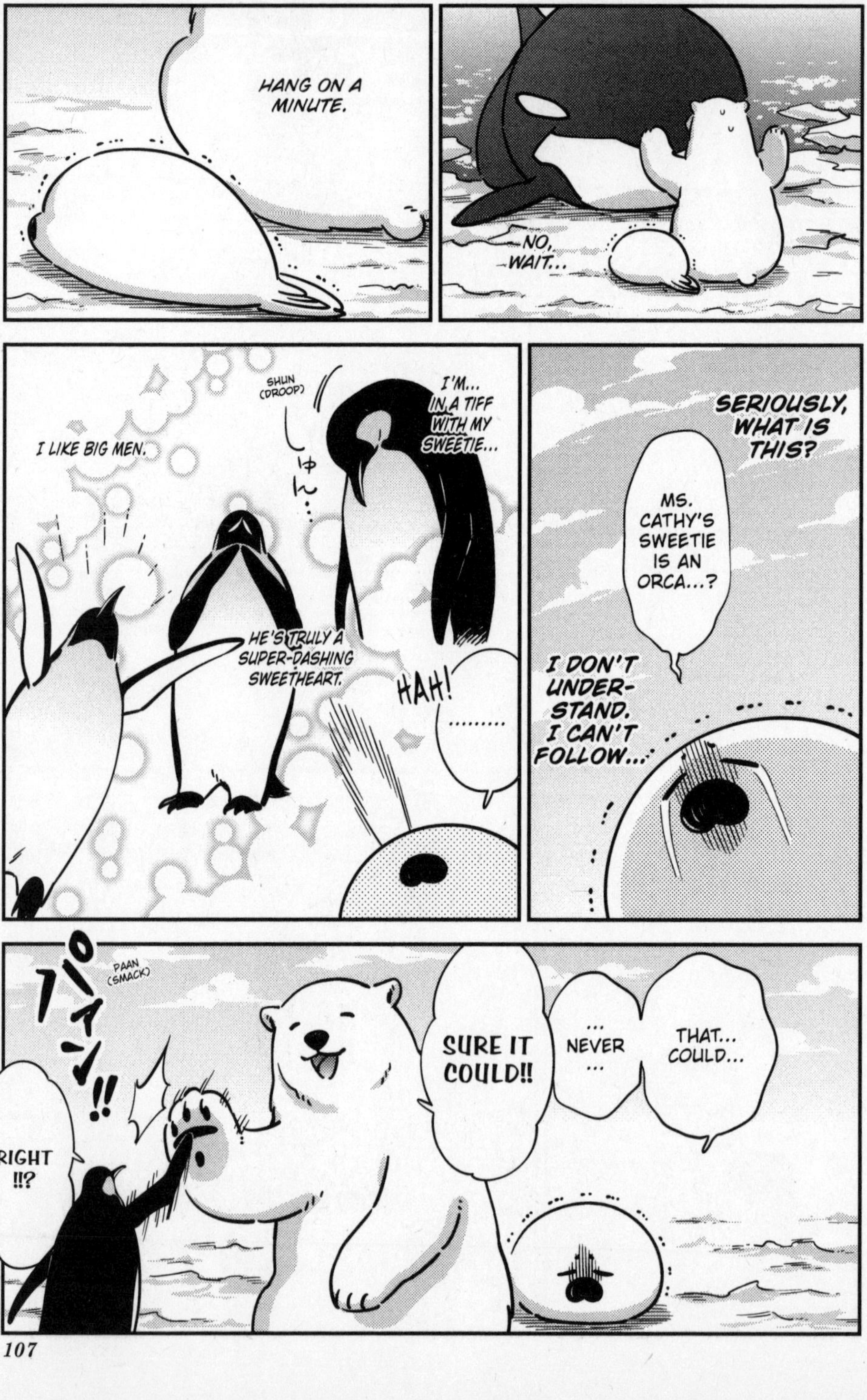
NO, WAIT...
HANG ON A MINUTE.
SERIOUSLY, WHAT IS THIS?
MS. CATHY'S SWEETIE IS AN ORCA...?
I DON'T UNDERSTAND. I CAN'T FOLLOW...
I'M... IN A TIFF WITH MY SWEETIE...
SHUN (DROOP)
しゅん…
I LIKE BIG MEN.
HE'S TRULY A SUPER-DASHING SWEETHEART.
HAH!
....
THAT... COULD...
... NEVER ...
SURE IT COULD!!
PAAN (SMACK)
パァン!!
RIGHT !!?

IDENTICAL

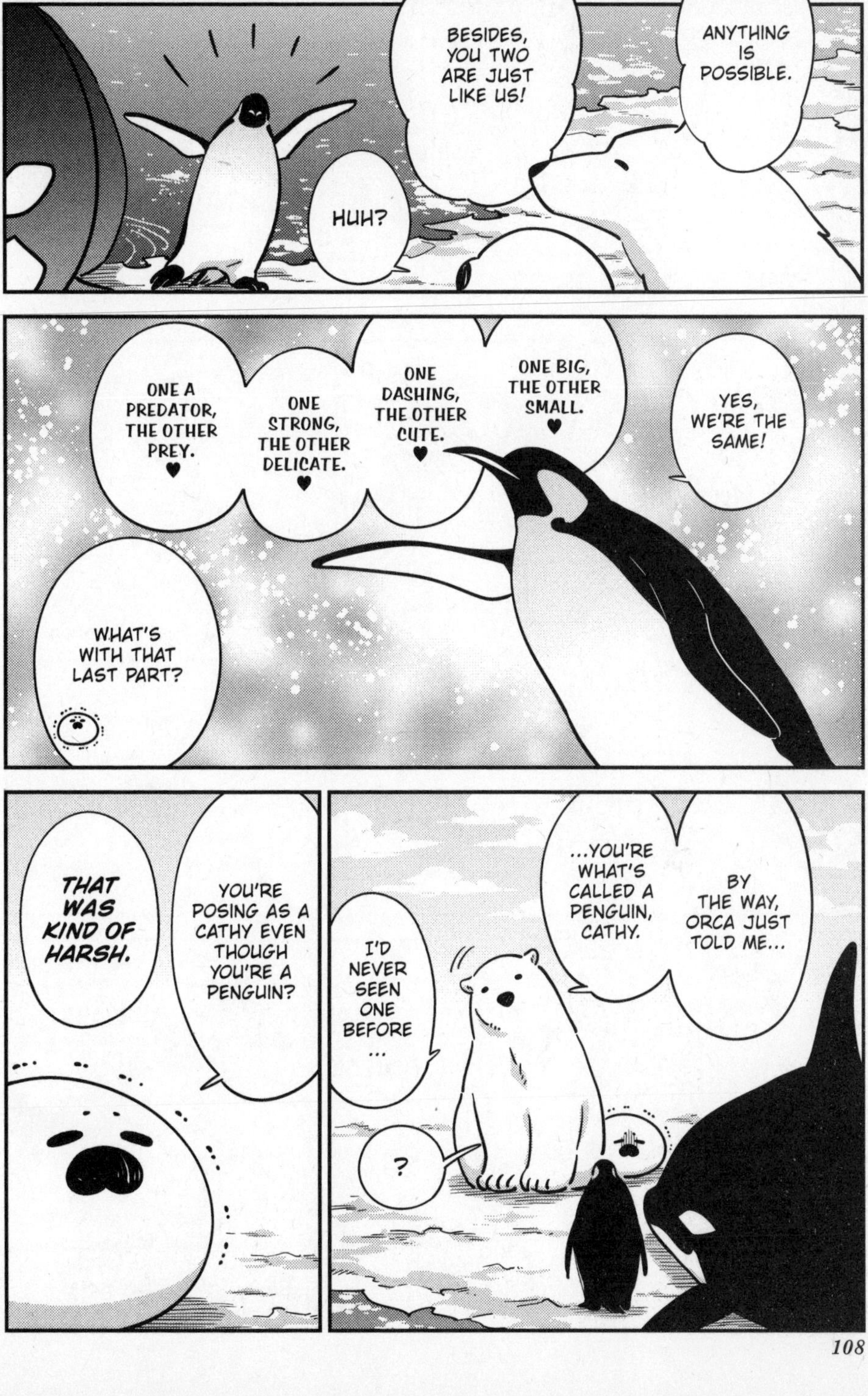
ANYTHING IS POSSIBLE.
BESIDES, YOU TWO ARE JUST LIKE US!
HUH?
YES, WE'RE THE SAME!
ONE BIG, THE OTHER SMALL. ♥
ONE DASHING, THE OTHER CUTE. ♥
ONE STRONG, THE OTHER DELICATE. ♥
ONE A PREDATOR, THE OTHER PREY. ♥
WHAT'S WITH THAT LAST PART?
BY THE WAY, ORCA JUST TOLD ME...
...YOU'RE WHAT'S CALLED A PENGUIN, CATHY.
I'D NEVER SEEN ONE BEFORE...
?
YOU'RE POSING AS A CATHY EVEN THOUGH YOU'RE A PENGUIN?
THAT WAS KIND OF HARSH.

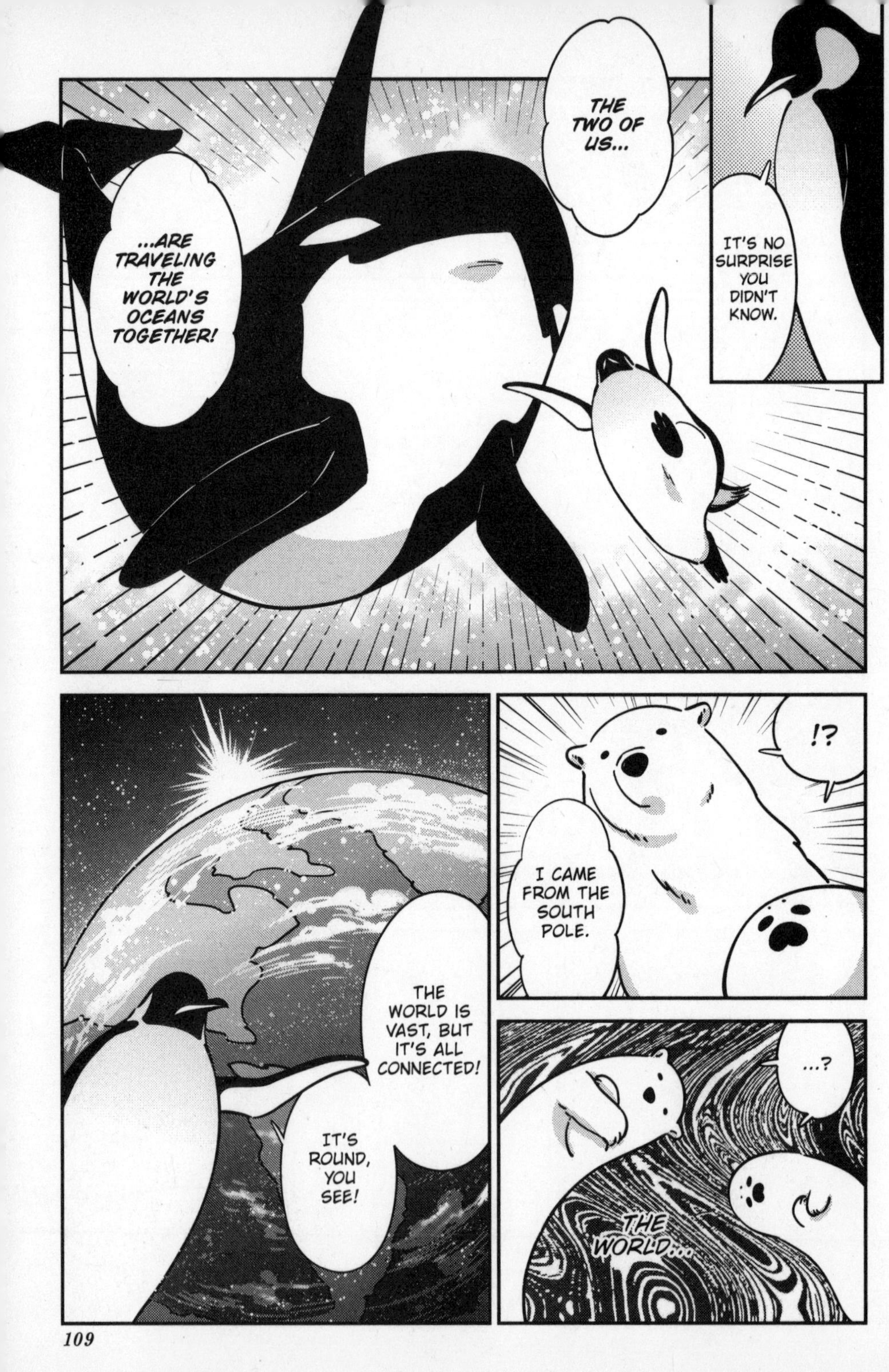
IT'S NO SURPRISE YOU DIDN'T KNOW.
THE TWO OF US...
...ARE TRAVELING THE WORLD'S OCEANS TOGETHER!
!?
I CAME FROM THE SOUTH POLE.
...?
THE WORLD...
THE WORLD IS VAST, BUT IT'S ALL CONNECTED!
IT'S ROUND, YOU SEE!

THE WORLD IS ROUND

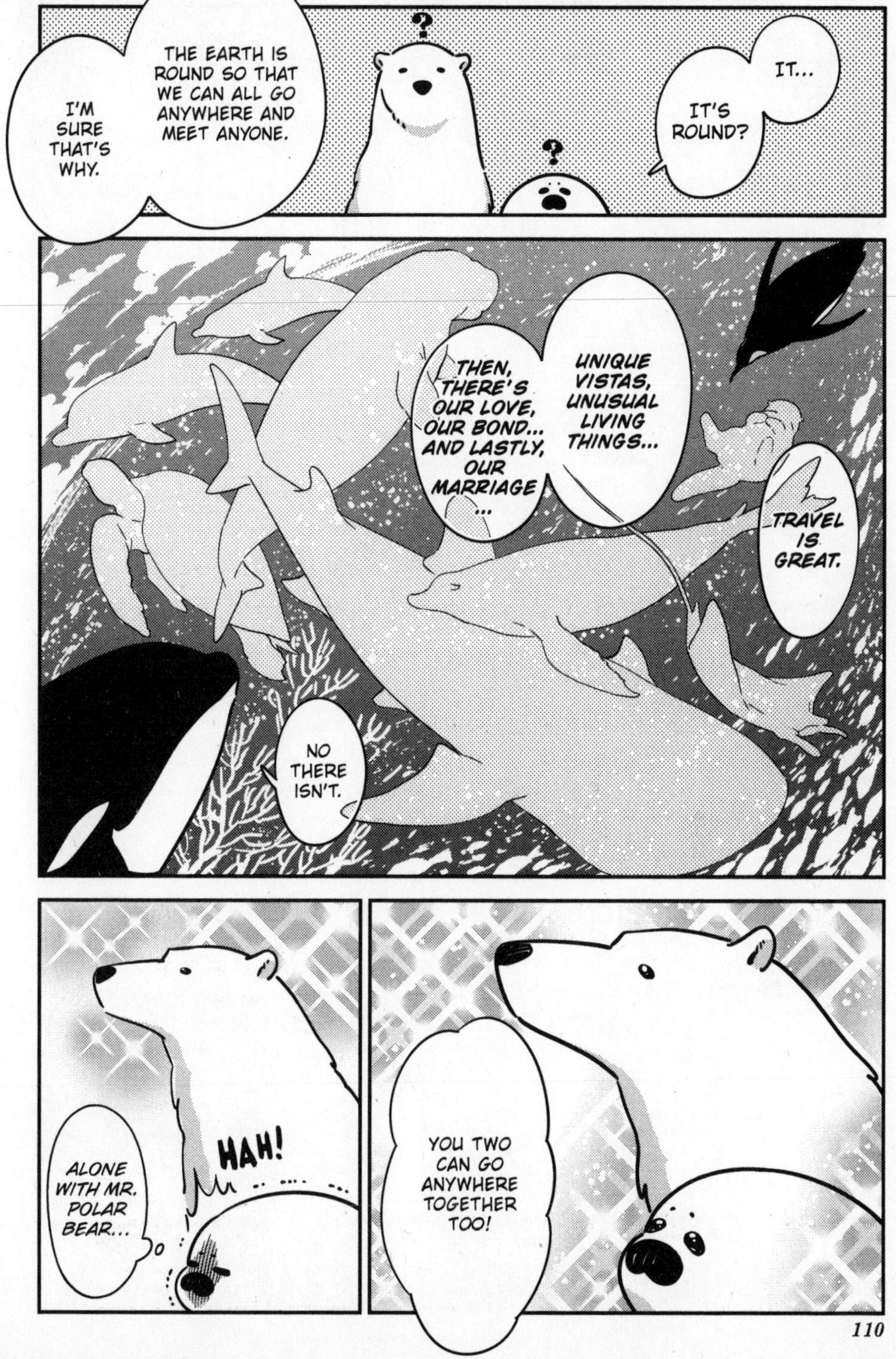
IT...
IT'S ROUND?
THE EARTH IS ROUND SO THAT WE CAN ALL GO ANYWHERE AND MEET ANYONE.
I'M SURE THAT'S WHY.
TRAVEL IS GREAT.
UNIQUE VISTAS, UNUSUAL LIVING THINGS...
THEN, THERE'S OUR LOVE, OUR BOND... AND LASTLY, OUR MARRIAGE...
NO THERE ISN'T.
YOU TWO CAN GO ANYWHERE TOGETHER TOO!
HAH!
ALONE WITH MR. POLAR BEAR...

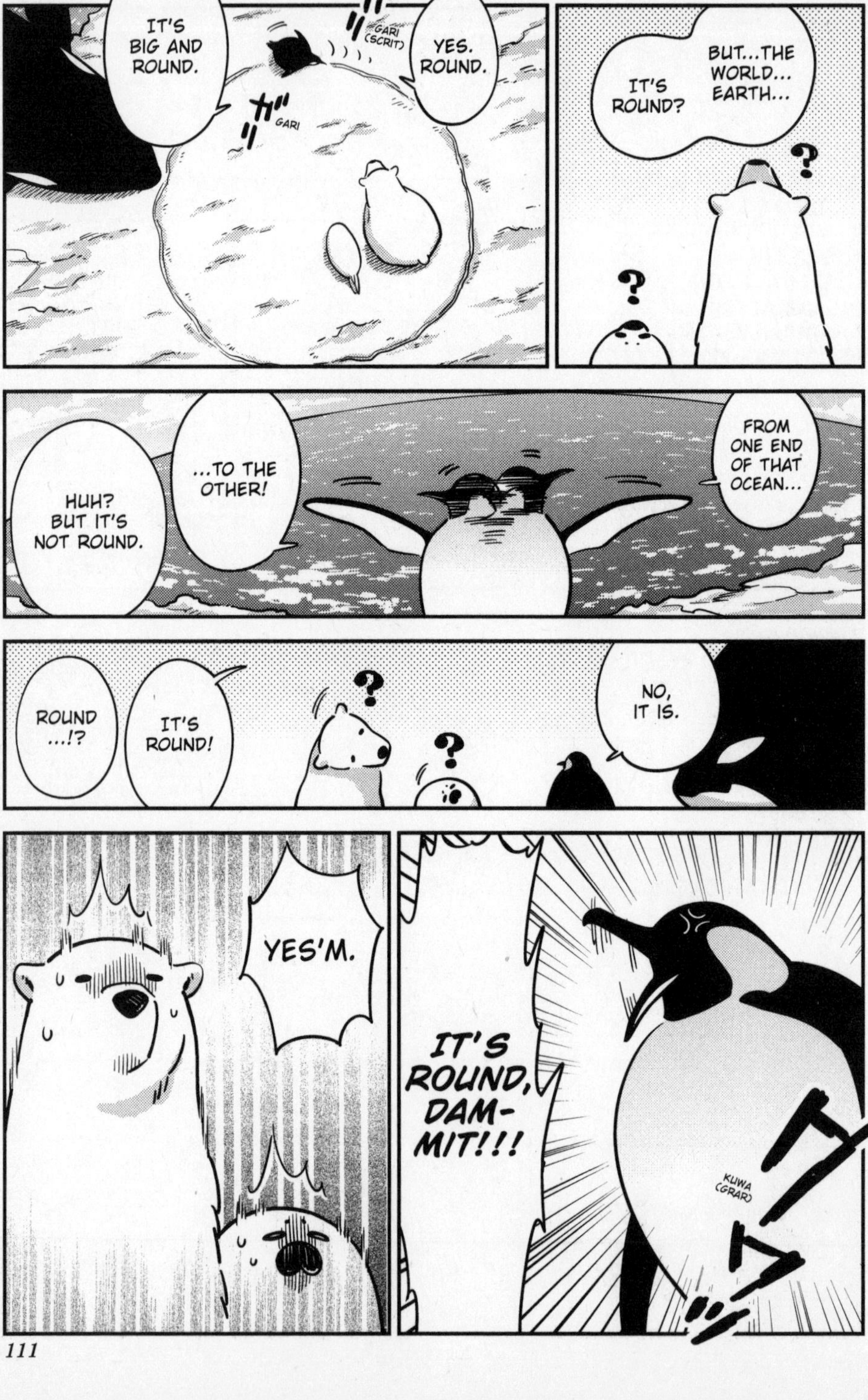
BUT...THE WORLD... EARTH...
IT'S ROUND?
YES. ROUND.
GARI (SCRIT)
IT'S BIG AND ROUND.
GARI
FROM ONE END OF THAT OCEAN...
...TO THE OTHER!
HUH? BUT IT'S NOT ROUND.
NO, IT IS.
IT'S ROUND!
ROUND ...!?
KUWA (GRAR)
IT'S ROUND, DAM-MIT!!!
YES'M.

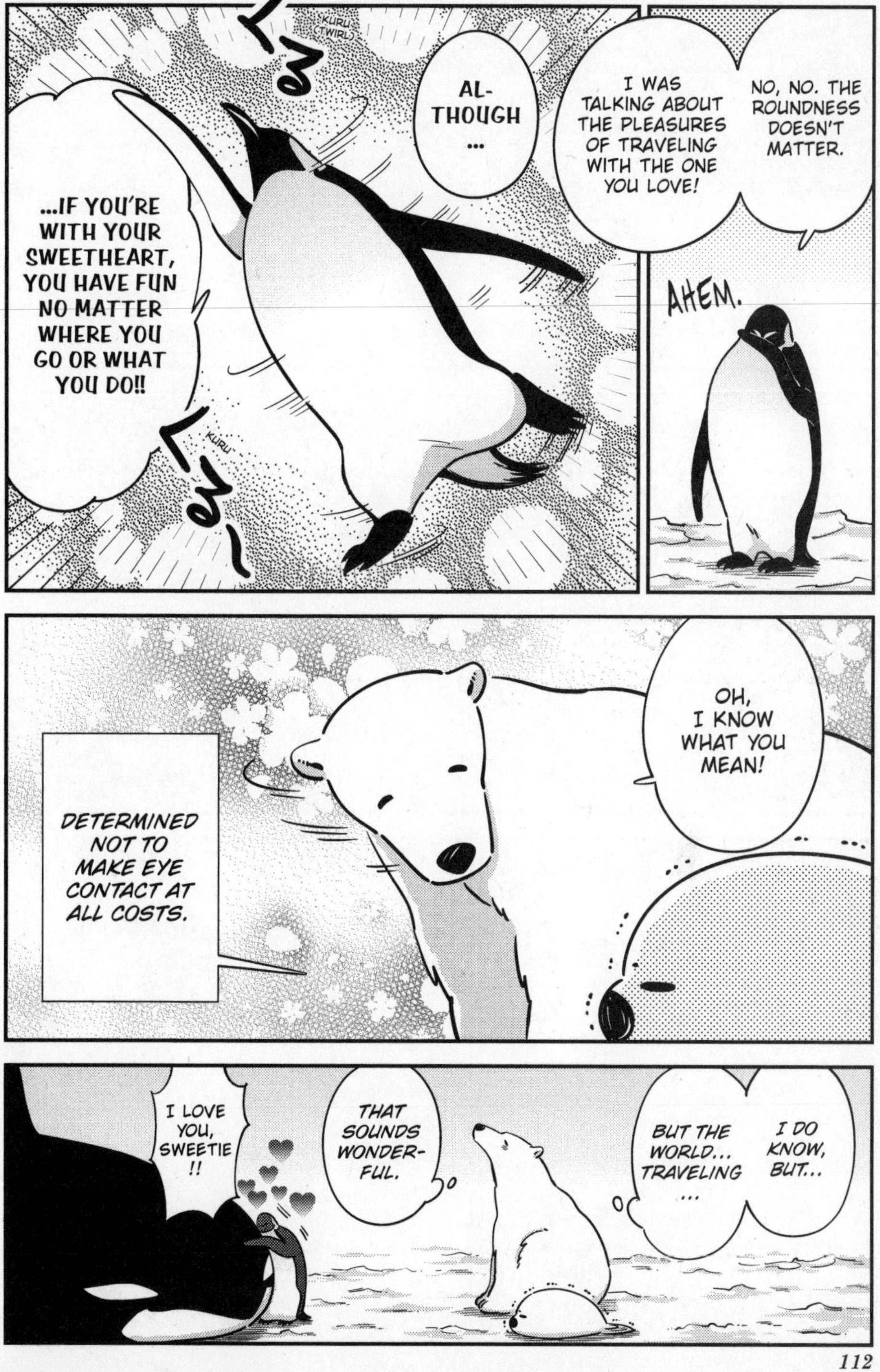
NO, NO. THE ROUNDNESS DOESN'T MATTER.
I WAS TALKING ABOUT THE PLEASURES OF TRAVELING WITH THE ONE YOU LOVE!
AHEM.
KURU (TWIRL)
AL-THOUGH ...
...IF YOU'RE WITH YOUR SWEETHEART, YOU HAVE FUN NO MATTER WHERE YOU GO OR WHAT YOU DO!!
KURU
OH, I KNOW WHAT YOU MEAN!
DETERMINED NOT TO MAKE EYE CONTACT AT ALL COSTS.
I DO KNOW, BUT...
BUT THE WORLD... TRAVELING ...
THAT SOUNDS WONDER-FUL.
I LOVE YOU, SWEETIE !!

THE TRUTH AND SEAL RAP

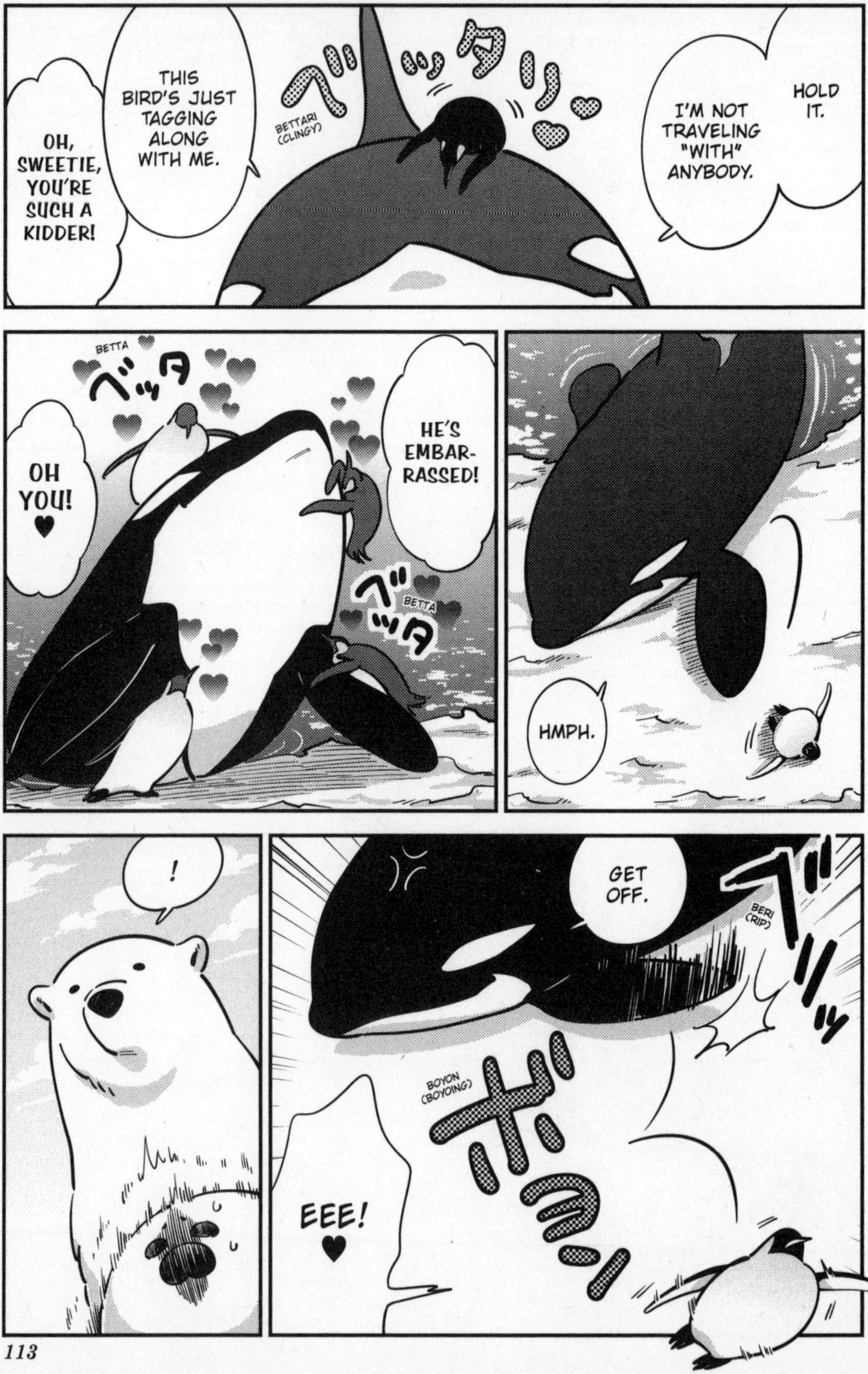
HOLD IT.
I'M NOT TRAVELING "WITH" ANYBODY.
ベッタリ
BETTARI (CLINGY)
THIS BIRD'S JUST TAGGING ALONG WITH ME.
OH, SWEETIE, YOU'RE SUCH A KIDDER!
HMPH.
HE'S EMBARRASSED!
ベッタ
BETTA
ベッタ
BETTA
OH YOU! ♥
GET OFF.
ベリッ
BERI (RIP)
ボヨーン
BOYON (BOYOING)
EEE! ♥
!

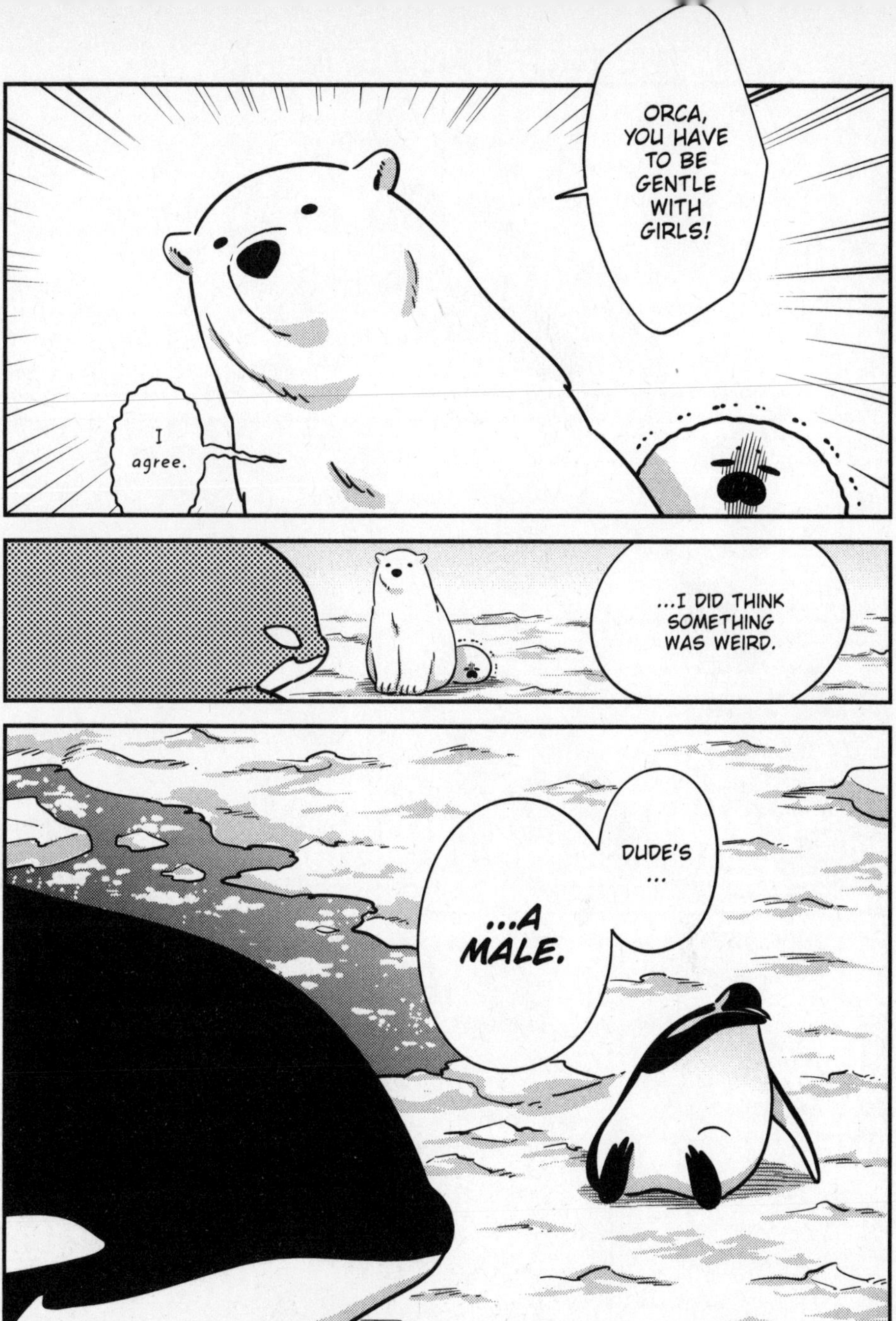
ORCA, YOU HAVE TO BE GENTLE WITH GIRLS!
I agree.
...I DID THINK SOMETHING WAS WEIRD.
DUDE'S ...
...A MALE.

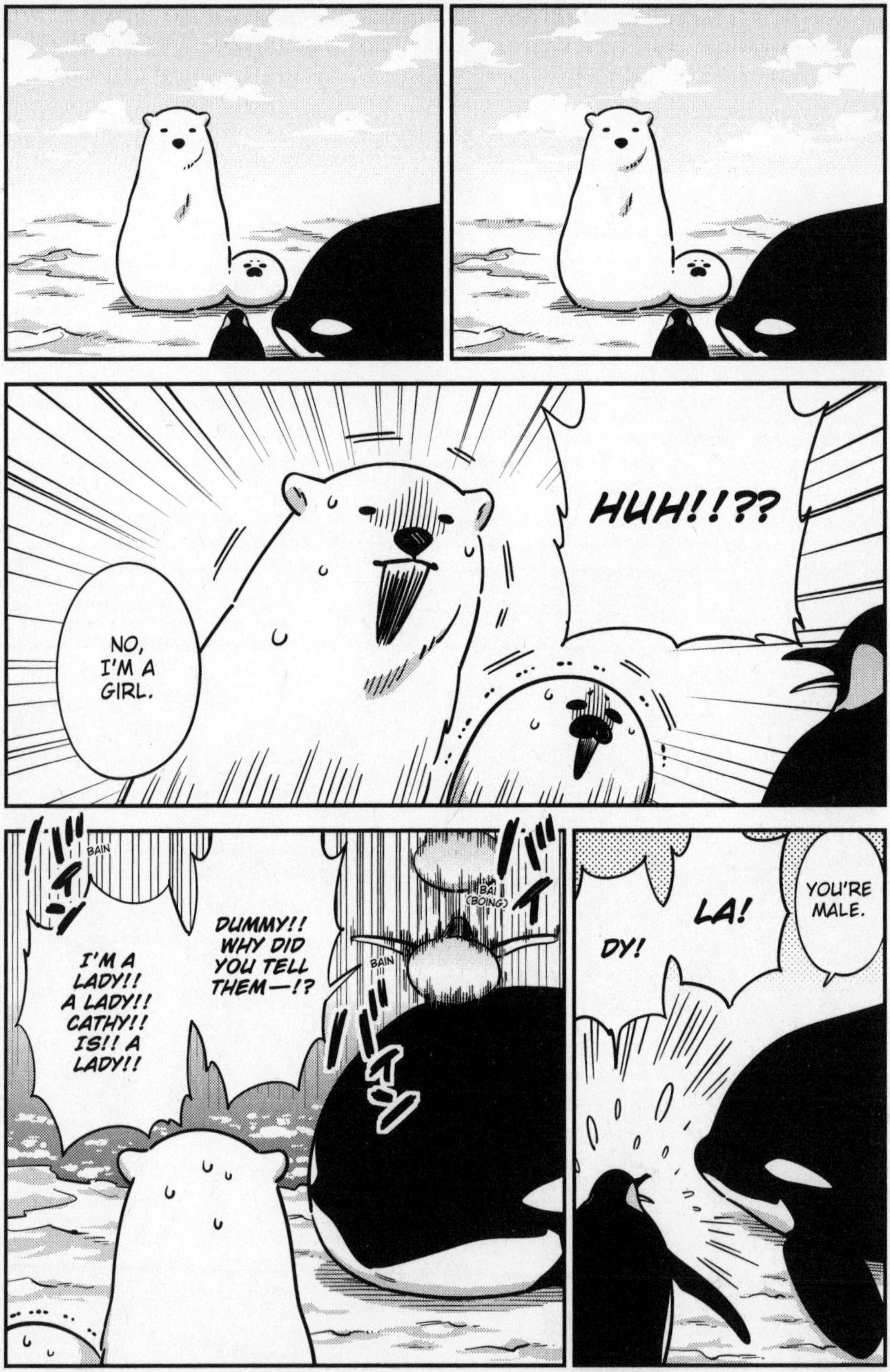
HUH!!??
NO, I'M A GIRL.
YOU'RE MALE.
LA!
DY!
BAI (BOING)
DUMMY!! WHY DID YOU TELL THEM—!?
BAIN
BAIN
I'M A LADY!! A LADY!! CATHY!! IS!! A LADY!!

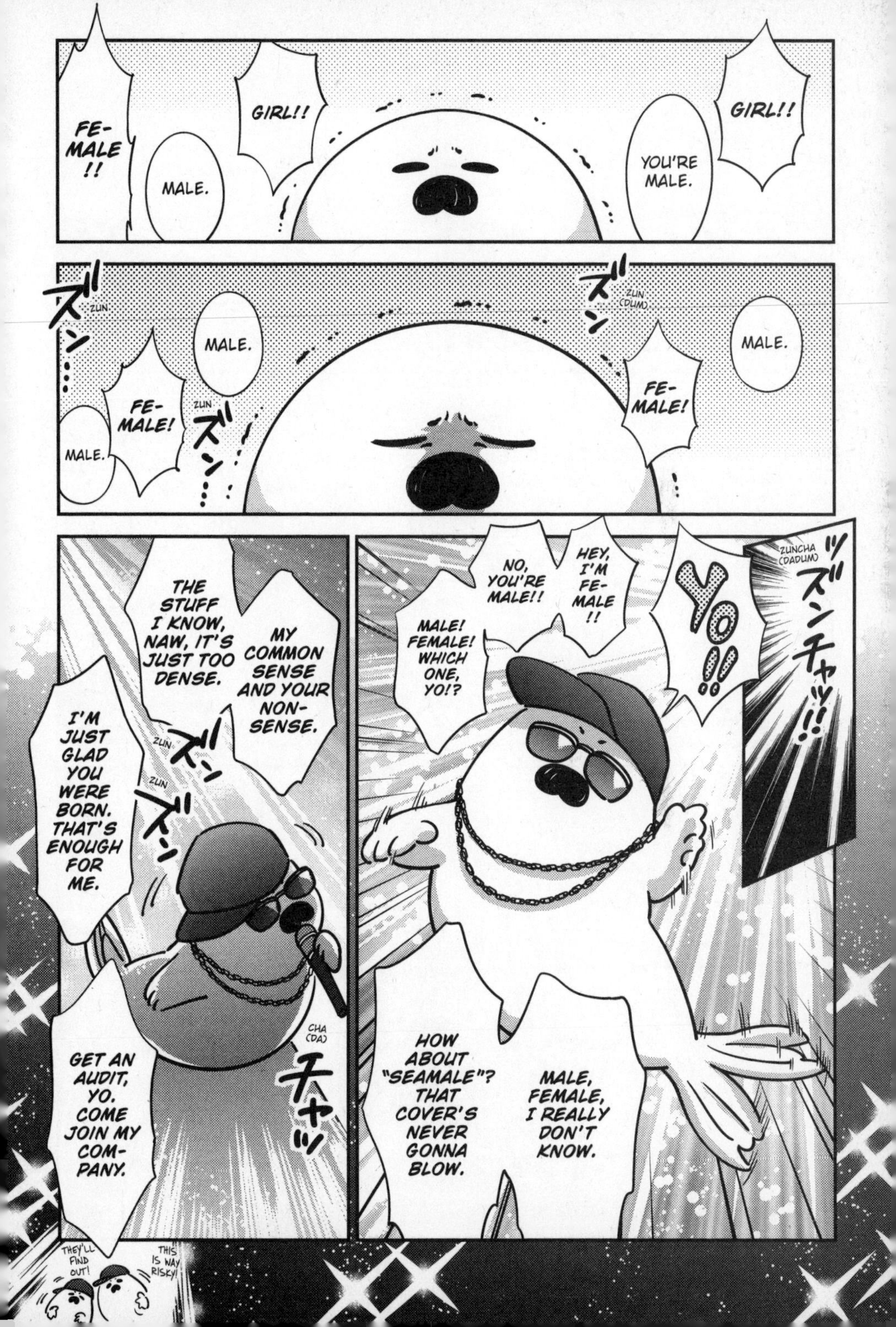
GIRL!!
YOU'RE MALE.
GIRL!!
MALE.
FE-MALE!!
MALE.
ズン
ZUN (DUM)
FE-MALE!
MALE.
ズン
ZUN
FE-MALE!
MALE.
ズン
ZUN
ツズンチャッ!!
ZUNCHA (DADUM)
YO!!
HEY, I'M FE-MALE!!
NO, YOU'RE MALE!!
MALE! FEMALE! WHICH ONE, YO!?
MALE, FEMALE, I REALLY DON'T KNOW.
HOW ABOUT "SEAMALE"? THAT COVER'S NEVER GONNA BLOW.
MY COMMON SENSE AND YOUR NON-SENSE.
THE STUFF I KNOW, NAW, IT'S JUST TOO DENSE.
ズン
ZUN
ズン
ZUN
I'M JUST GLAD YOU WERE BORN. THAT'S ENOUGH FOR ME.
チャッ
CHA (DA)
GET AN AUDIT, YO. COME JOIN MY COM-PANY.
THIS IS WAY RISKY!
THEY'LL FIND OUT!

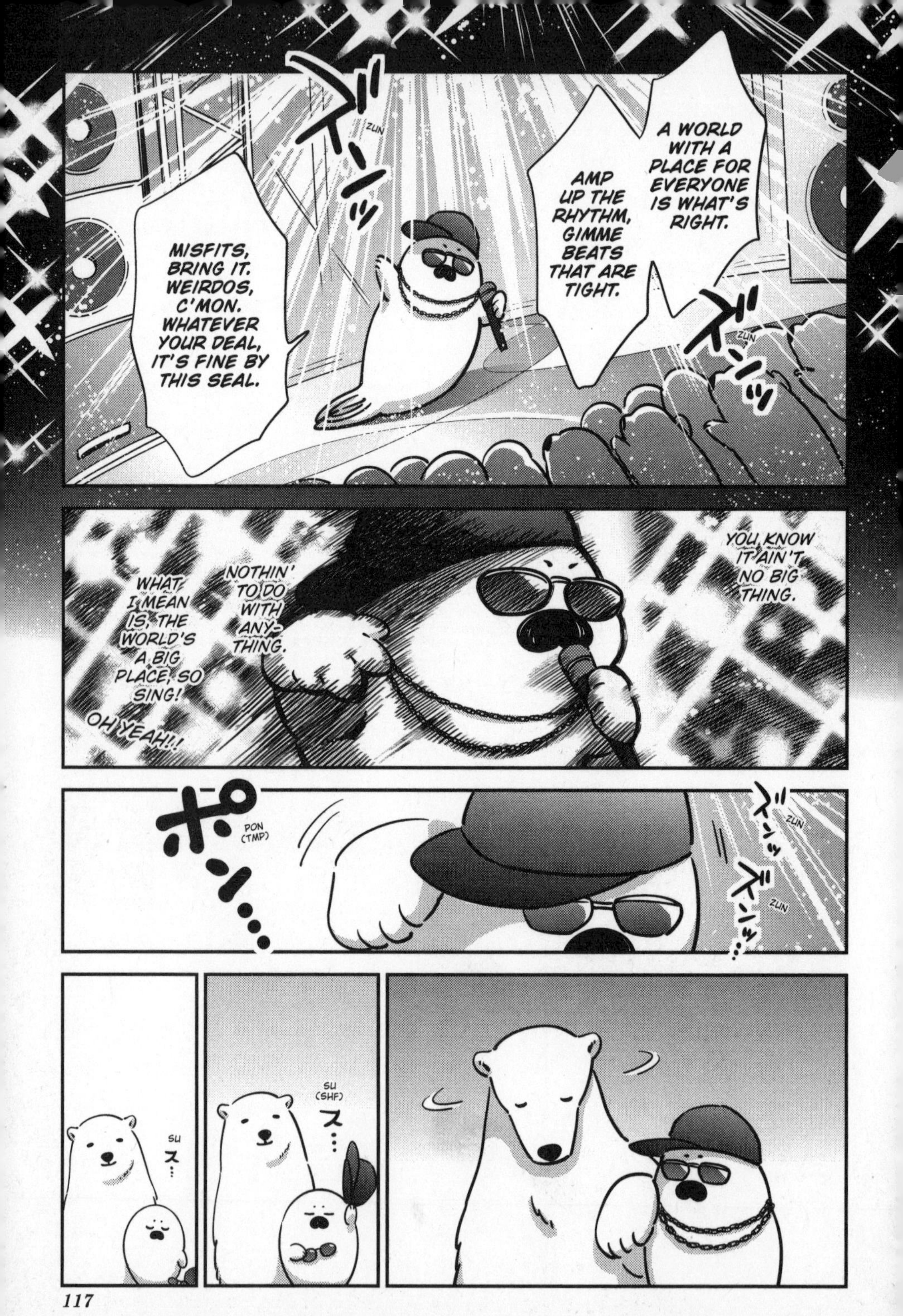
A WORLD WITH A PLACE FOR EVERYONE IS WHAT'S RIGHT.
AMP UP THE RHYTHM, GIMME BEATS THAT ARE TIGHT.
ZUN
ZUN
MISFITS, BRING IT. WEIRDOS, C'MON. WHATEVER YOUR DEAL, IT'S FINE BY THIS SEAL.
YOU KNOW IT AIN'T NO BIG THING.
NOTHIN' TO DO WITH ANYTHING.
WHAT I MEAN IS, THE WORLD'S A BIG PLACE, SO SING!
OH YEAH!!
ZUN
ZUN
PON (TMP)
SU (SHF)
SU

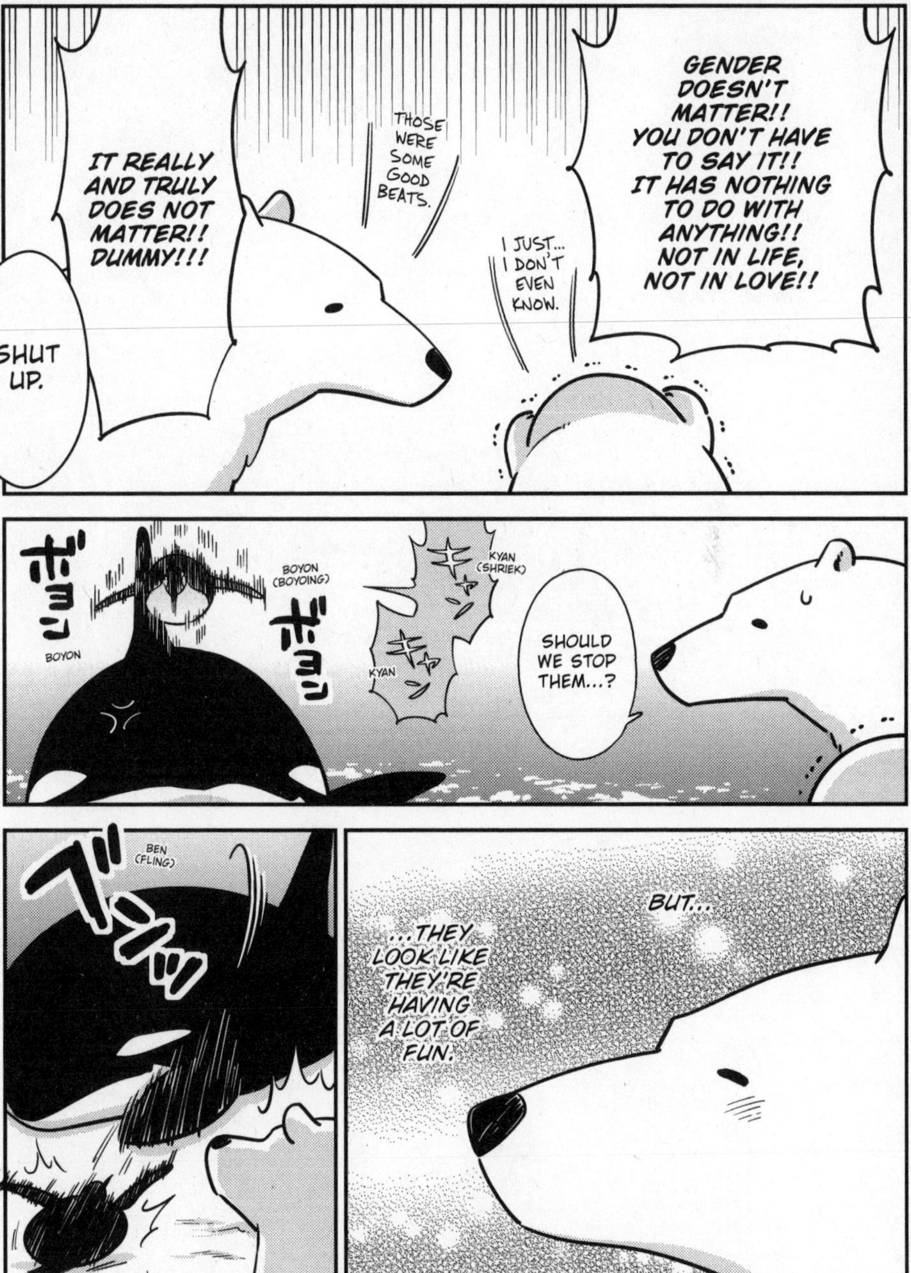
GENDER DOESN'T MATTER!! YOU DON'T HAVE TO SAY IT!! IT HAS NOTHING TO DO WITH ANYTHING!! NOT IN LIFE, NOT IN LOVE!!
I JUST... I DON'T EVEN KNOW.
THOSE WERE SOME GOOD BEATS.
IT REALLY AND TRULY DOES NOT MATTER!! DUMMY!!!
SHUT UP.
SHOULD WE STOP THEM...?
キャン
KYAN (SHRIEK)
キャン
KYAN
ボヨン
BOYON (BOYOING)
ボヨン
BOYON
BUT...
...THEY LOOK LIKE THEY'RE HAVING A LOT OF FUN.
ブンッ
BEN (FLING)

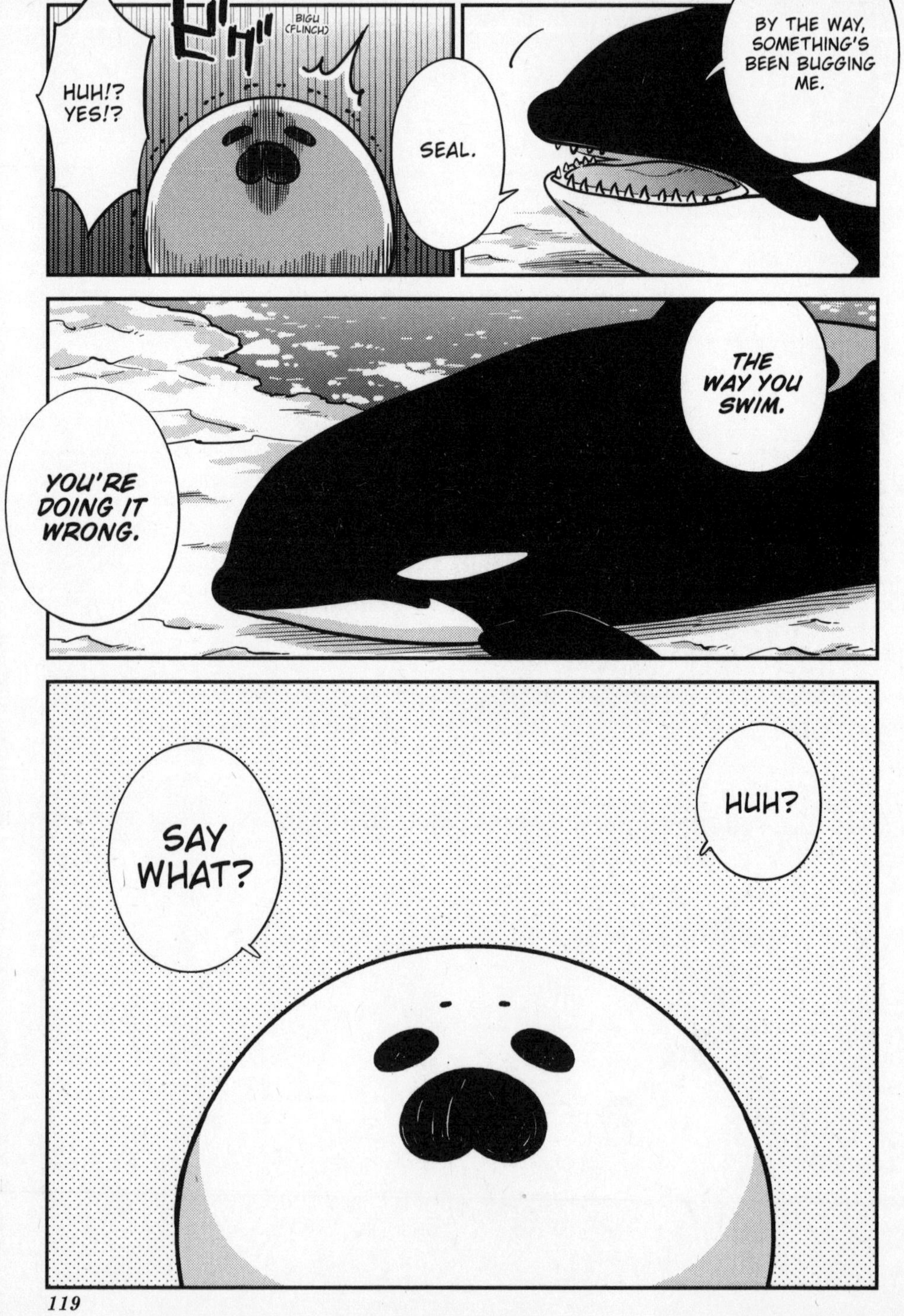
BY THE WAY, SOMETHING'S BEEN BUGGING ME.
SEAL.
BIGU (FLINCH)
HUH!? YES!?
THE WAY YOU SWIM.
YOU'RE DOING IT WRONG.
HUH?
SAY WHAT?

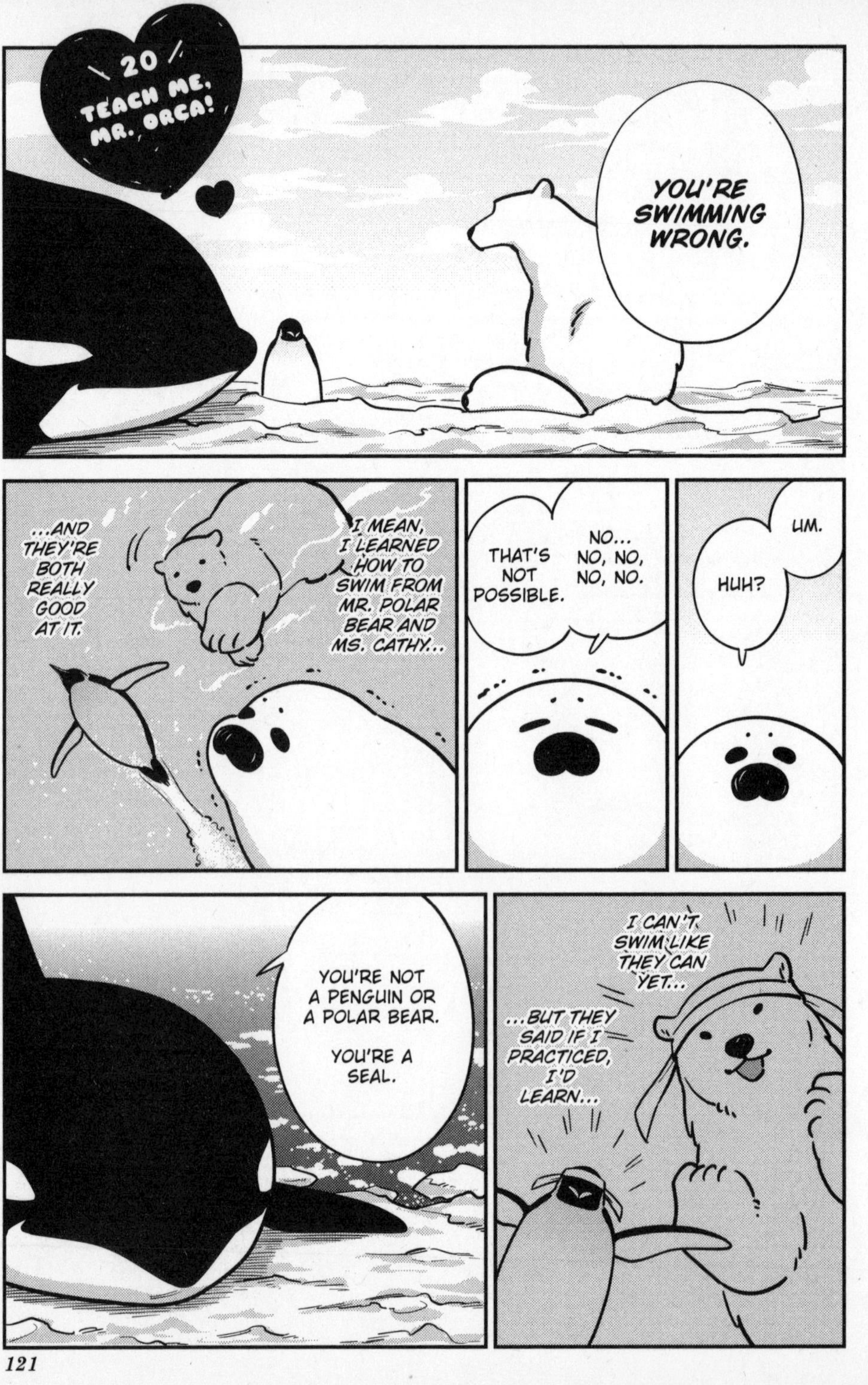
20
TEACH ME, MR. ORCA!
YOU'RE SWIMMING WRONG.
UM.
HUH?
NO... NO, NO, NO, NO.
THAT'S NOT POSSIBLE.
I MEAN, I LEARNED HOW TO SWIM FROM MR. POLAR BEAR AND MS. CATHY...
...AND THEY'RE BOTH REALLY GOOD AT IT.
I CAN'T SWIM LIKE THEY CAN YET...
...BUT THEY SAID IF I PRACTICED, I'D LEARN...
YOU'RE NOT A PENGUIN OR A POLAR BEAR.
YOU'RE A SEAL.

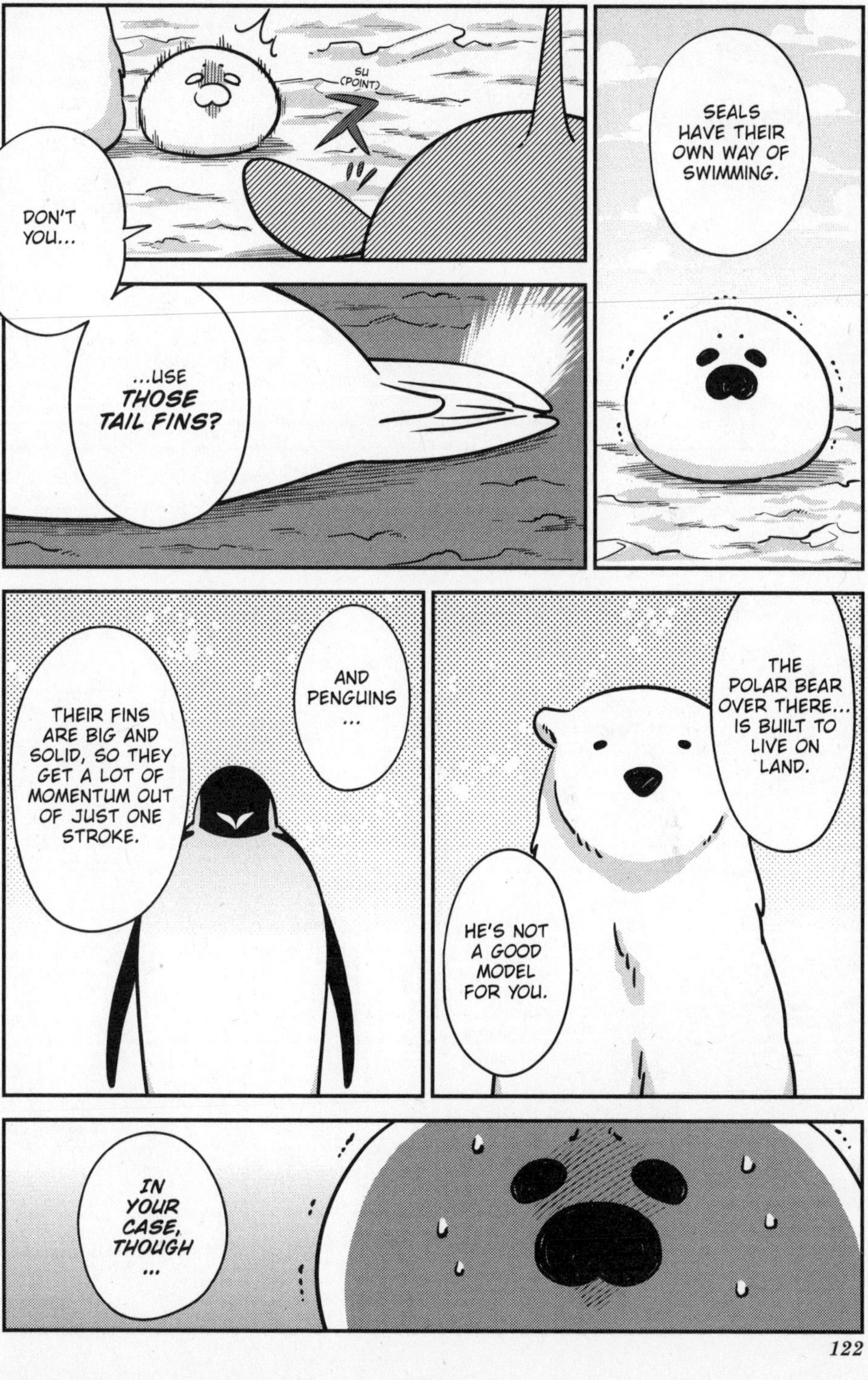
SEALS HAVE THEIR OWN WAY OF SWIMMING.
SU (POINT)
DON'T YOU...
...USE *THOSE TAIL FINS?*
THE POLAR BEAR OVER THERE... IS BUILT TO LIVE ON LAND.
HE'S NOT A GOOD MODEL FOR YOU.
AND PENGUINS...
THEIR FINS ARE BIG AND SOLID, SO THEY GET A LOT OF MOMENTUM OUT OF JUST ONE STROKE.
IN YOUR CASE, THOUGH...

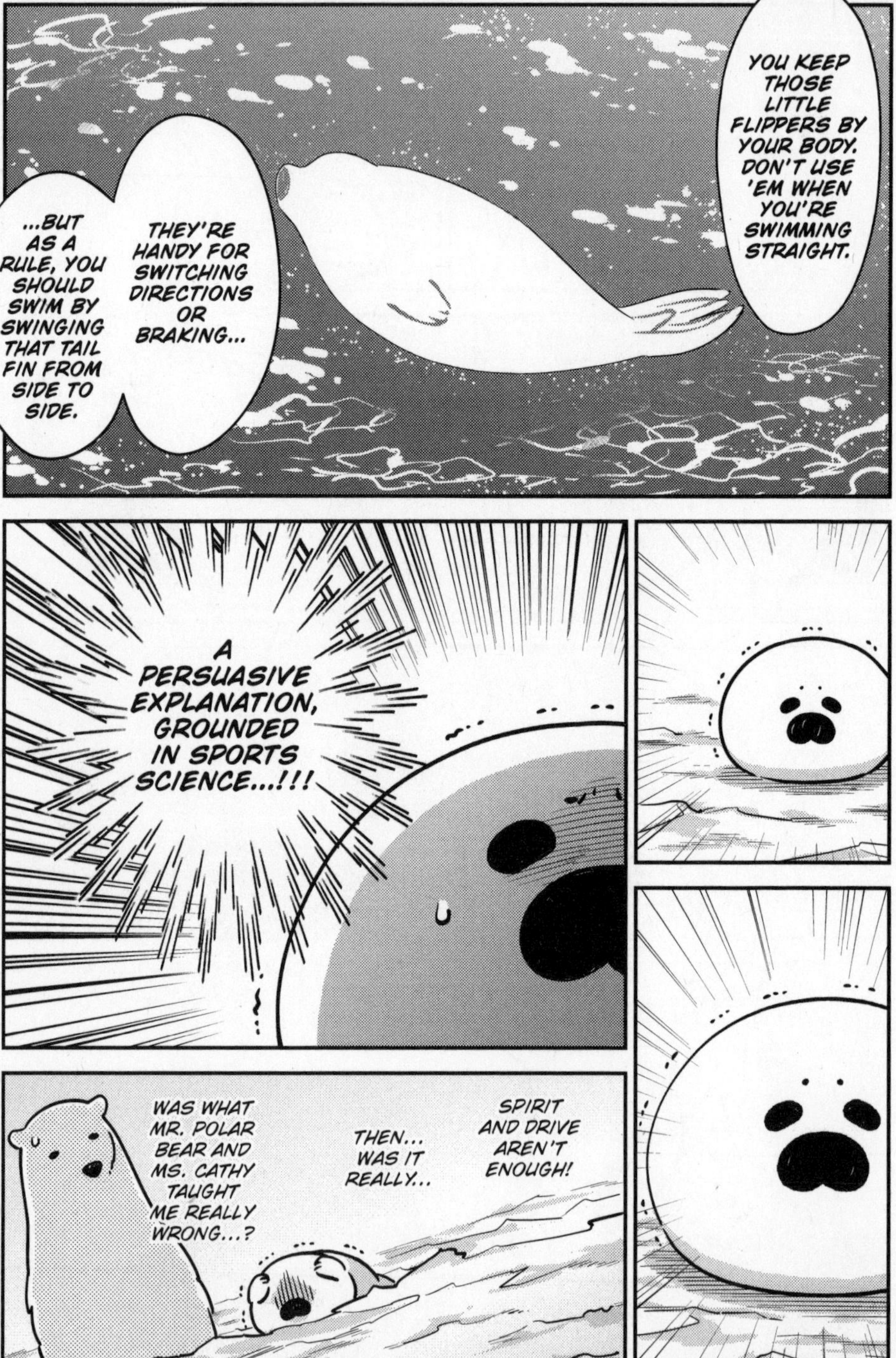
YOU KEEP THOSE LITTLE FLIPPERS BY YOUR BODY. DON'T USE 'EM WHEN YOU'RE SWIMMING STRAIGHT.
THEY'RE HANDY FOR SWITCHING DIRECTIONS OR BRAKING...
...BUT AS A RULE, YOU SHOULD SWIM BY SWINGING THAT TAIL FIN FROM SIDE TO SIDE.
A PERSUASIVE EXPLANATION, GROUNDED IN SPORTS SCIENCE...!!!
SPIRIT AND DRIVE AREN'T ENOUGH!
THEN... WAS IT REALLY...
WAS WHAT MR. POLAR BEAR AND MS. CATHY TAUGHT ME REALLY WRONG...?

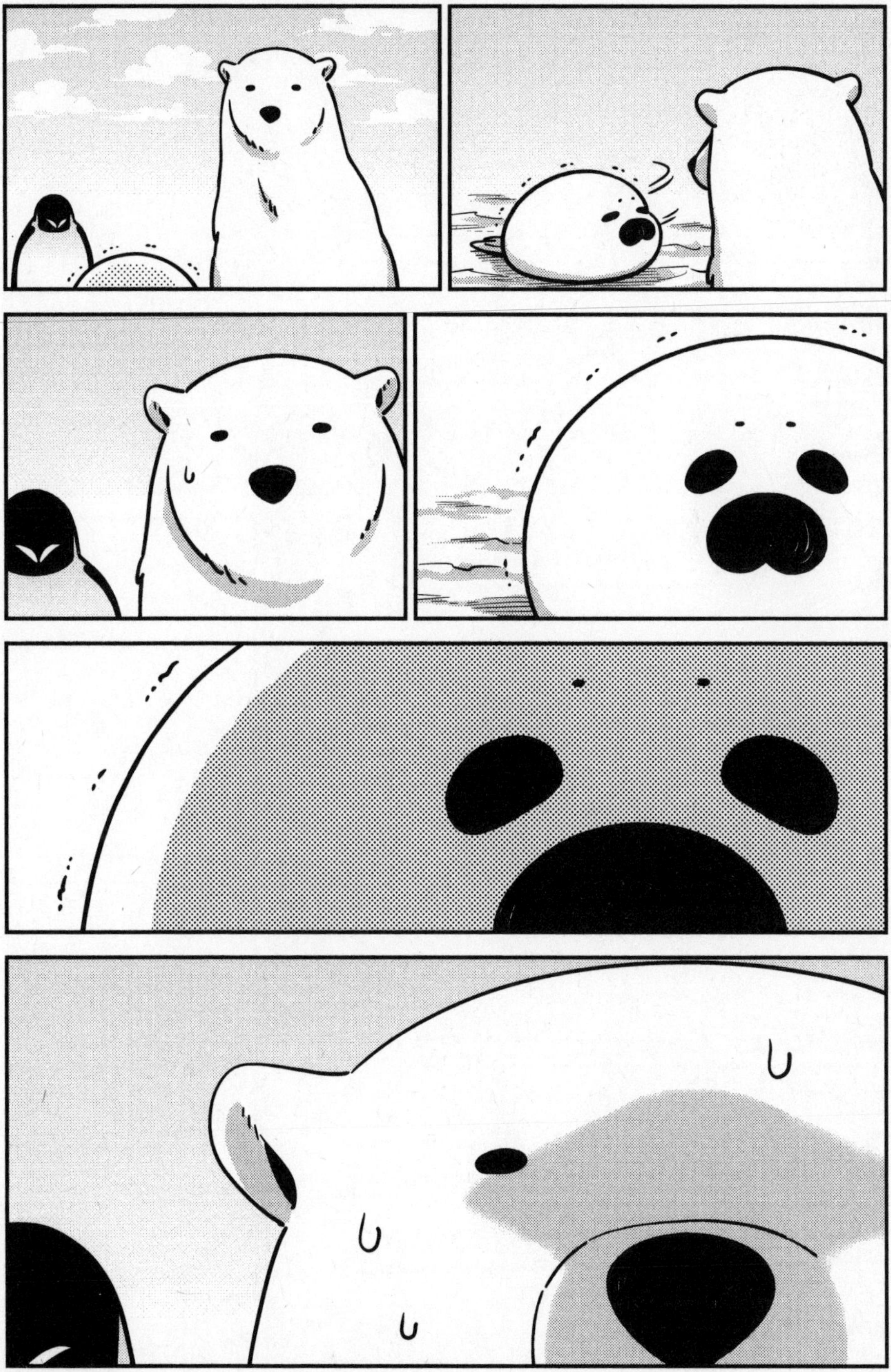

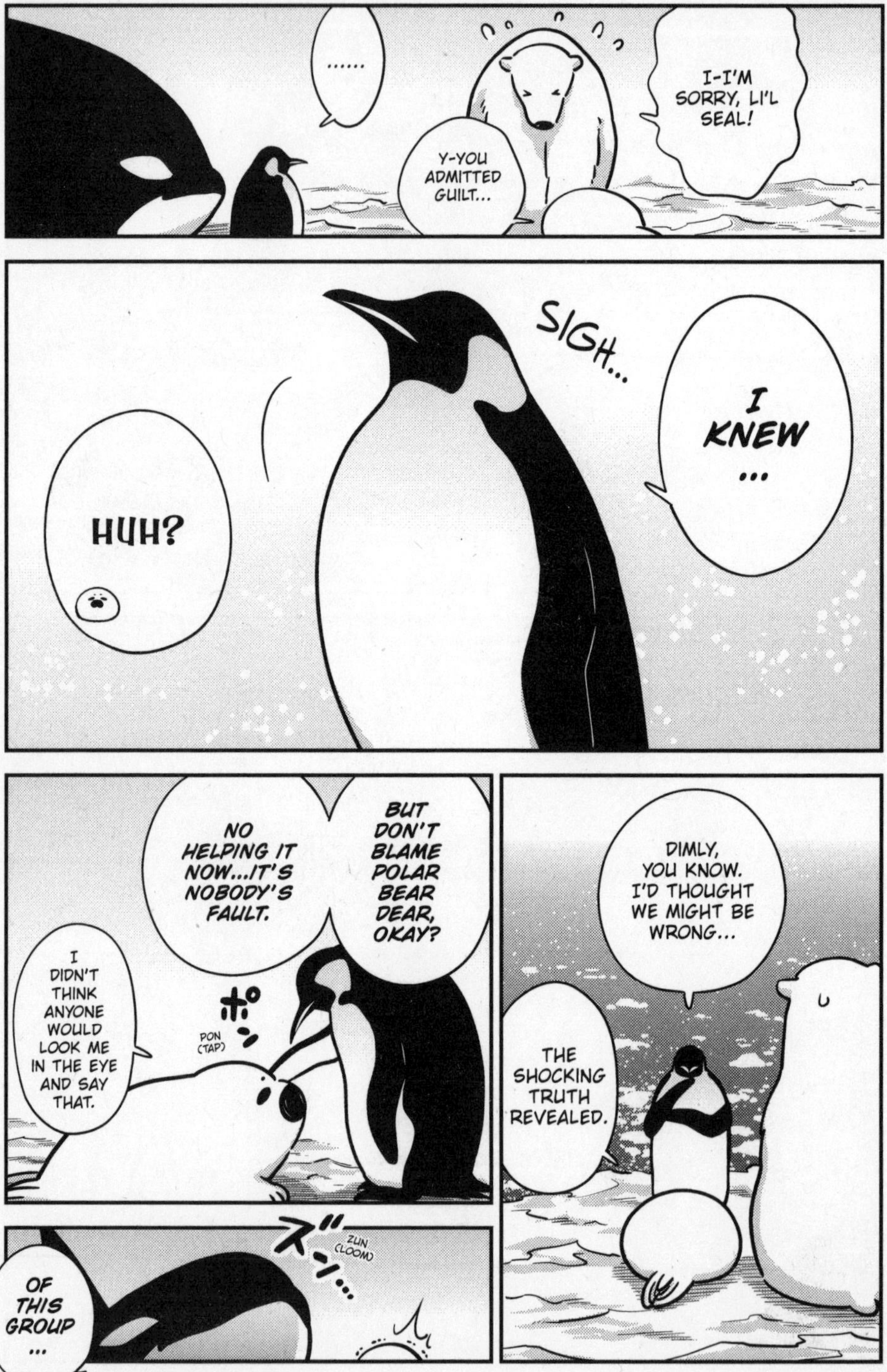
I-I'M SORRY, LI'L SEAL!
......
Y-YOU ADMITTED GUILT...
SIGH...
I KNEW...
HUH?
DIMLY, YOU KNOW. I'D THOUGHT WE MIGHT BE WRONG...
THE SHOCKING TRUTH REVEALED.
BUT DON'T BLAME POLAR BEAR DEAR, OKAY?
NO HELPING IT NOW...IT'S NOBODY'S FAULT.
ポン
PON (TAP)
I DIDN'T THINK ANYONE WOULD LOOK ME IN THE EYE AND SAY THAT.
ズーン...
ZUN (LOOM)
OF THIS GROUP...

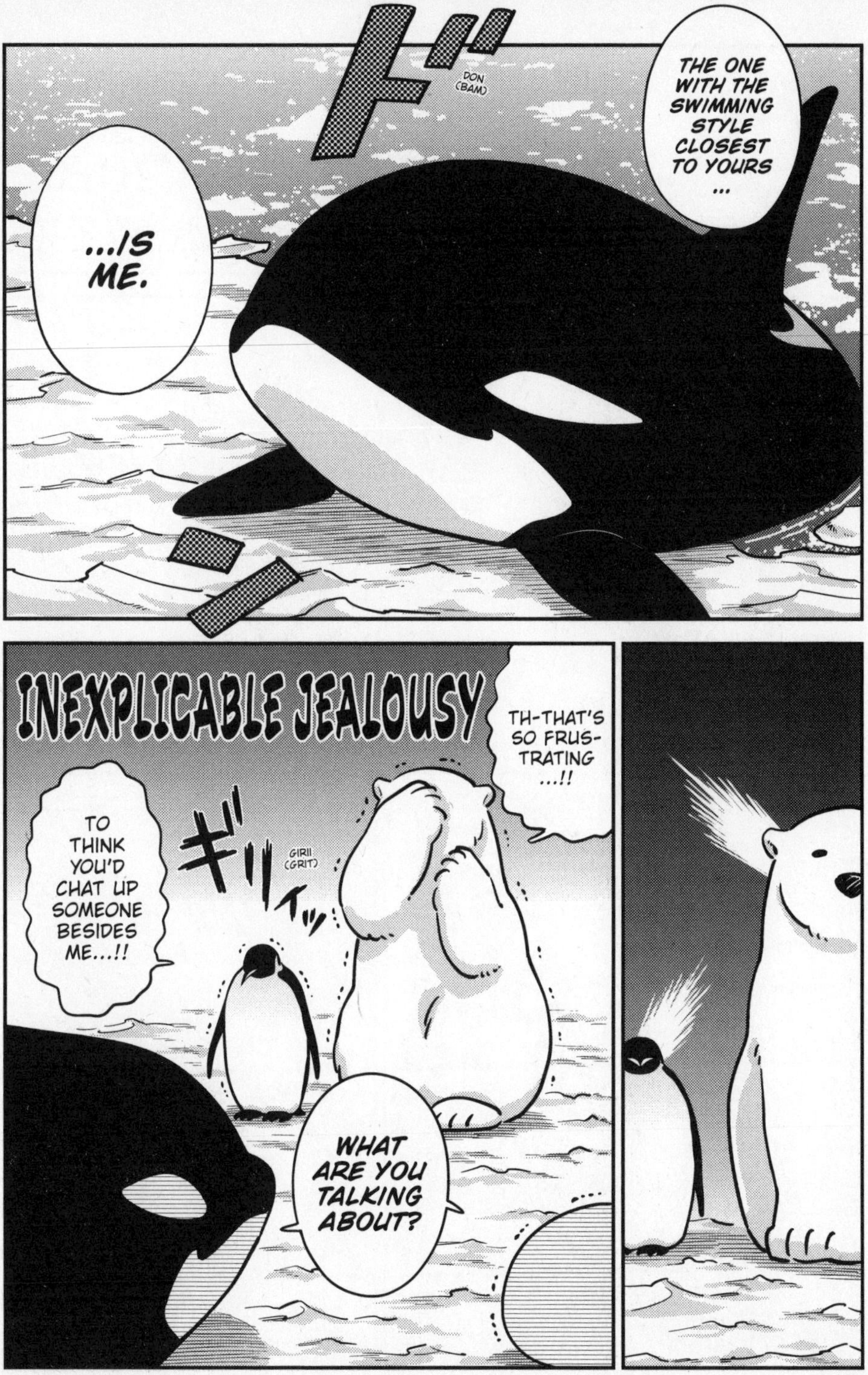
THE ONE WITH THE SWIMMING STYLE CLOSEST TO YOURS ...
DON (BAM)
...IS ME.
INEXPLICABLE JEALOUSY
TH-THAT'S SO FRUS-TRATING ...!!
GIRII (GRIT)
TO THINK YOU'D CHAT UP SOMEONE BESIDES ME...!!
WHAT ARE YOU TALKING ABOUT?

GENDER

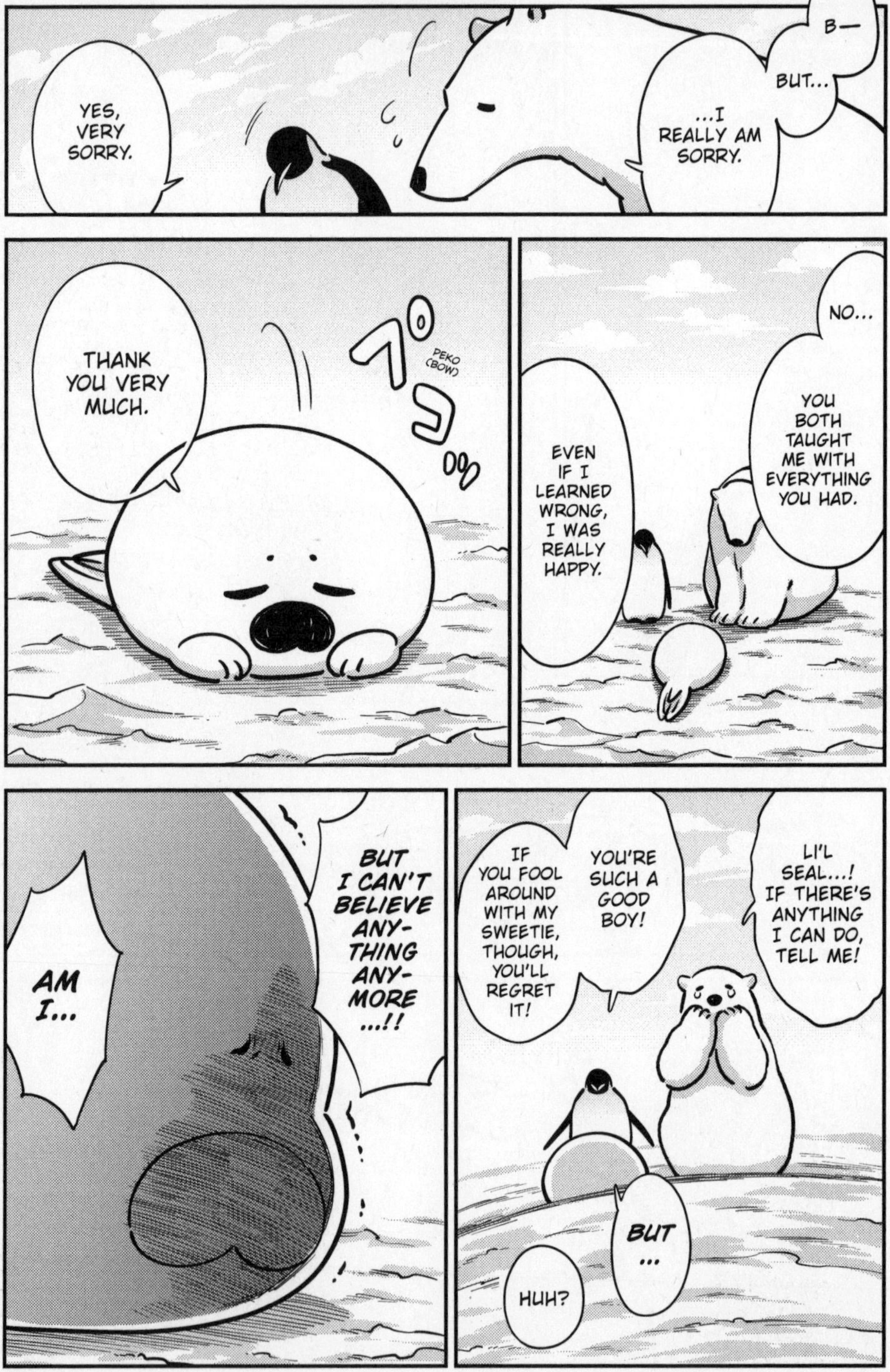

B—
BUT...
...I REALLY AM SORRY.
YES, VERY SORRY.
NO...
YOU BOTH TAUGHT ME WITH EVERYTHING YOU HAD.
EVEN IF I LEARNED WRONG, I WAS REALLY HAPPY.
PEKO (BOW)
THANK YOU VERY MUCH.
LI'L SEAL...! IF THERE'S ANYTHING I CAN DO, TELL ME!
YOU'RE SUCH A GOOD BOY!
IF YOU FOOL AROUND WITH MY SWEETIE, THOUGH, YOU'LL REGRET IT!
BUT...
HUH?
BUT I CAN'T BELIEVE ANY-THING ANY-MORE...!!
AM I...

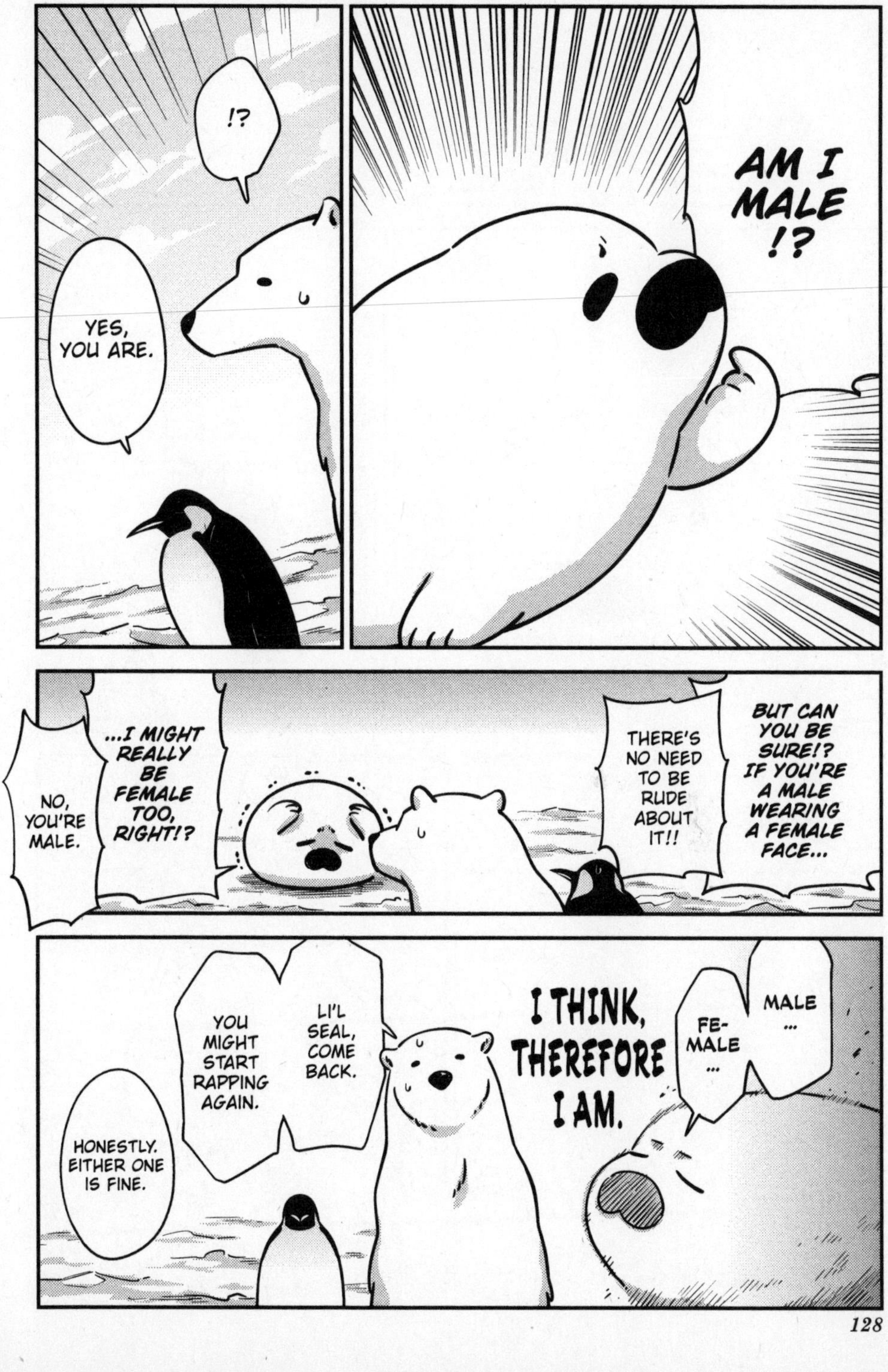
AM I MALE !?
!?
YES, YOU ARE.
BUT CAN YOU BE SURE!? IF YOU'RE A MALE WEARING A FEMALE FACE...
THERE'S NO NEED TO BE RUDE ABOUT IT!!
...I MIGHT REALLY BE FEMALE TOO, RIGHT!?
NO, YOU'RE MALE.
MALE ...
FE-MALE ...
I THINK, THEREFORE I AM.
LI'L SEAL, COME BACK.
YOU MIGHT START RAPPING AGAIN.
HONESTLY. EITHER ONE IS FINE.

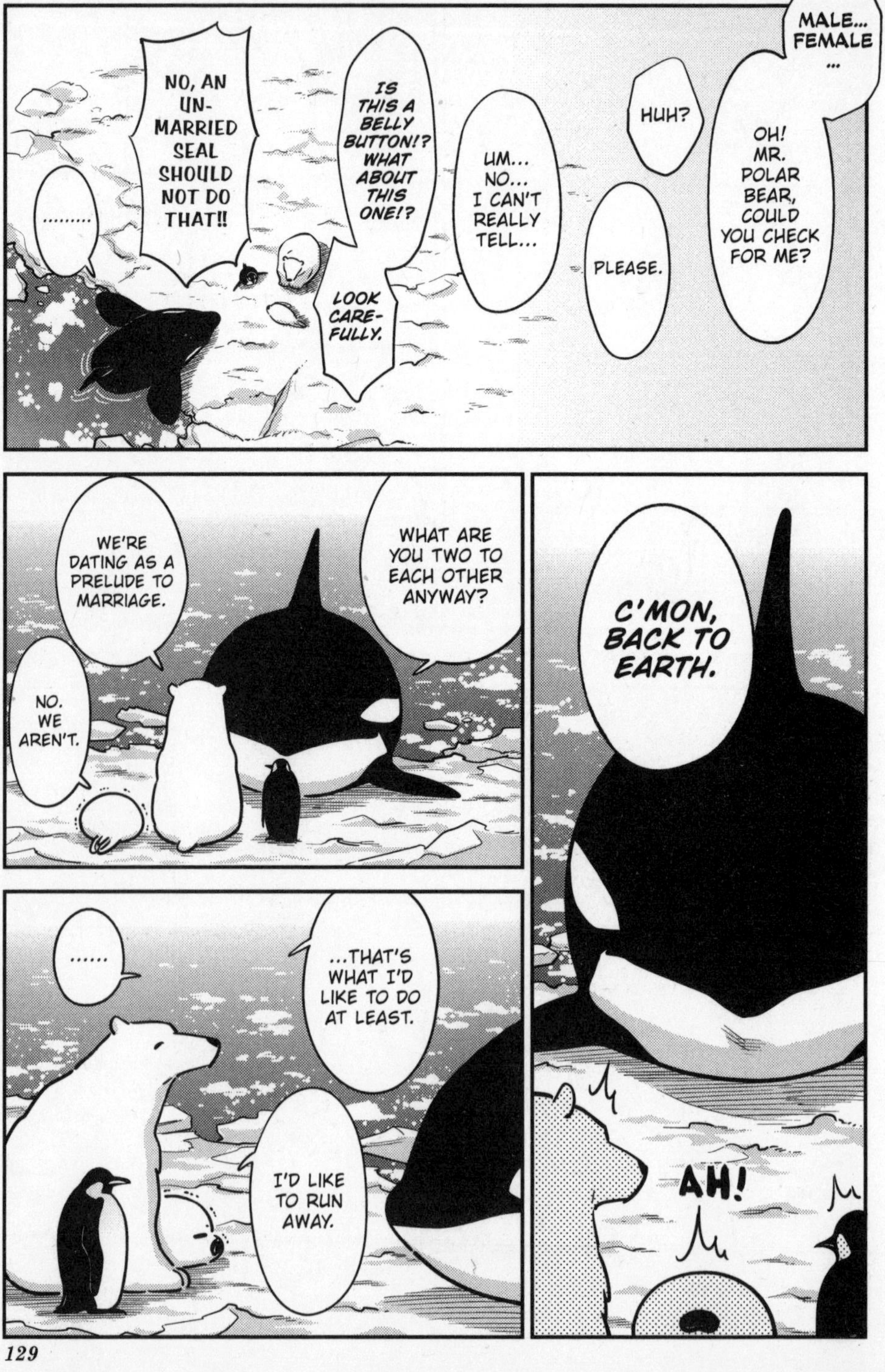
MALE... FEMALE ...
OH! MR. POLAR BEAR, COULD YOU CHECK FOR ME?
HUH?
PLEASE.
UM... NO... I CAN'T REALLY TELL...
IS THIS A BELLY BUTTON!? WHAT ABOUT THIS ONE!?
LOOK CARE-FULLY.
NO, AN UN-MARRIED SEAL SHOULD NOT DO THAT!!
....
C'MON, BACK TO EARTH.
AH!
WHAT ARE YOU TWO TO EACH OTHER ANYWAY?
WE'RE DATING AS A PRELUDE TO MARRIAGE.
NO. WE AREN'T.
...THAT'S WHAT I'D LIKE TO DO AT LEAST.
......
I'D LIKE TO RUN AWAY.

LOVE OR DEATH

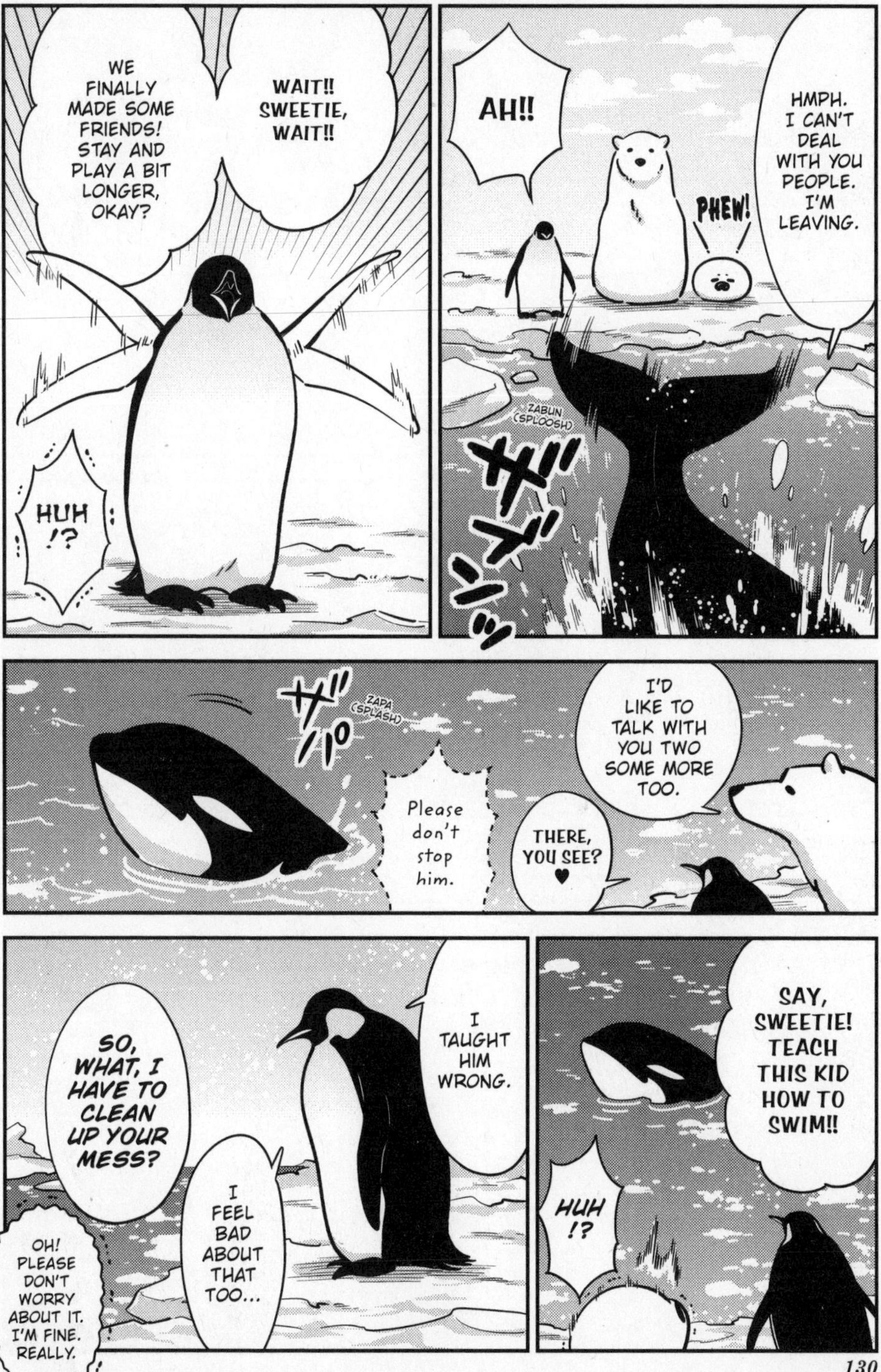
HMPH. I CAN'T DEAL WITH YOU PEOPLE. I'M LEAVING.
AH!!
PHEW!
ZABUN (SPLOOSH)
WAIT!! SWEETIE, WAIT!!
WE FINALLY MADE SOME FRIENDS! STAY AND PLAY A BIT LONGER, OKAY?
HUH!?
I'D LIKE TO TALK WITH YOU TWO SOME MORE TOO.
THERE, YOU SEE? ♥
Please don't stop him.
ZAPA (SPLASH)
SAY, SWEETIE! TEACH THIS KID HOW TO SWIM!!
HUH!?
I TAUGHT HIM WRONG.
SO, WHAT, I HAVE TO CLEAN UP YOUR MESS?
I FEEL BAD ABOUT THAT TOO...
OH! PLEASE DON'T WORRY ABOUT IT. I'M FINE. REALLY.

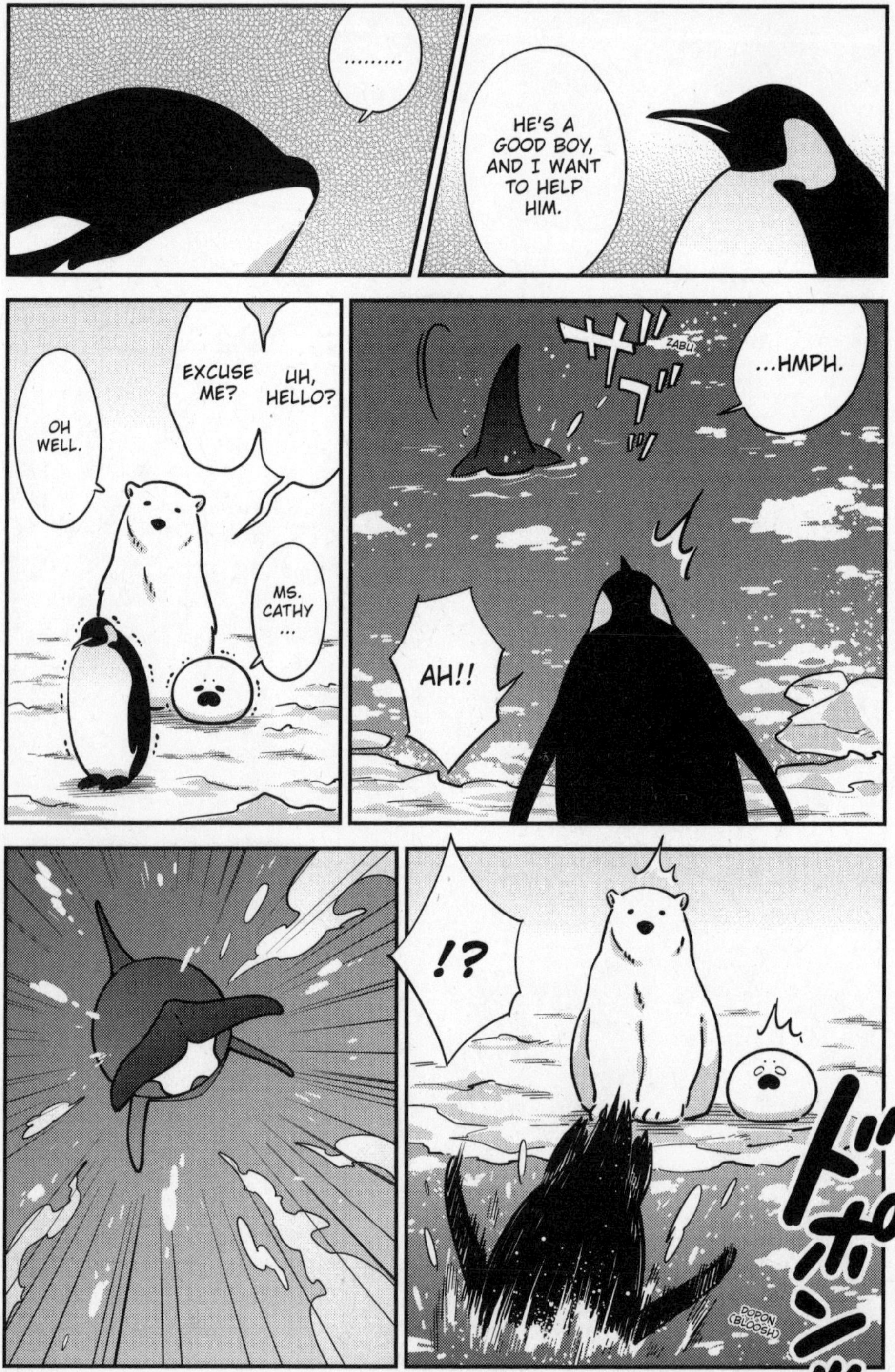
HE'S A GOOD BOY, AND I WANT TO HELP HIM.
....
...HMPH.
ZABU
AH!!
UH, HELLO?
EXCUSE ME?
MS. CATHY ...
OH WELL.
!?
DOPON (BLOOSH)

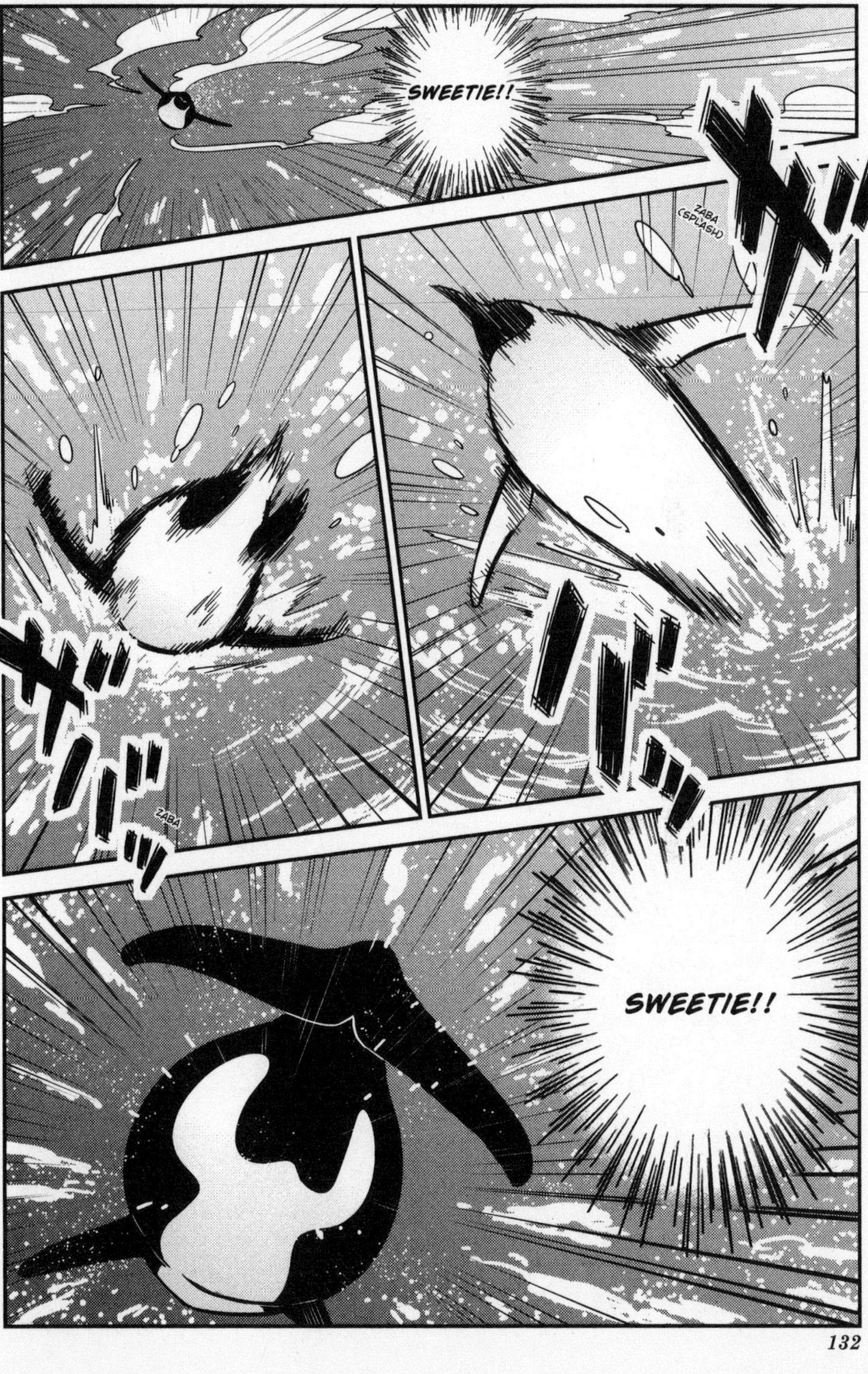
SWEETIE!!
ZABA (SPLASH)
ZABA
SWEETIE!!

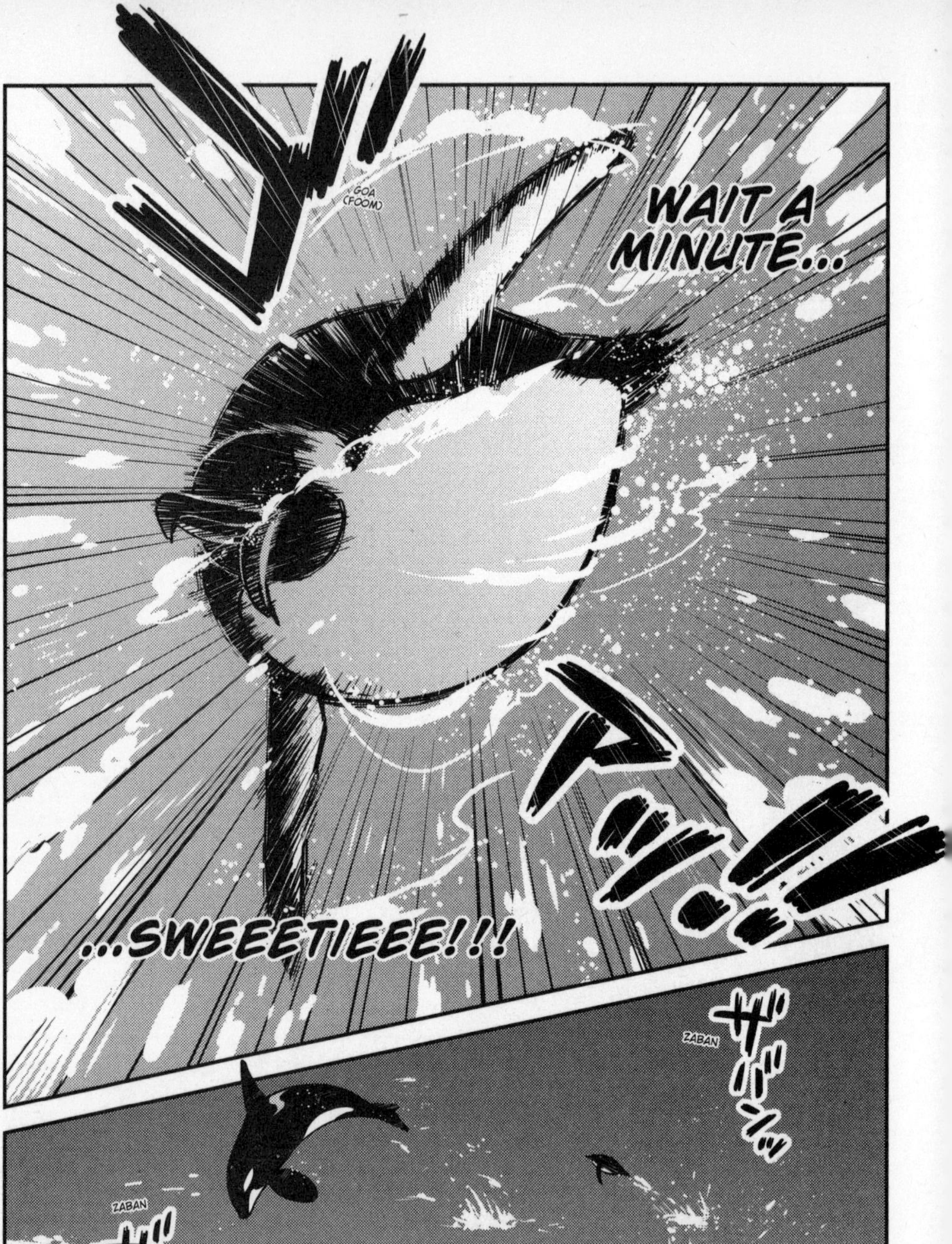
WAIT A MINUTE...
GOA (FOOM)
...SWEEETIEEE!!!
ZABAN
ZABAN

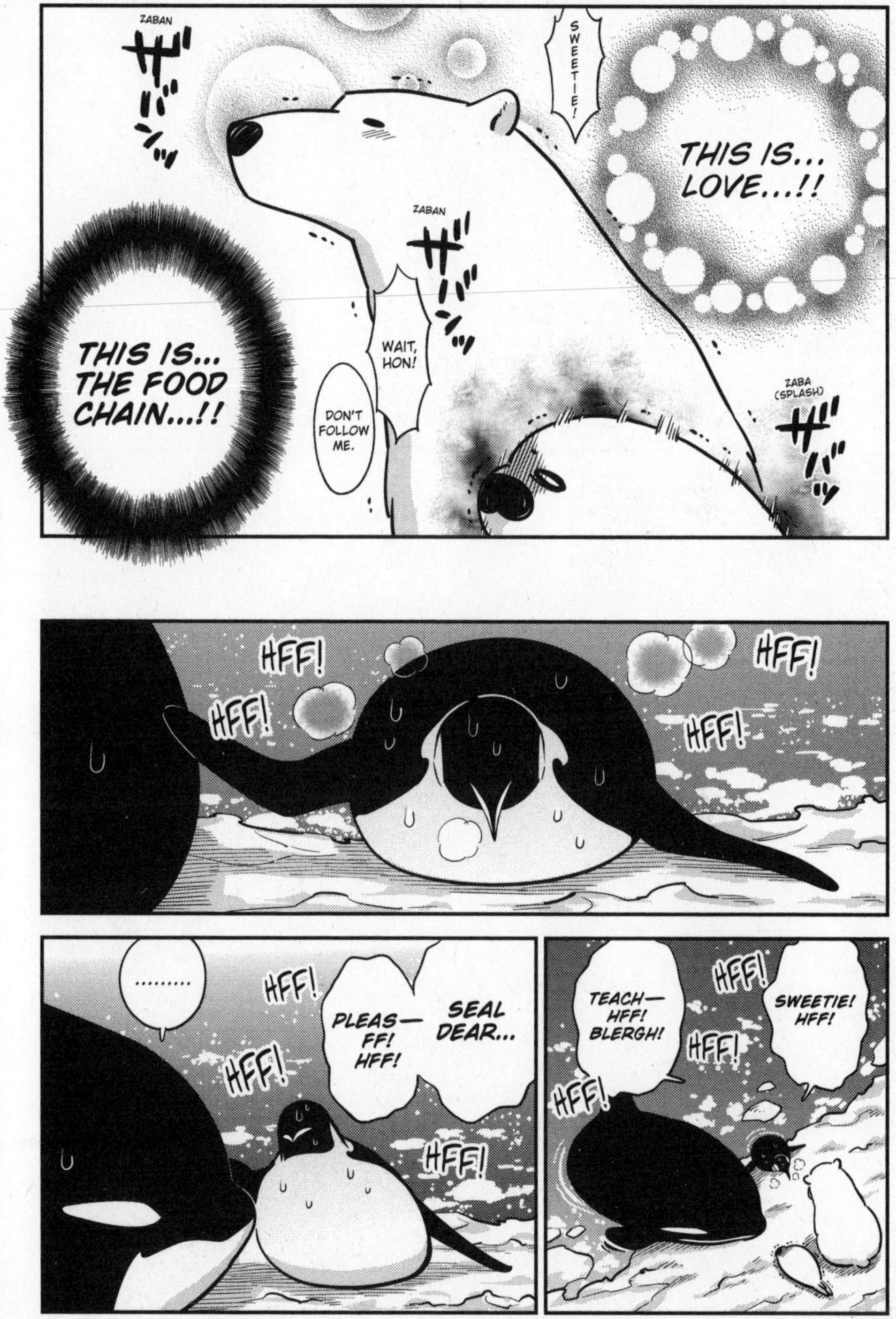
SWEETIE!
THIS IS... LOVE...!!
ZABA (SPLASH)
ZABAN
WAIT, HON!
DON'T FOLLOW ME.
ZABAN
THIS IS... THE FOOD CHAIN...!!
HFF!
HFF!
HFF!
HFF!
SWEETIE! HFF!
HFF!
TEACH— HFF! BLERGH!
HFF!
HFF!
SEAL DEAR...
PLEAS— FF! HFF!
HFF!
....
HFF!

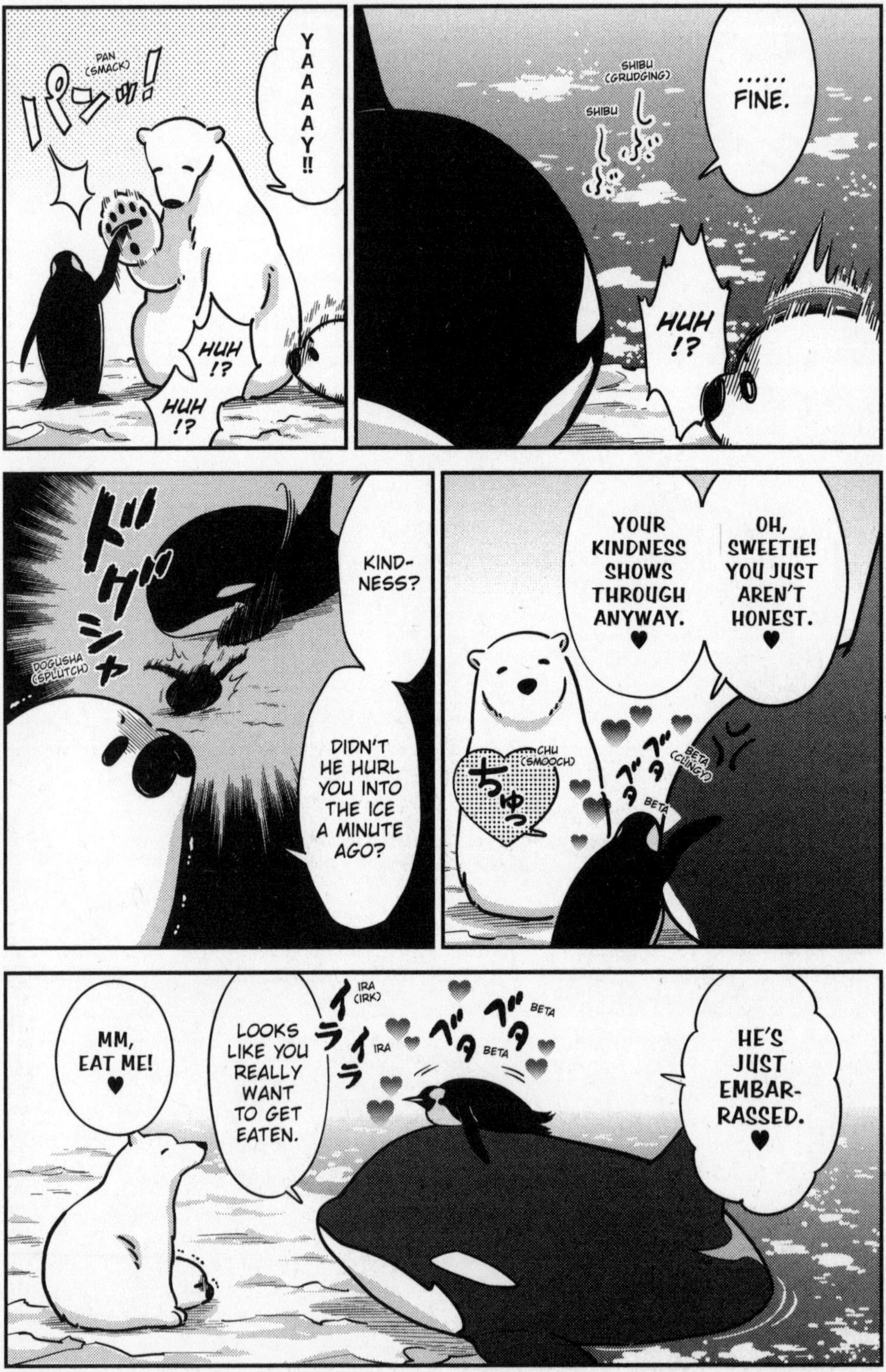

...... FINE.
SHIBU (GRUDGING)
SHIBU
しぶしぶ
HUH !?
YAAAAAY!!
PAN (SMACK)
パンッ!
HUH !?
HUH !?
OH, SWEETIE! YOU JUST AREN'T HONEST. ♥
YOUR KINDNESS SHOWS THROUGH ANYWAY. ♥
BETA (CLINGY)
BETA
ベタベタ
CHU (SMOOCH)
ちゅっ
KIND- NESS?
DIDN'T HE HURL YOU INTO THE ICE A MINUTE AGO?
ドグシャ
DOGUSHA (SPLUTCH)
HE'S JUST EMBAR- RASSED. ♥
BETA
BETA
ベタベタ
IRA (IRK)
IRA
イライラ
LOOKS LIKE YOU REALLY WANT TO GET EATEN.
MM, EAT ME! ♥

WHY I FOLLOWED YOU

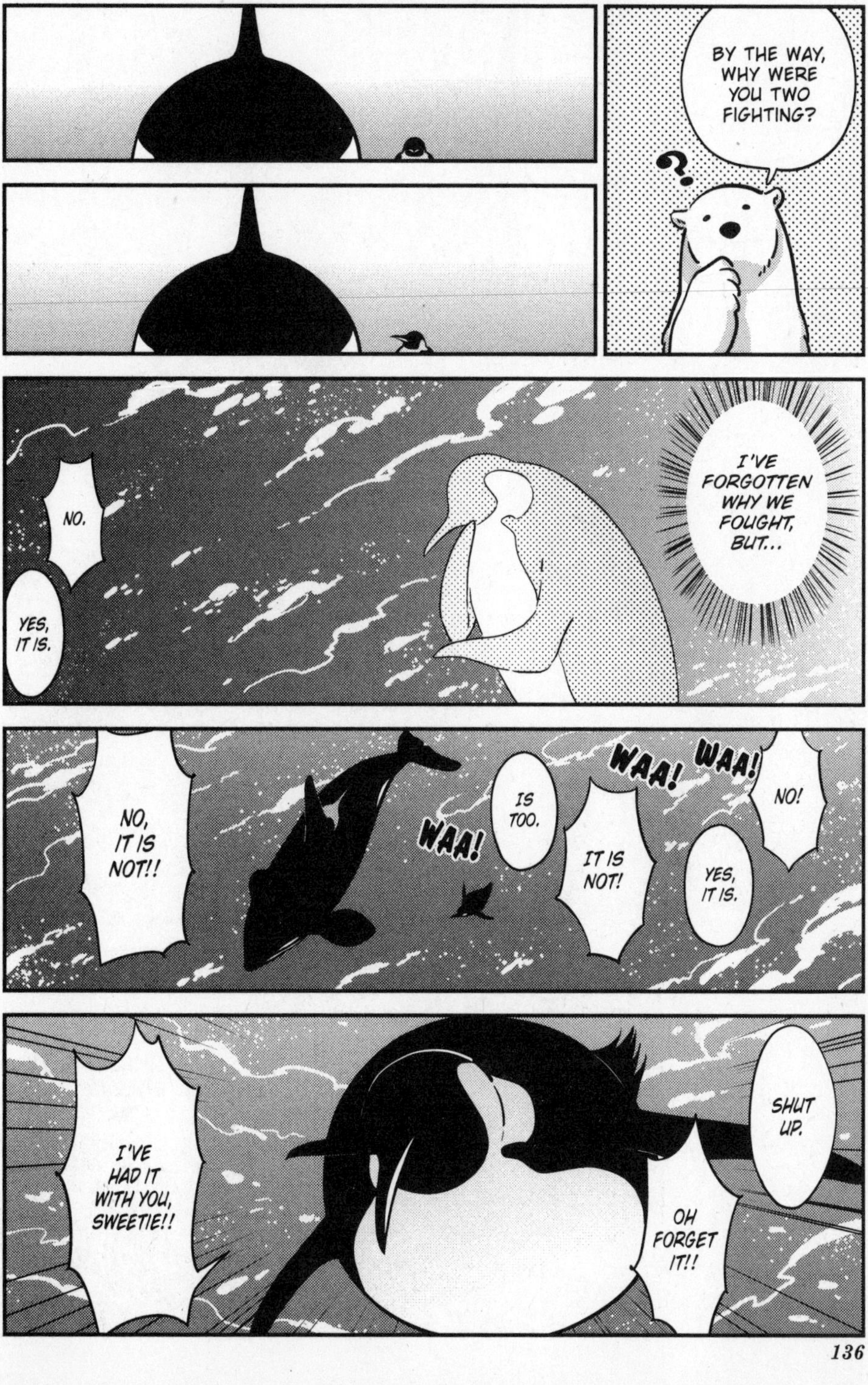
BY THE WAY, WHY WERE YOU TWO FIGHTING?
?
I'VE FORGOTTEN WHY WE FOUGHT, BUT...
NO.
YES, IT IS.
NO!
WAA!
WAA!
YES, IT IS.
IT IS NOT!
IS TOO.
WAA!
NO, IT IS NOT!!
SHUT UP.
OH FORGET IT!!
I'VE HAD IT WITH YOU, SWEETIE!!

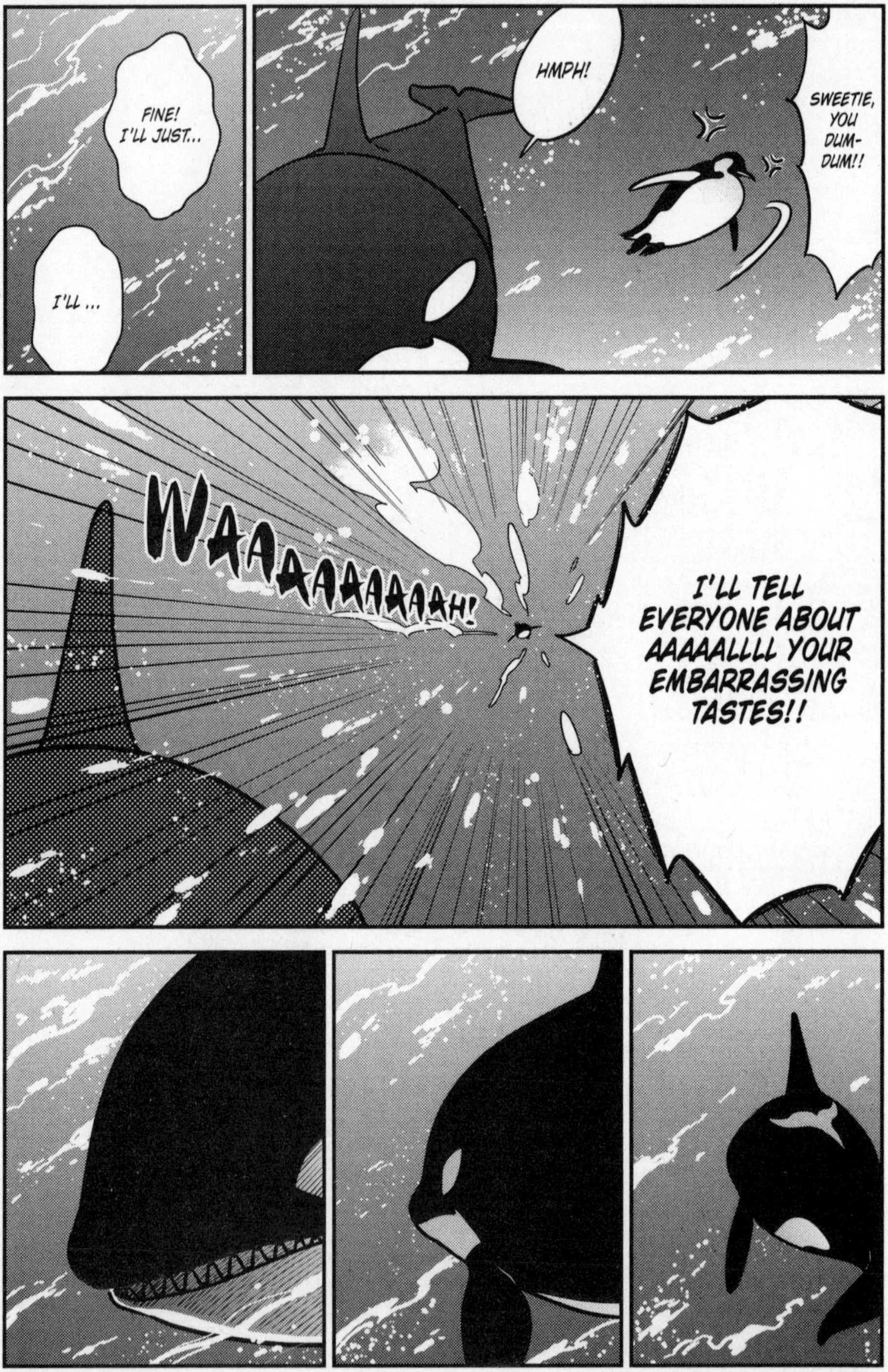
SWEETIE, YOU DUM-DUM!!
HMPH!
FINE! I'LL JUST...
I'LL ...
I'LL TELL EVERYONE ABOUT AAAAALLLL YOUR EMBARRASSING TASTES!!
WAAAAAAAAAAAH!

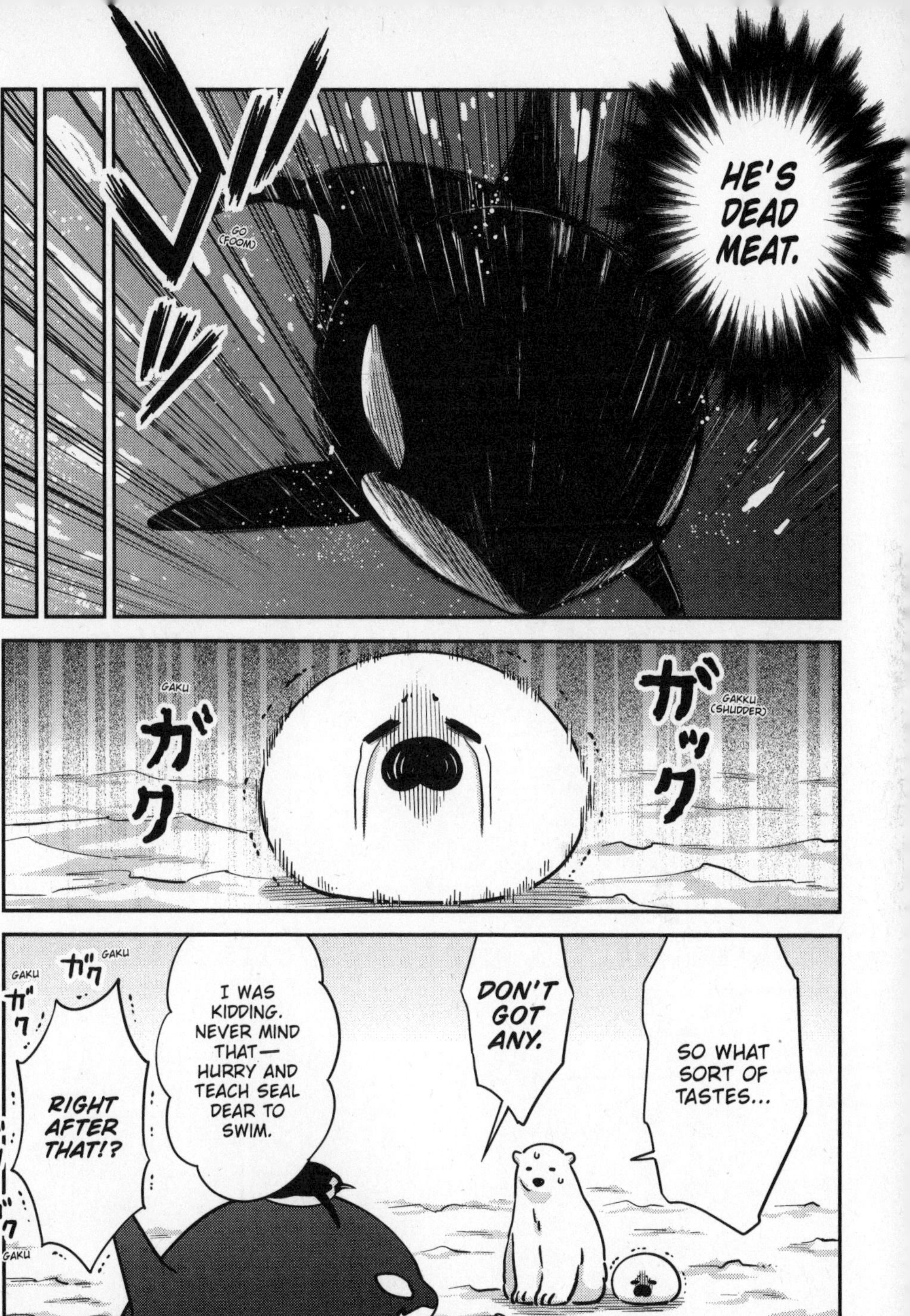
HE'S DEAD MEAT.
ゴッ
GO (FOOM)
ガック
GAKKU (SHUDDER)
ガク
GAKU
SO WHAT SORT OF TASTES...
DON'T GOT ANY.
I WAS KIDDING. NEVER MIND THAT— HURRY AND TEACH SEAL DEAR TO SWIM.
RIGHT AFTER THAT!?
ガク
GAKU
ガク
GAKU
ガク
GAKU
ガク
GAKU

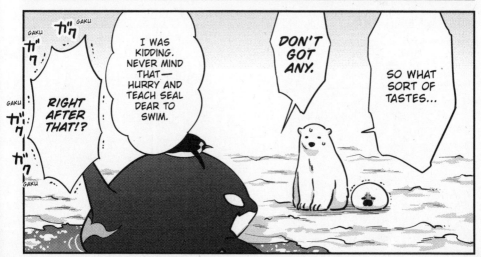

TO BE CONTINUED IN VOLUME 4 ♥

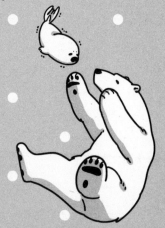

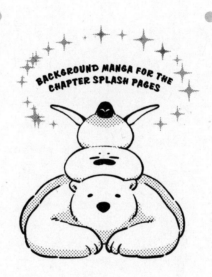

BACKGROUND MANGA FOR THE CHAPTER SPLASH PAGES

CALL ME BIG BROTHER

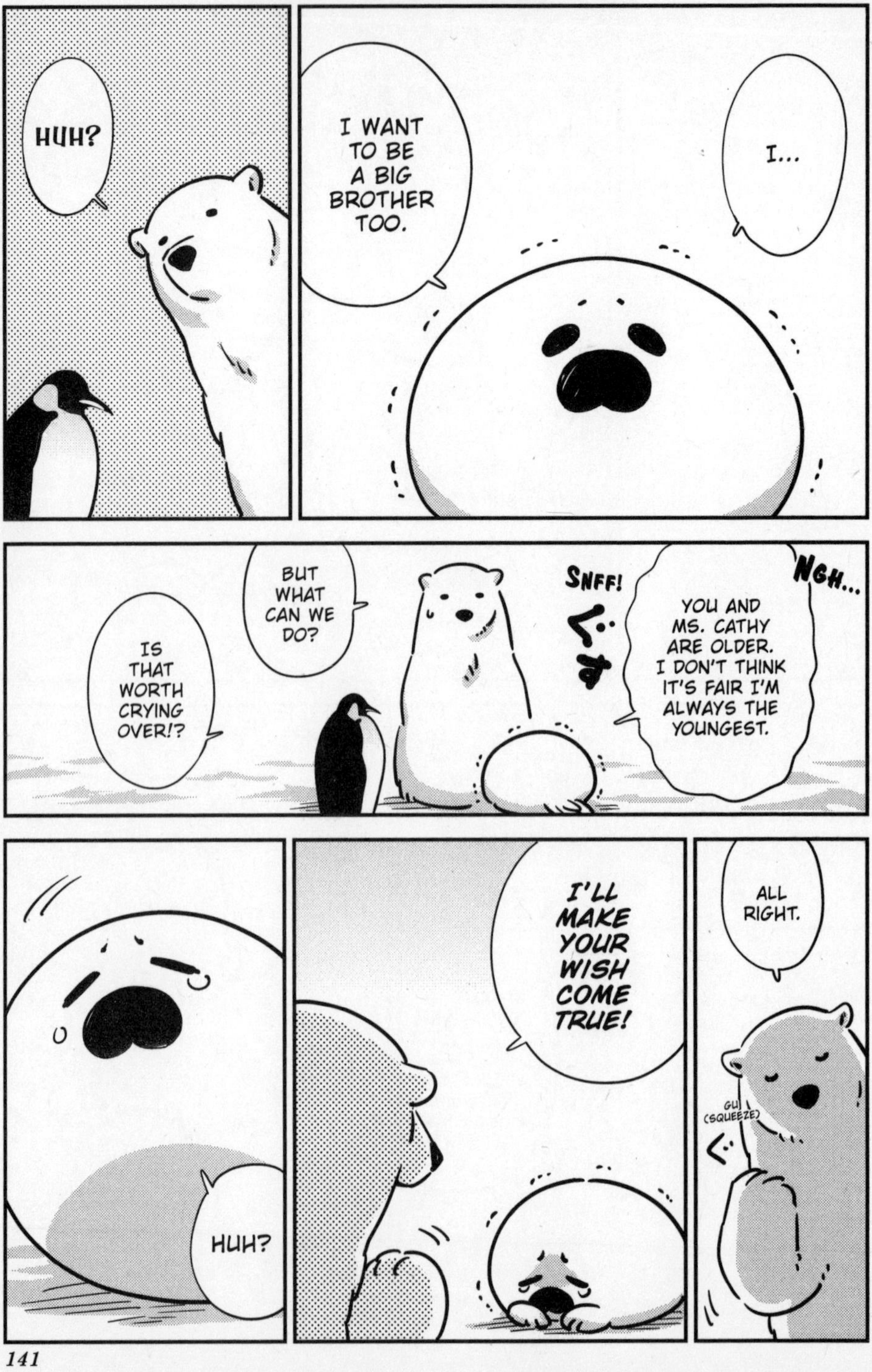
I...
I WANT TO BE A BIG BROTHER TOO.
HUH?
NGH...
YOU AND MS. CATHY ARE OLDER. I DON'T THINK IT'S FAIR I'M ALWAYS THE YOUNGEST.
SNFF!
ぐす
BUT WHAT CAN WE DO?
IS THAT WORTH CRYING OVER!?
ALL RIGHT.
GU (SQUEEZE)
ぐっ
I'LL MAKE YOUR WISH COME TRUE!
HUH?

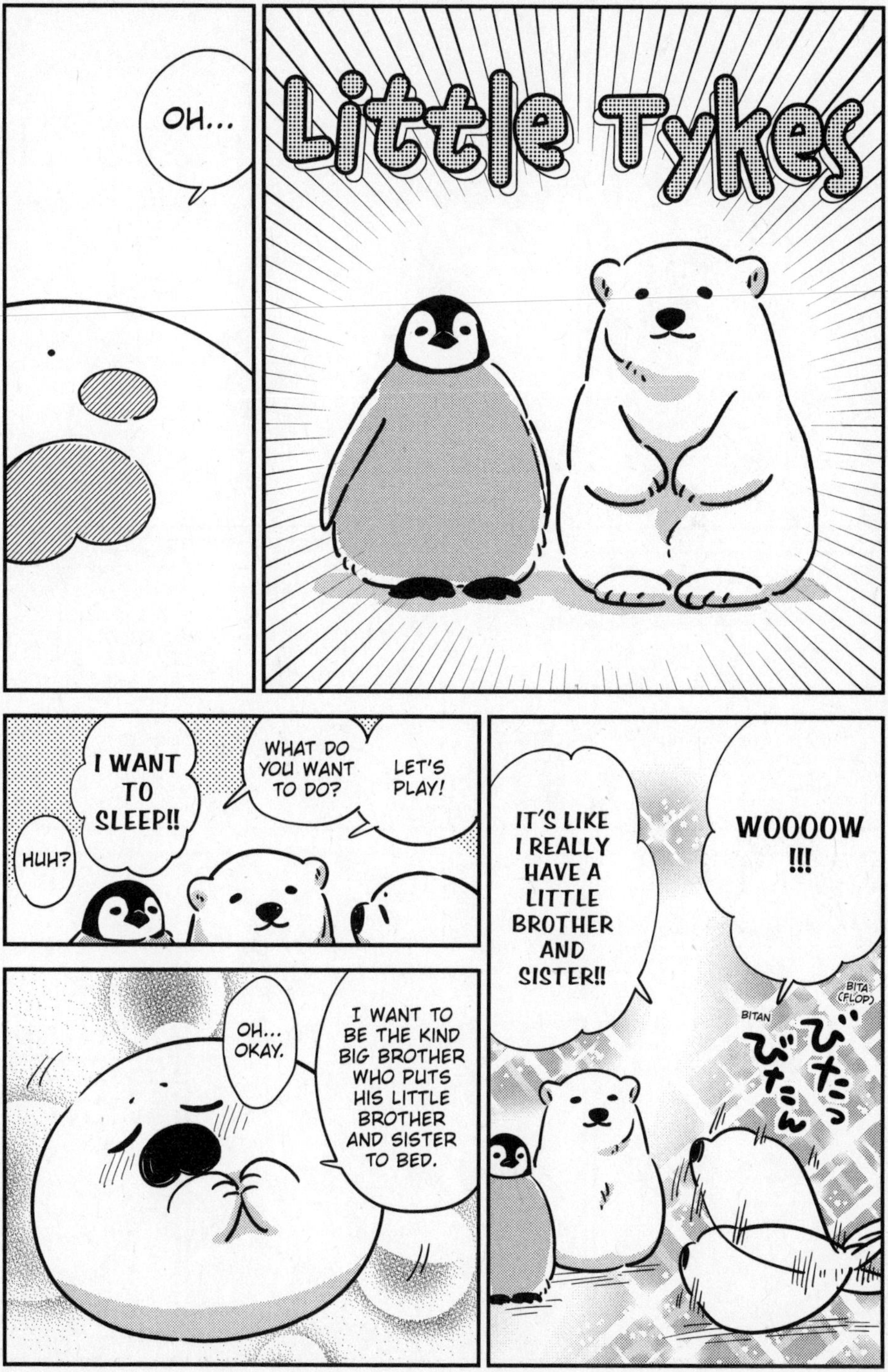
Little Tykes
OH...
WOOOOW!!!
IT'S LIKE I REALLY HAVE A LITTLE BROTHER AND SISTER!!
BITA (FLOP)
びたっ
BITAN
びたん
LET'S PLAY!
WHAT DO YOU WANT TO DO?
I WANT TO SLEEP!!
HUH?
I WANT TO BE THE KIND BIG BROTHER WHO PUTS HIS LITTLE BROTHER AND SISTER TO BED.
OH... OKAY.

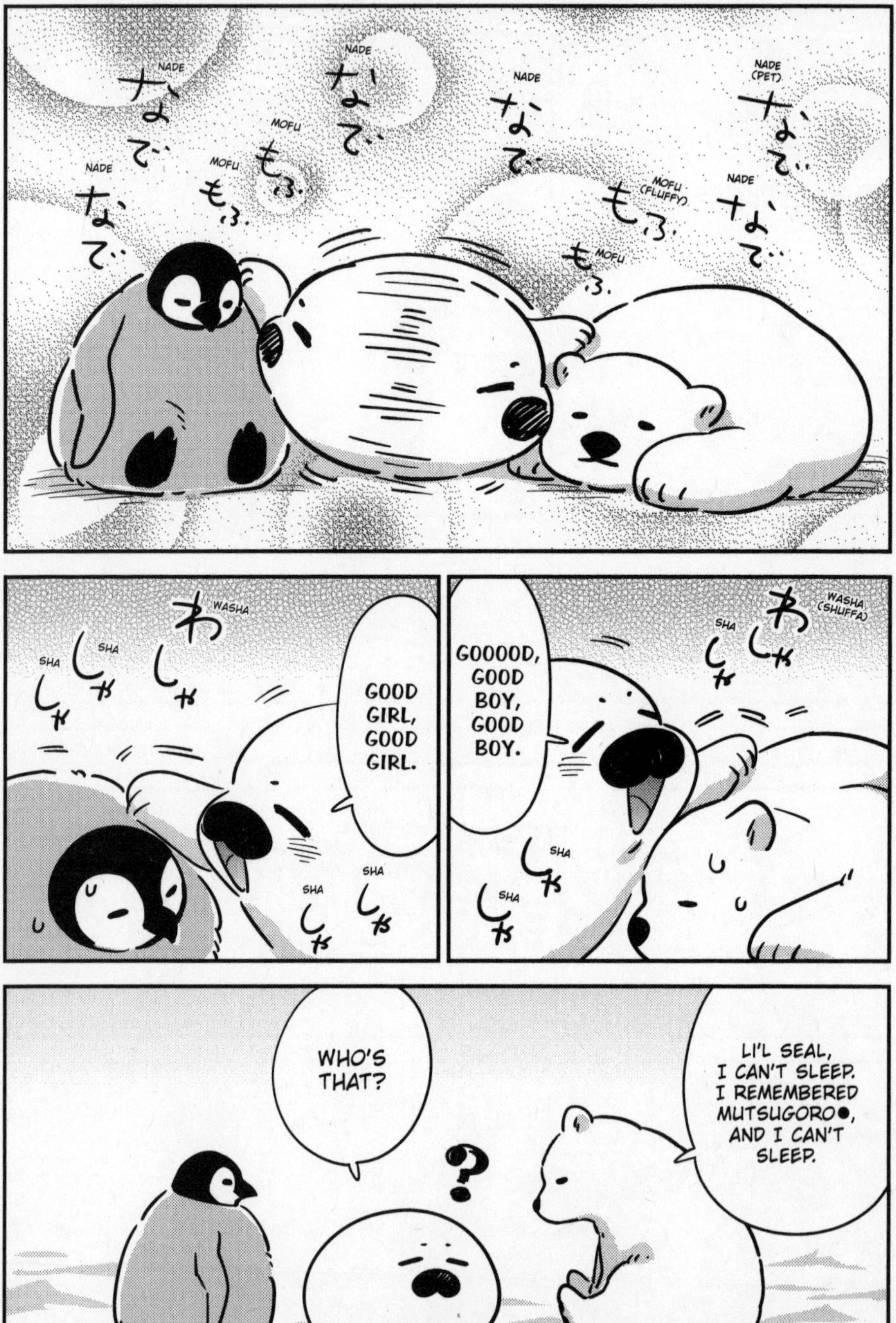
NADE (PET)
なで
NADE
なで
MOFU (FLUFFY)
もふ
MOFU
もふ
NADE
なで
MOFU
もふ
MOFU
もふ
NADE
なで
NADE
なで
NADE
なで
WASHA (SHUFFA)
わしゃ
SHA
しゃ
GOOOOD, GOOD BOY, GOOD BOY.
SHA
しゃ
SHA
しゃ
GOOD GIRL, GOOD GIRL.
WASHA
わしゃ
SHA
しゃ
SHA
しゃ
SHA
しゃ
SHA
しゃ
LI'L SEAL, I CAN'T SLEEP. I REMEMBERED MUTSUGORO●, AND I CAN'T SLEEP.
?
WHO'S THAT?

TAG

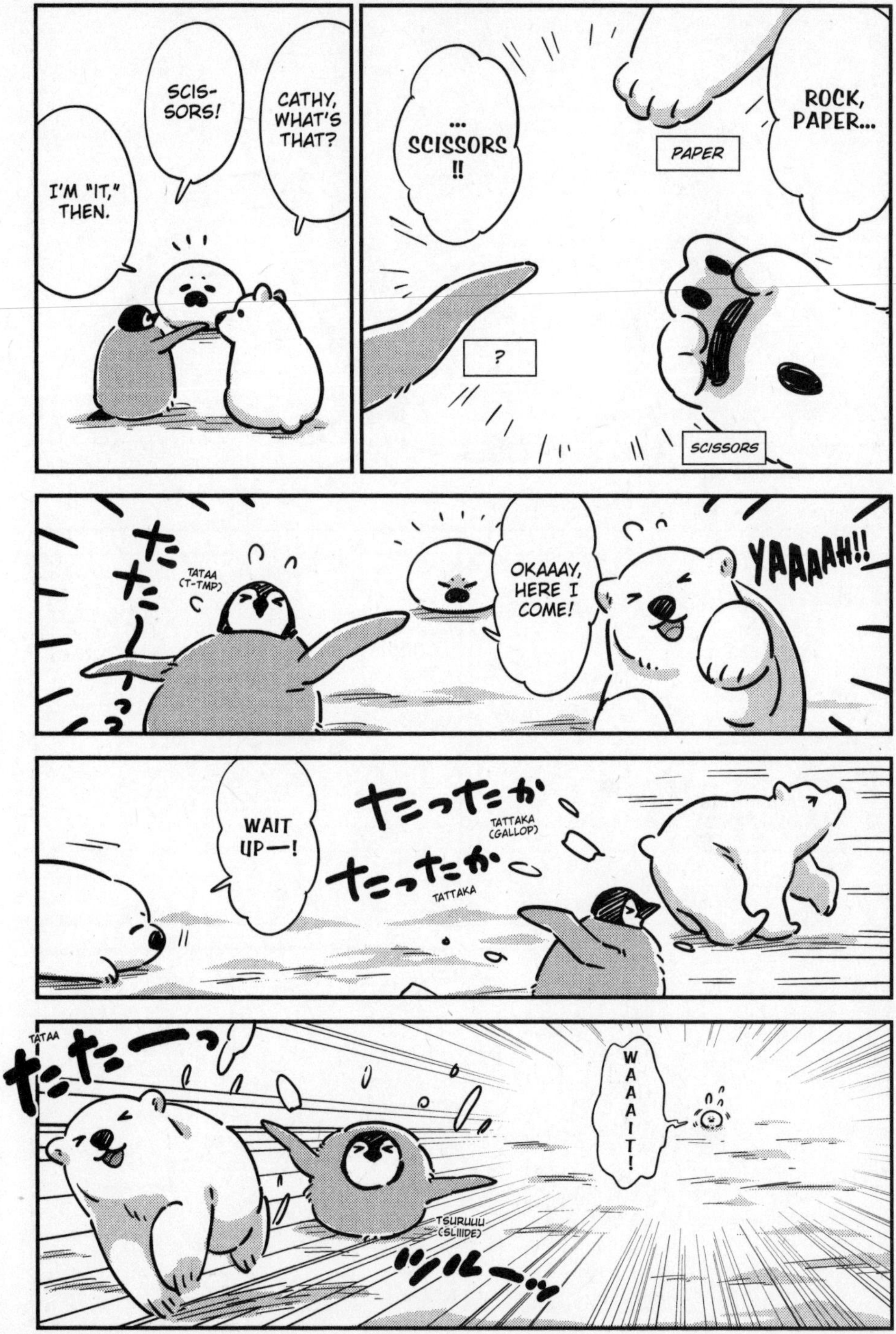

ROCK, PAPER...
PAPER
... SCISSORS !!
?
SCISSORS
CATHY, WHAT'S THAT?
SCIS-SORS!
I'M "IT," THEN.
YAAAAH!!
OKAAAY, HERE I COME!
TATAA (T-TMP)
TATTAKA (GALLOP)
TATTAKA
WAIT UP—!
WAAAIT!
TSURUUU (SLIIIDE)
TATAA

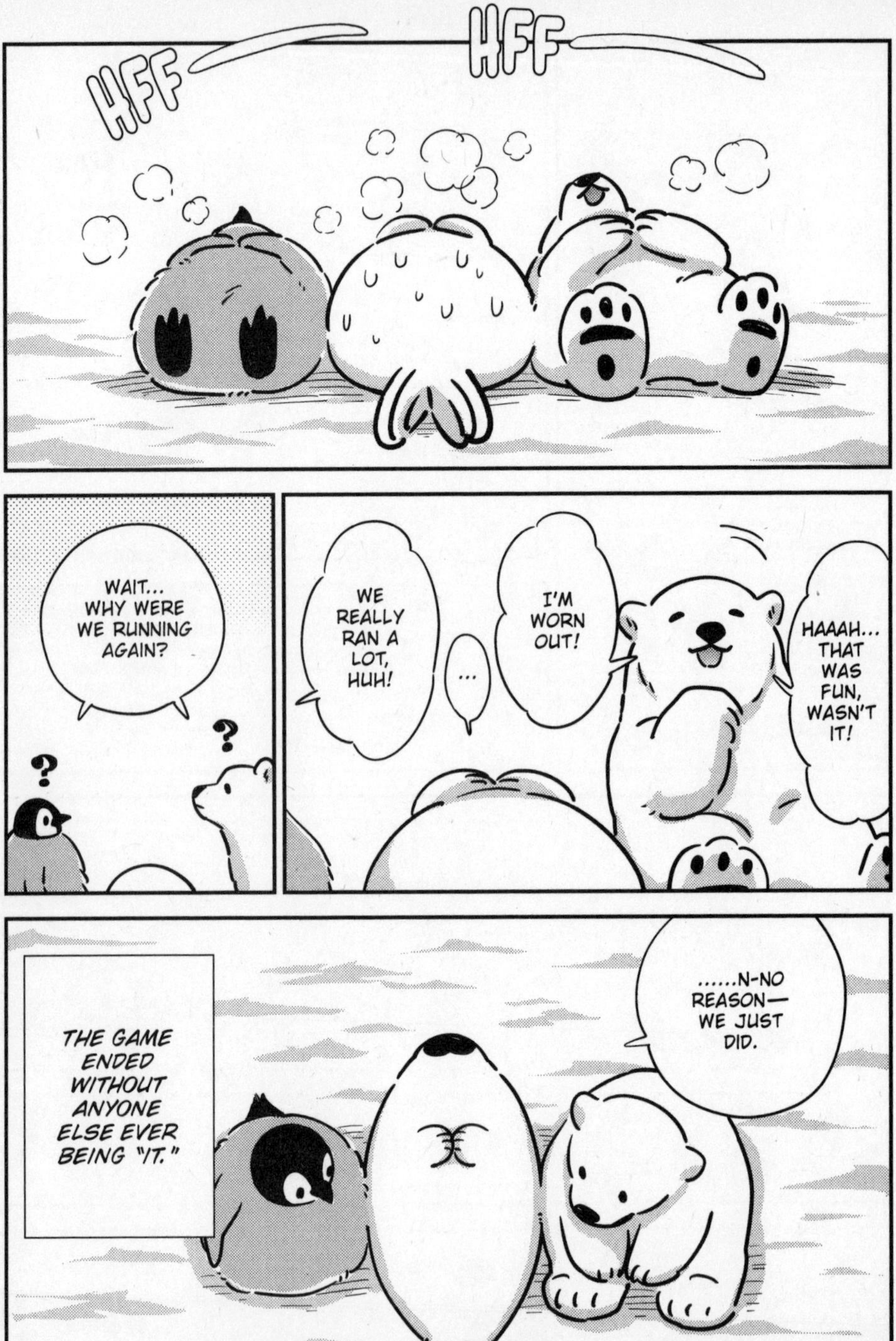
HFF
HFF
HAAAH... THAT WAS FUN, WASN'T IT!
I'M WORN OUT!
...
WE REALLY RAN A LOT, HUH!
WAIT... WHY WERE WE RUNNING AGAIN?
?
?
......N-NO REASON— WE JUST DID.
THE GAME ENDED WITHOUT ANYONE ELSE EVER BEING "IT."

SNOWMEN

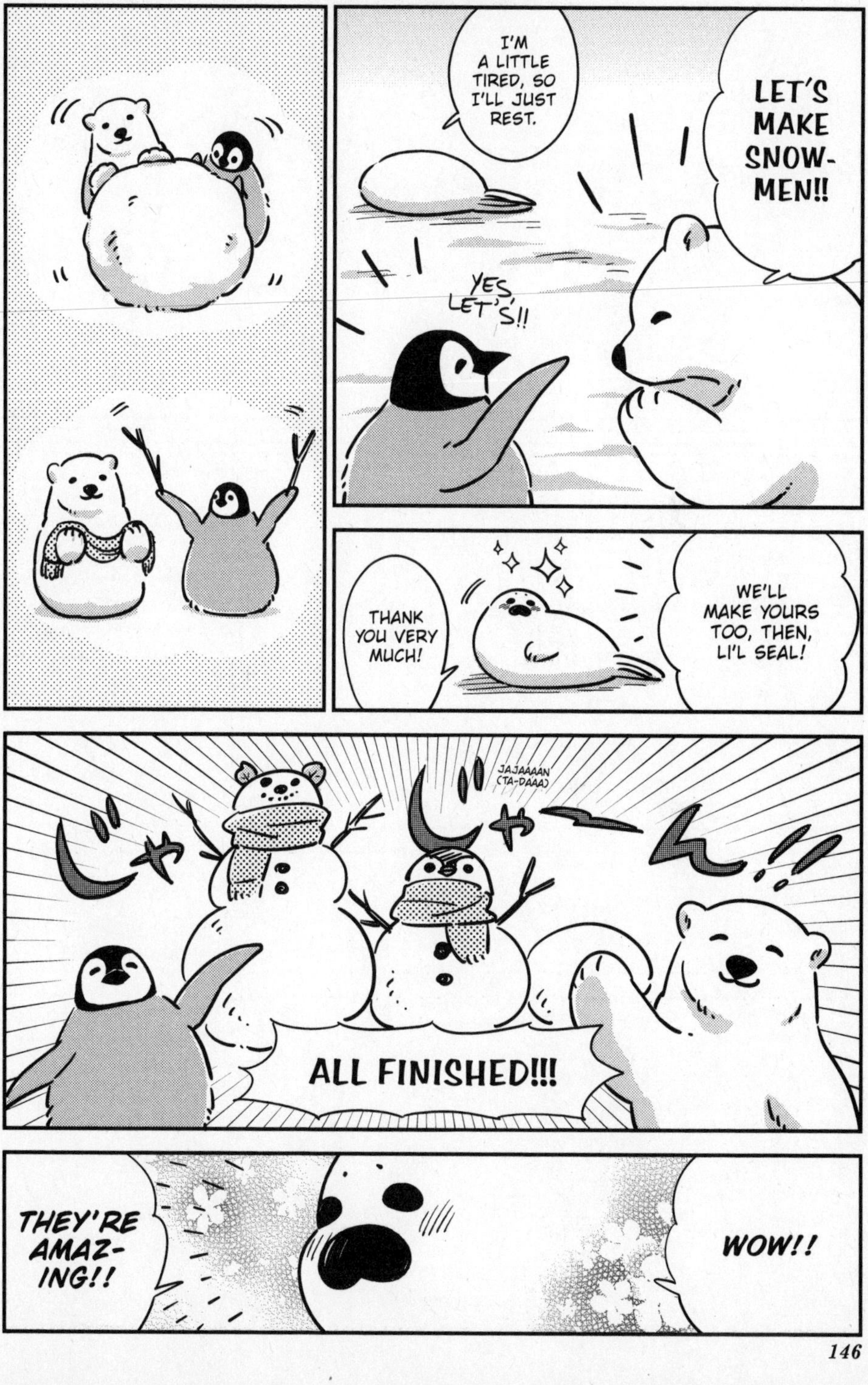
LET'S MAKE SNOW-MEN!!
I'M A LITTLE TIRED, SO I'LL JUST REST.
YES, LET'S!!
WE'LL MAKE YOURS TOO, THEN, LI'L SEAL!
THANK YOU VERY MUCH!
JAJAAAAN (TA-DAAA)
ALL FINISHED!!!
WOW!!
THEY'RE AMAZ-ING!!

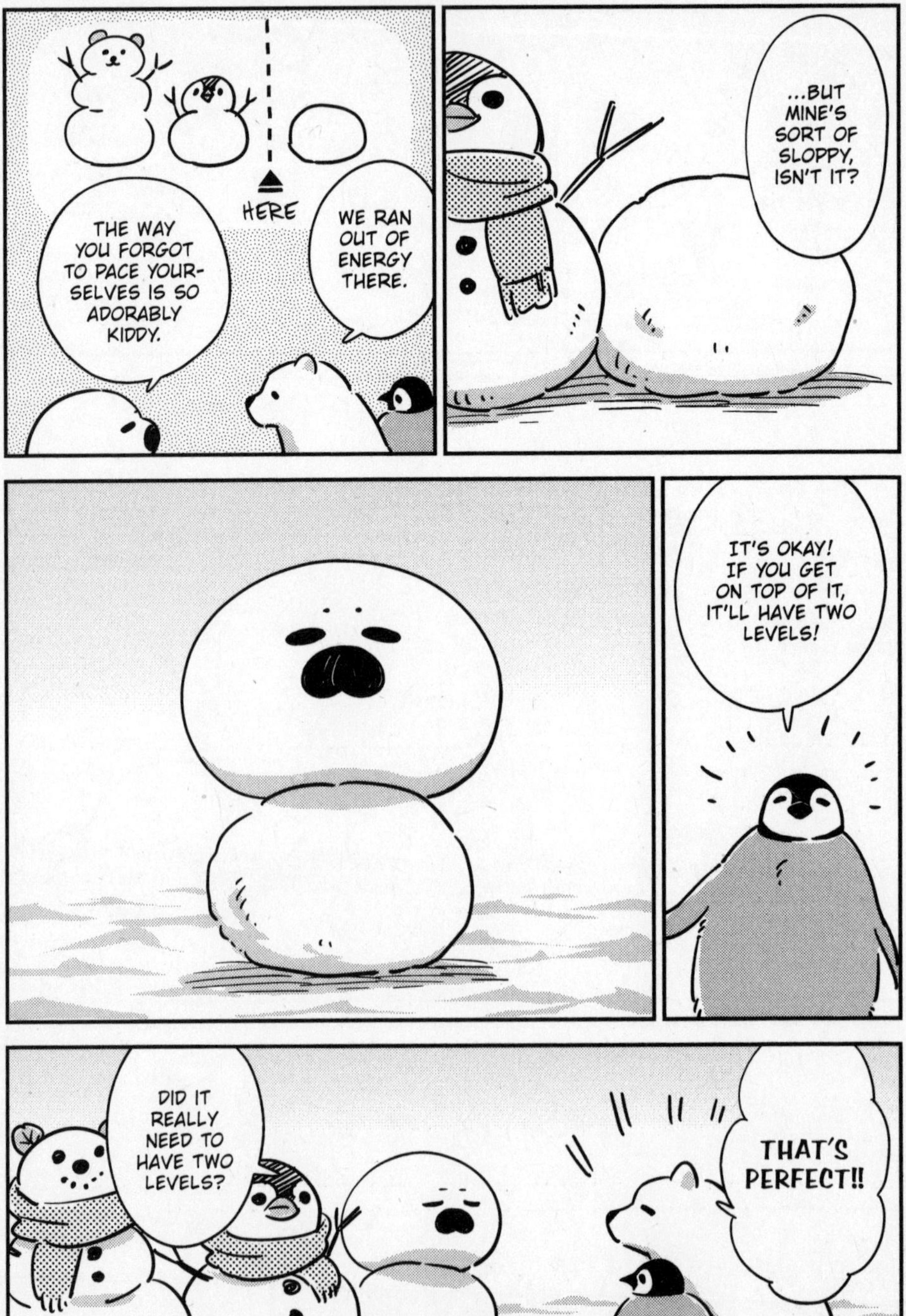
...BUT MINE'S SORT OF SLOPPY, ISN'T IT?
WE RAN OUT OF ENERGY THERE.
HERE
THE WAY YOU FORGOT TO PACE YOUR-SELVES IS SO ADORABLY KIDDY.
IT'S OKAY! IF YOU GET ON TOP OF IT, IT'LL HAVE TWO LEVELS!
THAT'S PERFECT!!
DID IT REALLY NEED TO HAVE TWO LEVELS?

SNOW HUT

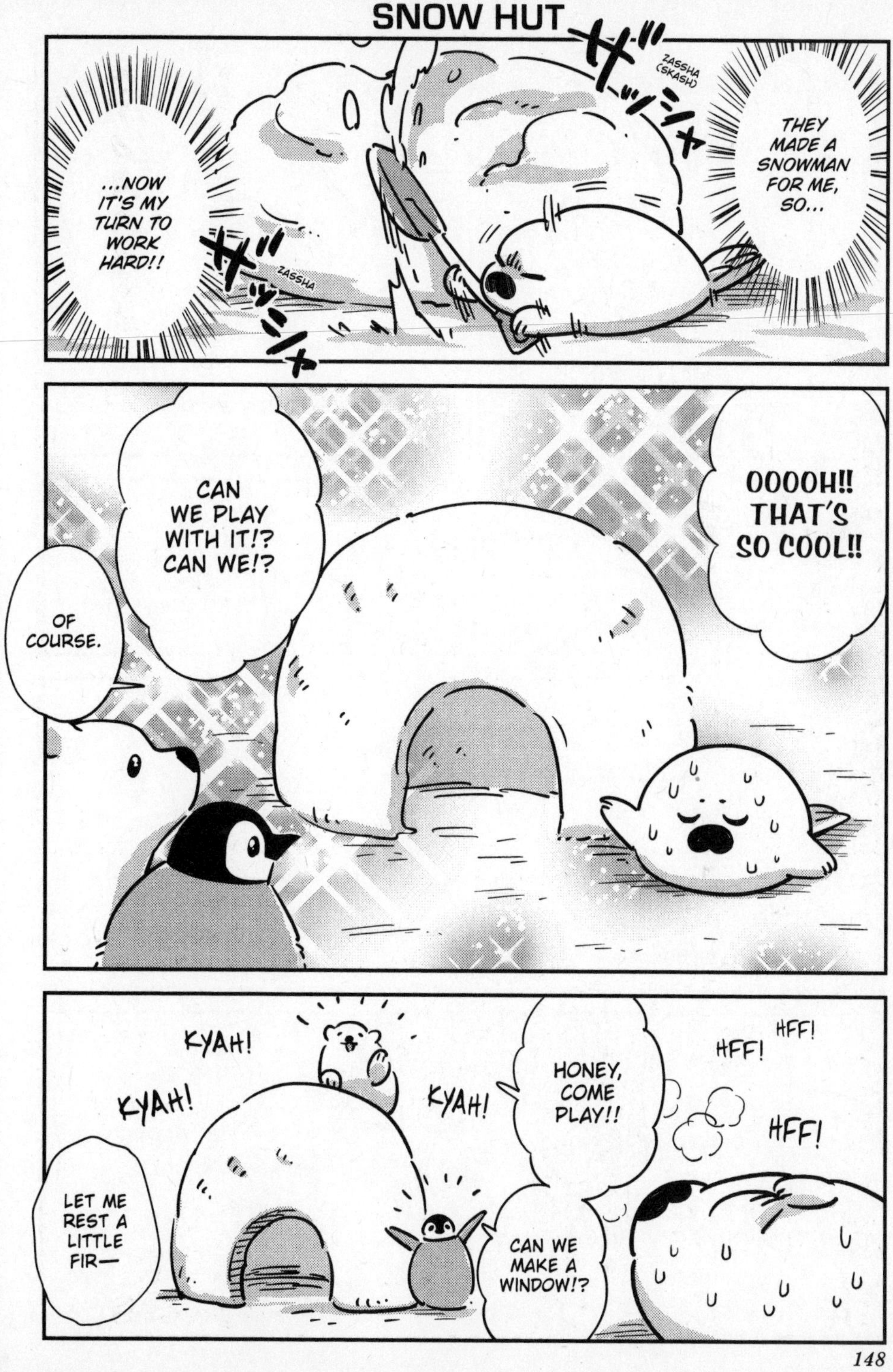
THEY MADE A SNOWMAN FOR ME, SO...
ZASSHA (SKASH)
...NOW IT'S MY TURN TO WORK HARD!!
ZASSHA
OOOOH!! THAT'S SO COOL!!
CAN WE PLAY WITH IT!? CAN WE!?
OF COURSE.
HFF!
HFF!
HFF!
HONEY, COME PLAY!!
CAN WE MAKE A WINDOW!?
KYAH!
KYAH!
KYAH!
LET ME REST A LITTLE FIR—

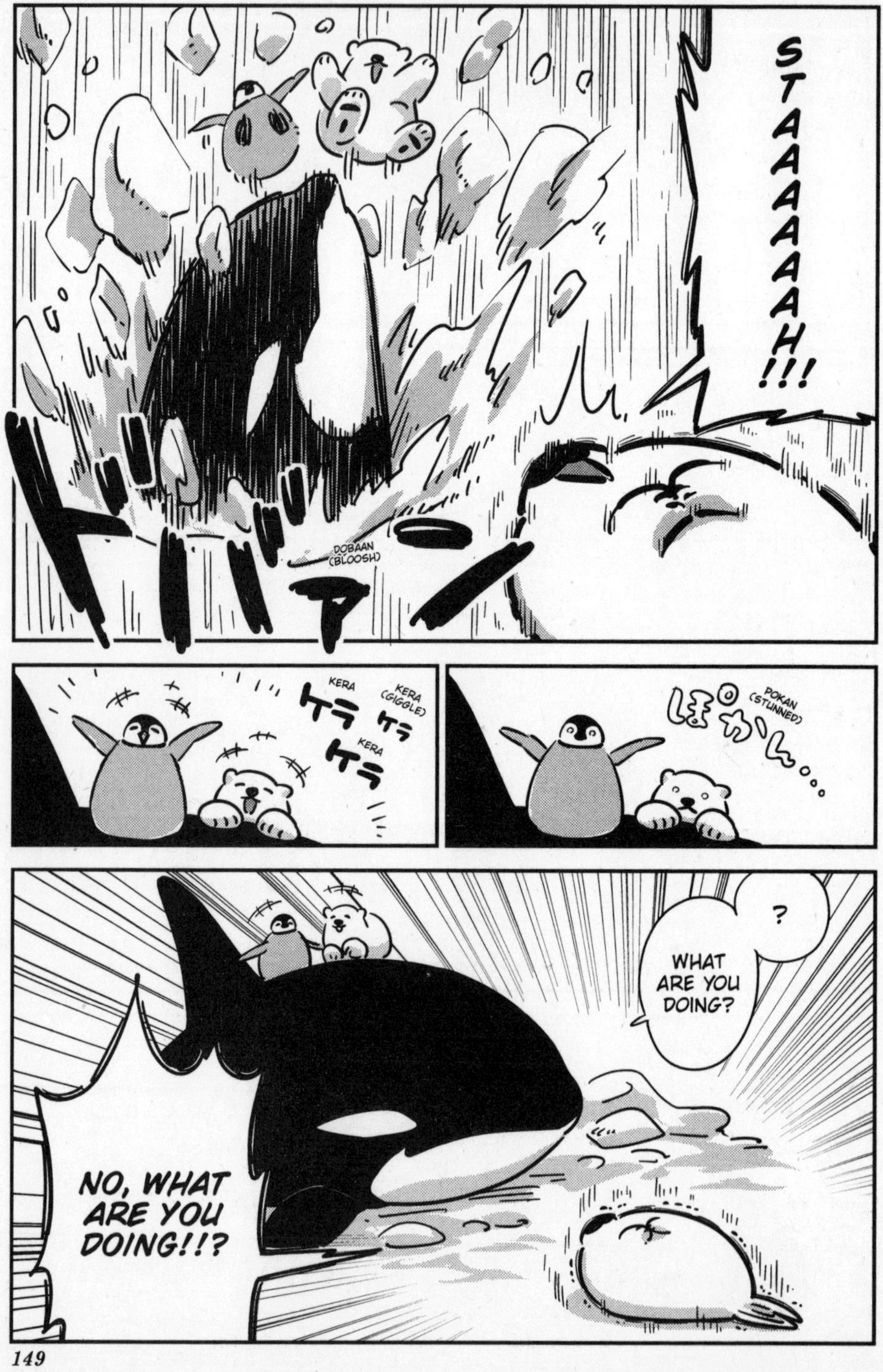
STAAAAAAAH!!!
DOBAAN (BLOOSH)
ぽかん…
POKAN (STUNNED)
ケラケラケラ
KERA KERA (GIGGLE) KERA
?
WHAT ARE YOU DOING?
NO, WHAT ARE YOU DOING!!?

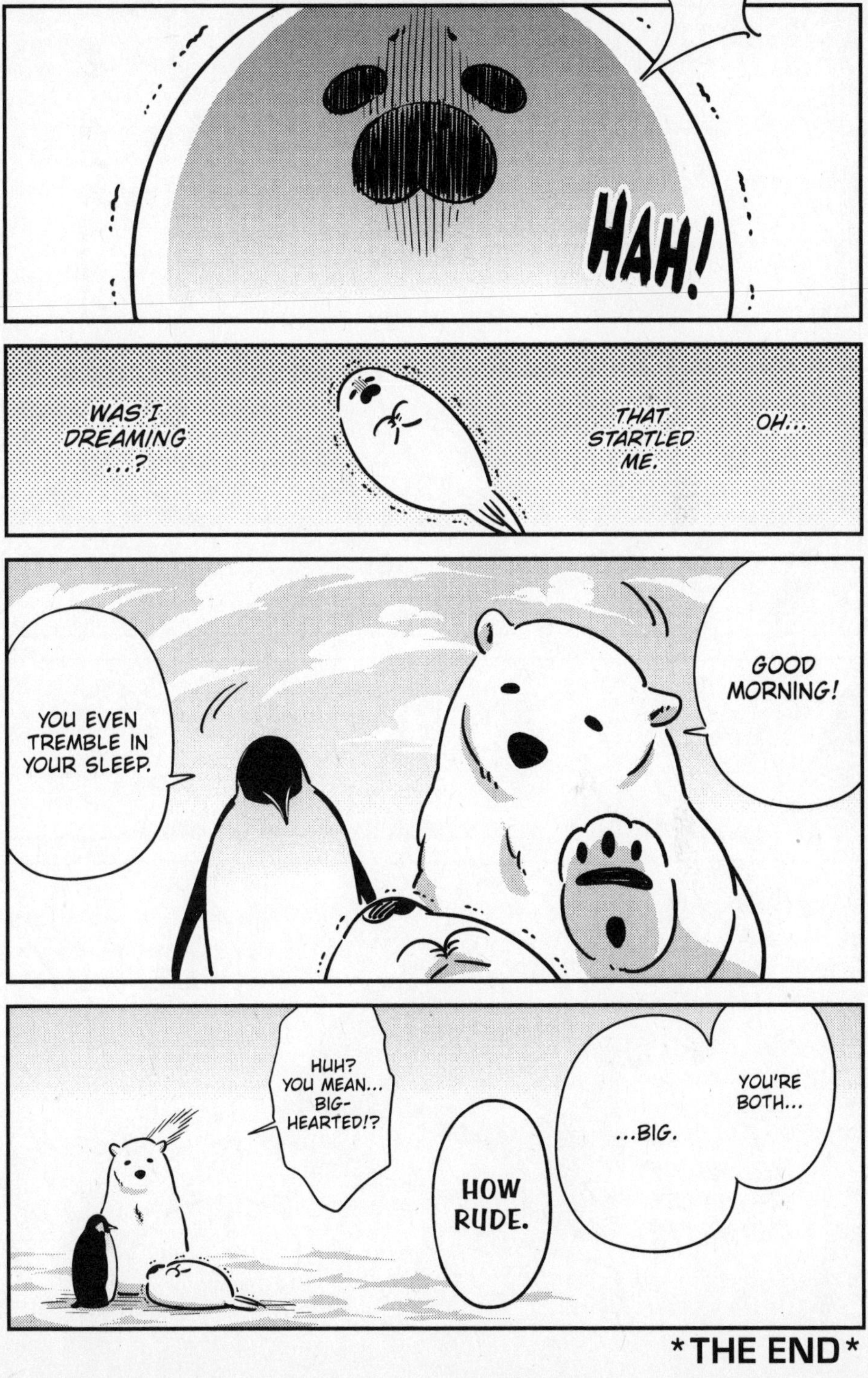
HAH!
OH...
THAT STARTLED ME.
WAS I DREAMING ...?
GOOD MORNING!
YOU EVEN TREMBLE IN YOUR SLEEP.
YOU'RE BOTH...
...BIG.
HOW RUDE.
HUH? YOU MEAN... BIG-HEARTED!?

THE END

\IT'S TRUE!/

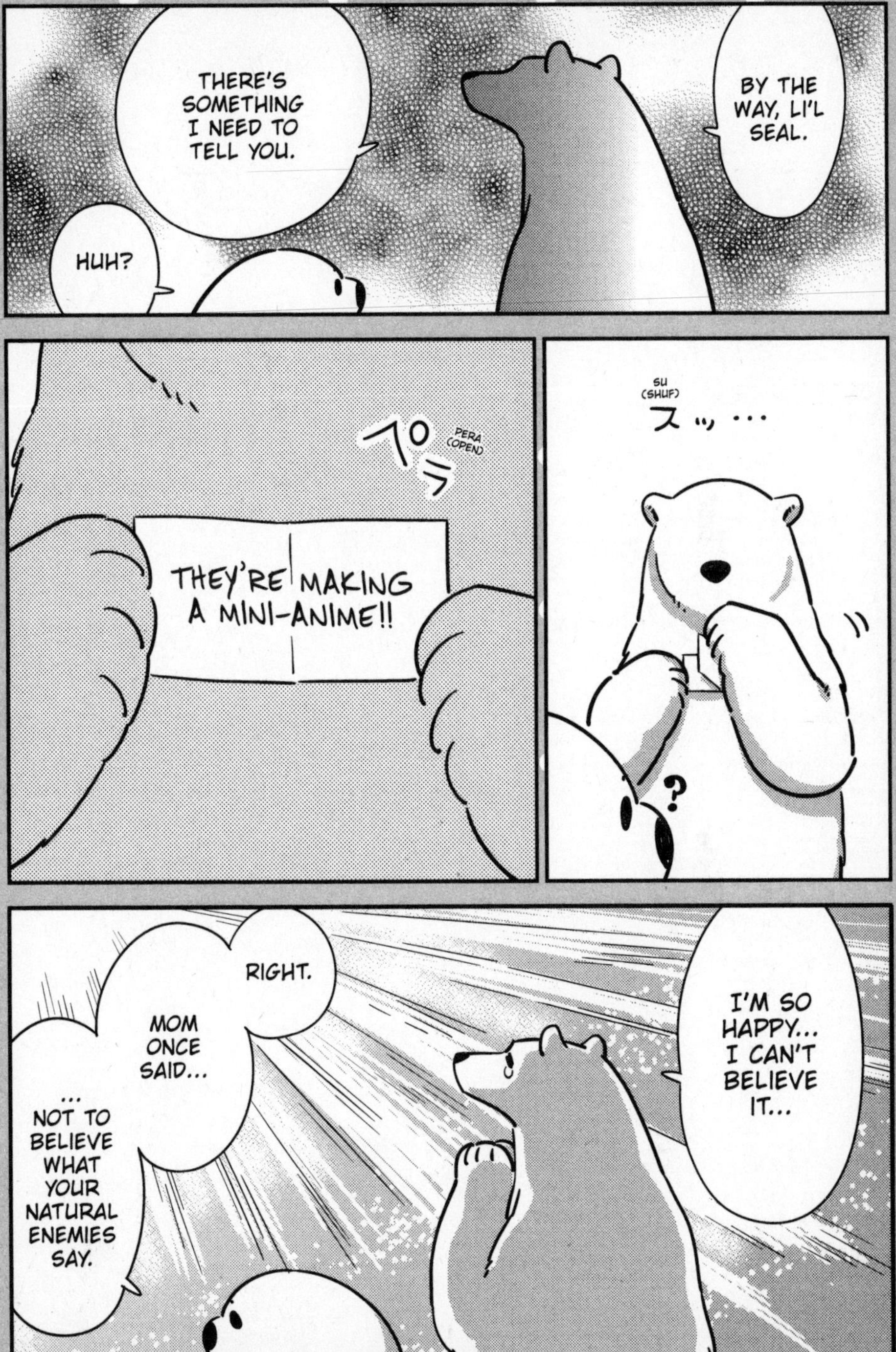
BY THE WAY, LI'L SEAL.
THERE'S SOMETHING I NEED TO TELL YOU.
HUH?
SU (SHUF)
スッ…
ペラ
PERA (OPEN)
THEY'RE MAKING A MINI-ANIME!!
I'M SO HAPPY... I CAN'T BELIEVE IT...
RIGHT.
MOM ONCE SAID...
...NOT TO BELIEVE WHAT YOUR NATURAL ENEMIES SAY.

VOICE-RECORDING REPORT MANGA

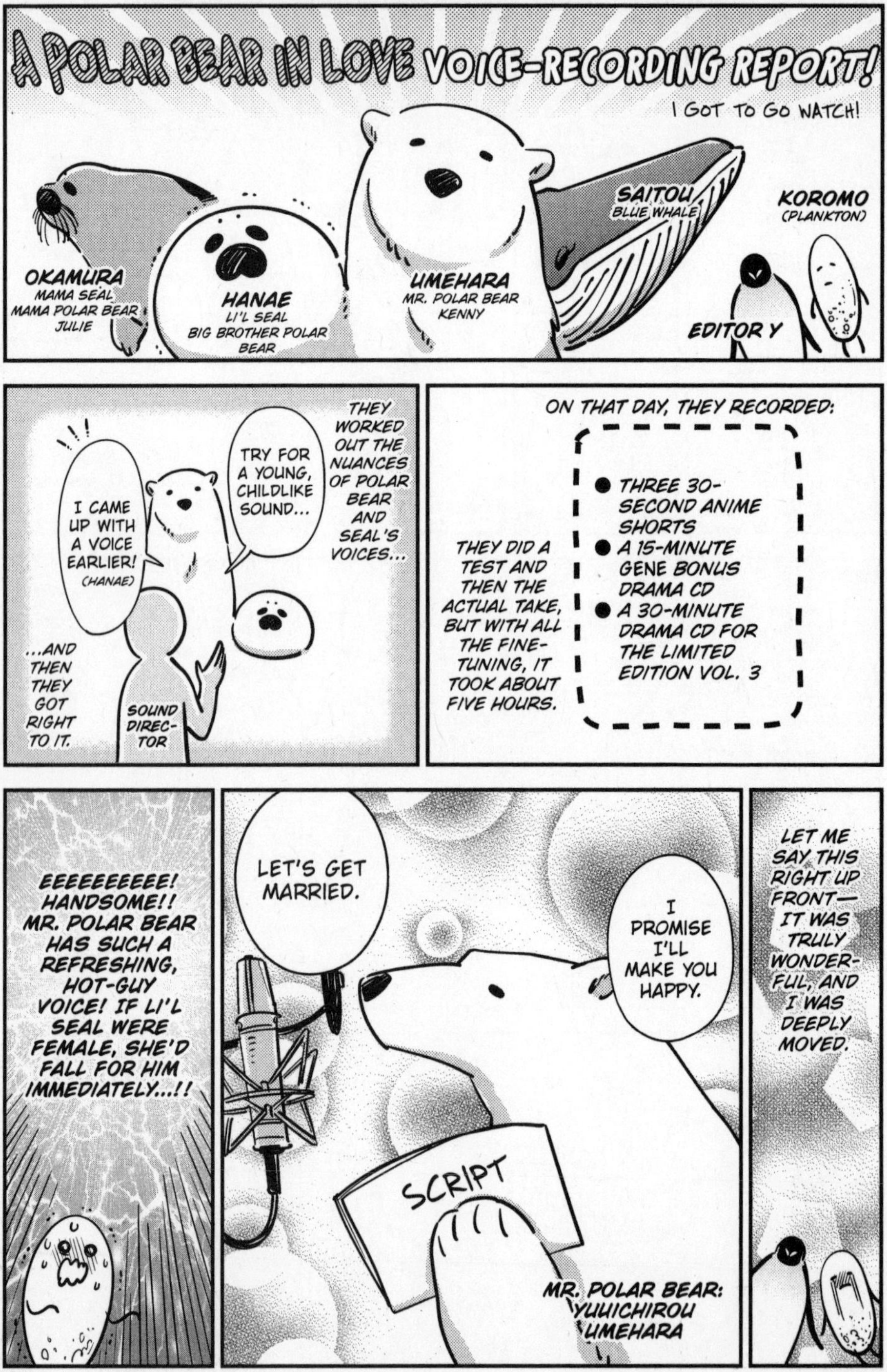

A POLAR BEAR IN LOVE VOICE-RECORDING REPORT!
I GOT TO GO WATCH!
KOROMO (PLANKTON)
EDITOR Y
SAITOU BLUE WHALE
UMEHARA MR. POLAR BEAR KENNY
HANAE LI'L SEAL BIG BROTHER POLAR BEAR
OKAMURA MAMA SEAL MAMA POLAR BEAR JULIE
ON THAT DAY, THEY RECORDED:
● THREE 30-SECOND ANIME SHORTS
● A 15-MINUTE GENE BONUS DRAMA CD
● A 30-MINUTE DRAMA CD FOR THE LIMITED EDITION VOL. 3
THEY DID A TEST AND THEN THE ACTUAL TAKE, BUT WITH ALL THE FINE-TUNING, IT TOOK ABOUT FIVE HOURS.
THEY WORKED OUT THE NUANCES OF POLAR BEAR AND SEAL'S VOICES...
TRY FOR A YOUNG, CHILDLIKE SOUND...
I CAME UP WITH A VOICE EARLIER! (HANAE)
...AND THEN THEY GOT RIGHT TO IT.
SOUND DIRECTOR
LET ME SAY THIS RIGHT UP FRONT—IT WAS TRULY WONDERFUL, AND I WAS DEEPLY MOVED.
LET'S GET MARRIED.
I PROMISE I'LL MAKE YOU HAPPY.
SCRIPT
MR. POLAR BEAR: YUUICHIROU UMEHARA
EEEEEEEEE! HANDSOME!! MR. POLAR BEAR HAS SUCH A REFRESHING, HOT-GUY VOICE! IF LI'L SEAL WERE FEMALE, SHE'D FALL FOR HIM IMMEDIATELY...!!

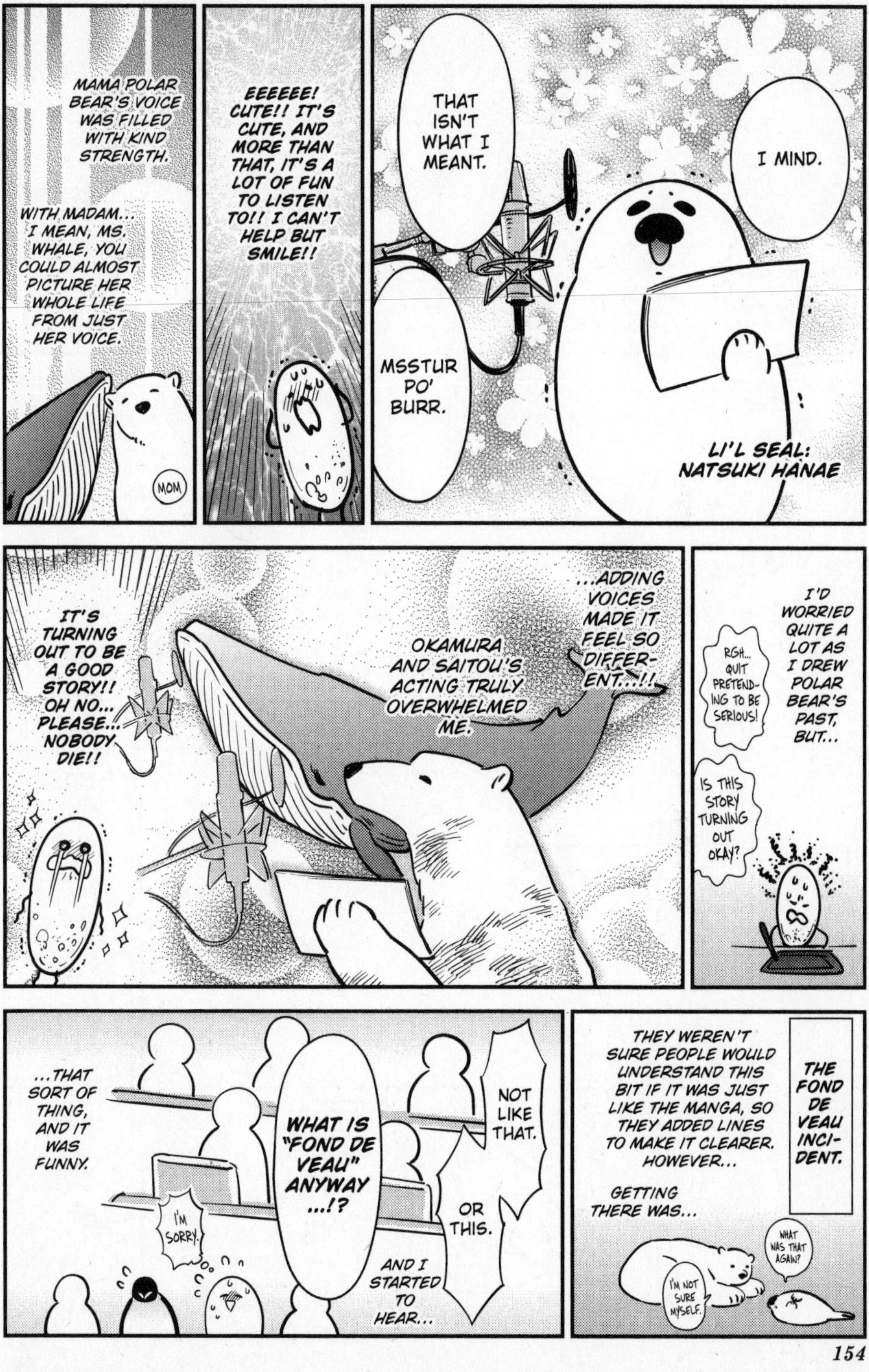
I MIND.
THAT ISN'T WHAT I MEANT.
MSSTUR PO' BURR.
LI'L SEAL: NATSUKI HANAE
EEEEEE! CUTE!! IT'S CUTE, AND MORE THAN THAT, IT'S A LOT OF FUN TO LISTEN TO!! I CAN'T HELP BUT SMILE!!
MAMA POLAR BEAR'S VOICE WAS FILLED WITH KIND STRENGTH.
WITH MADAM... I MEAN, MS. WHALE, YOU COULD ALMOST PICTURE HER WHOLE LIFE FROM JUST HER VOICE.
MOM
I'D WORRIED QUITE A LOT AS I DREW POLAR BEAR'S PAST, BUT...
RGH... QUIT PRETENDING TO BE SERIOUS!
IS THIS STORY TURNING OUT OKAY?
...ADDING VOICES MADE IT FEEL SO DIFFER-ENT...!!
OKAMURA AND SAITOU'S ACTING TRULY OVERWHELMED ME.
IT'S TURNING OUT TO BE A GOOD STORY!! OH NO... PLEASE... NOBODY DIE!!
THE FOND DE VEAU INCIDENT.
THEY WEREN'T SURE PEOPLE WOULD UNDERSTAND THIS BIT IF IT WAS JUST LIKE THE MANGA, SO THEY ADDED LINES TO MAKE IT CLEARER. HOWEVER...
GETTING THERE WAS...
WHAT WAS THAT AGAIN?
I'M NOT SURE MYSELF.
NOT LIKE THAT.
WHAT IS "FOND DE VEAU" ANYWAY...!?
OR THIS.
AND I STARTED TO HEAR...
...THAT SORT OF THING, AND IT WAS FUNNY.
I'M SORRY.

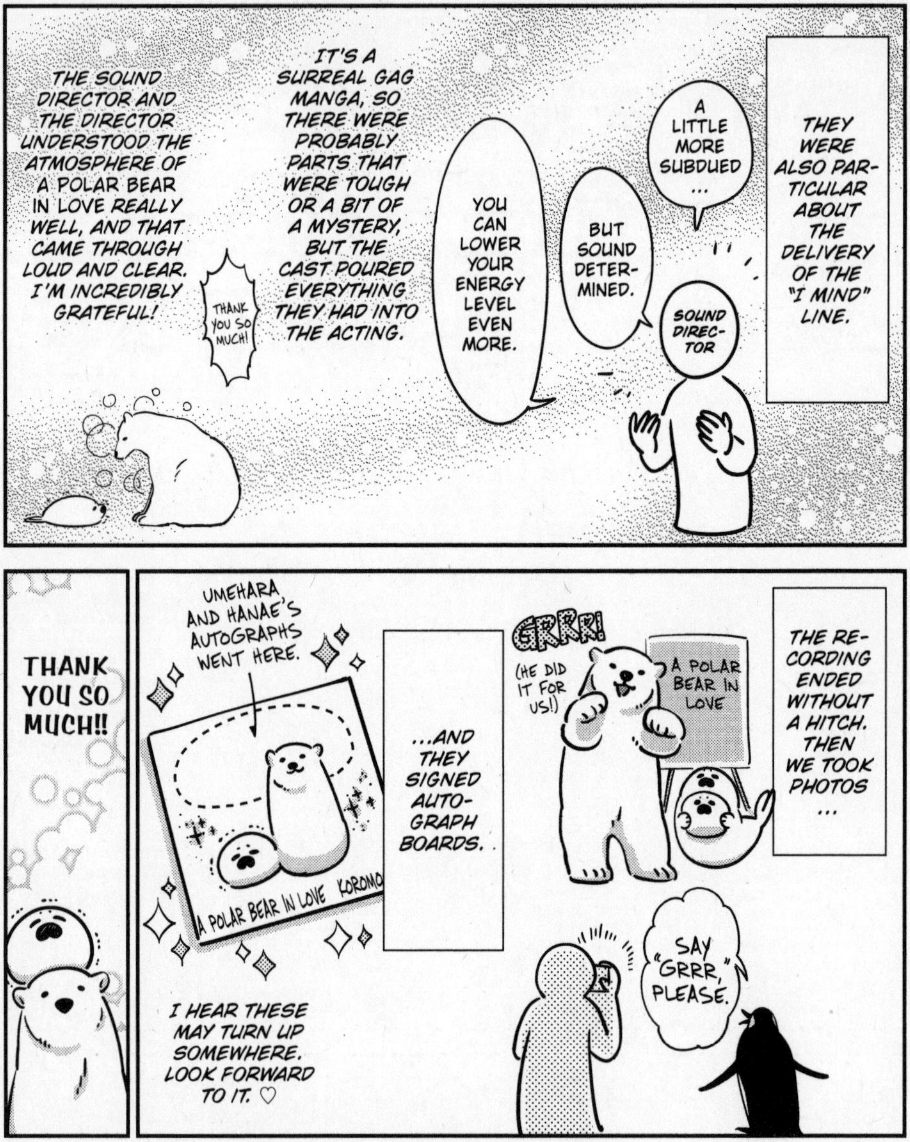
THEY WERE ALSO PARTICULAR ABOUT THE DELIVERY OF THE "I MIND" LINE.
A LITTLE MORE SUBDUED...
BUT SOUND DETERMINED.
YOU CAN LOWER YOUR ENERGY LEVEL EVEN MORE.
SOUND DIRECTOR
IT'S A SURREAL GAG MANGA, SO THERE WERE PROBABLY PARTS THAT WERE TOUGH OR A BIT OF A MYSTERY, BUT THE CAST POURED EVERYTHING THEY HAD INTO THE ACTING.
THANK YOU SO MUCH!
THE SOUND DIRECTOR AND THE DIRECTOR UNDERSTOOD THE ATMOSPHERE OF A POLAR BEAR IN LOVE REALLY WELL, AND THAT CAME THROUGH LOUD AND CLEAR. I'M INCREDIBLY GRATEFUL!
THE RECORDING ENDED WITHOUT A HITCH. THEN WE TOOK PHOTOS...
GRRR!
(HE DID IT FOR US!)
A POLAR BEAR IN LOVE
SAY "GRRR," PLEASE.
...AND THEY SIGNED AUTOGRAPH BOARDS.
UMEHARA AND HANAE'S AUTOGRAPHS WENT HERE.
A POLAR BEAR IN LOVE KOROMO
I HEAR THESE MAY TURN UP SOMEWHERE. LOOK FORWARD TO IT. ♡
THANK YOU SO MUCH!!

THIS WAS ALL THANKS TO EVERYONE WHO HAS READ *A POLAR BEAR IN LOVE!* THANK YOU VERY MUCH FOR PICKING UP VOLUME 3 AS WELL!

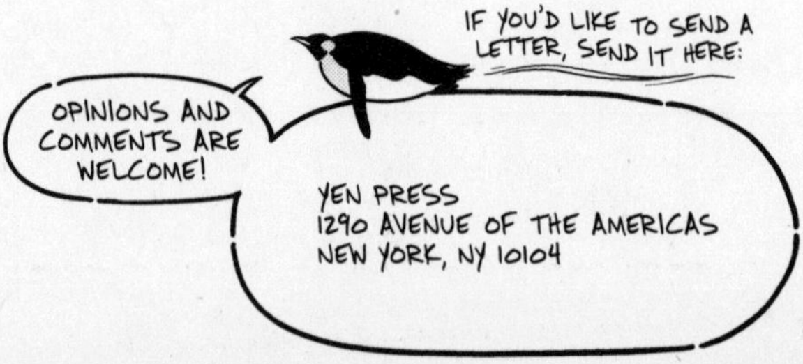
IF YOU'D LIKE TO SEND A LETTER, SEND IT HERE:
OPINIONS AND COMMENTS ARE WELCOME!
YEN PRESS
1290 AVENUE OF THE AMERICAS
NEW YORK, NY 10104

THE END

Let's all make...

Special Project

GENE COOKING ♪

Presenting a fun, delicious Li'l Seal recipe. ☆ Try it; it's easy!

A Polar Bear in Love

Chewy Li'l Seal Rice Flour Dumplings

Learn to make it! ☆

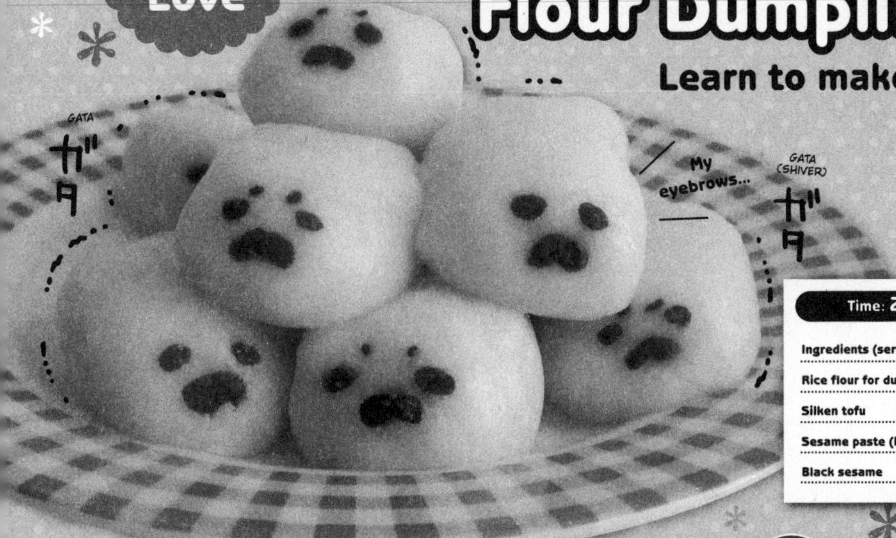

...
GATA
ガタ
My eyebrows...
GATA (SHIVER)
ガタ

Time: 20 min.	
Ingredients (serves 2–3 people)	
Rice flour for dumplings	100g
Silken tofu	1/3 block
Sesame paste (black)	2 Tbsp
Black sesame	To taste

1 Mix the rice flour and tofu. Make the mixture about as firm as your earlobes. Then set aside a bite-size piece on a separate dish.

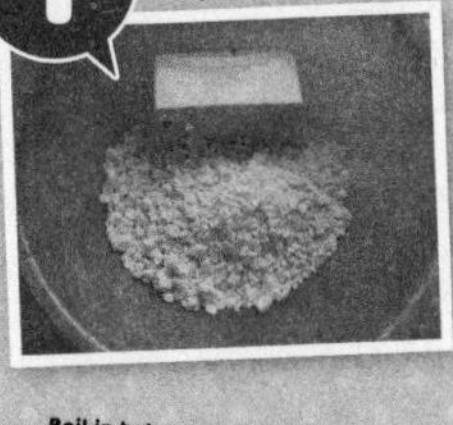

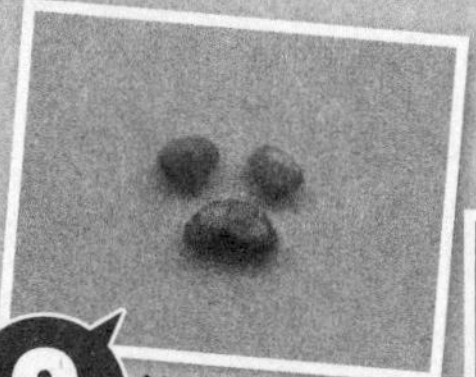

2 Add the sesame paste to the dough you set aside. Shape it into eyes and muzzles. Making them small is key.

3 Take a bite-size piece of the remaining dough. Form it into an oval, and pinch one end into a tail shape. It's okay to make the dumpling perfectly round too.

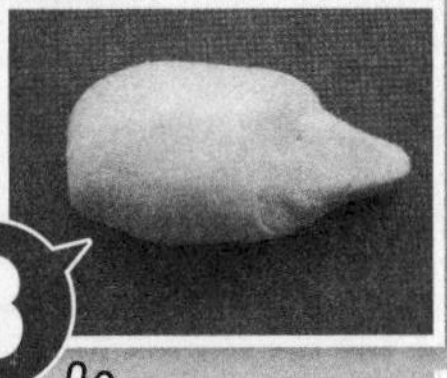

4 Use kitchen shears to make a cut in the tail. Then lightly press on eyes and a muzzle. Add two grains of black sesame for the eyebrows.

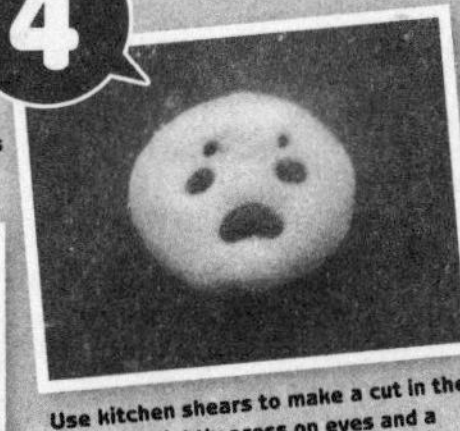

5 Boil in hot water. When they float to the top, drop them into cold water to cool.

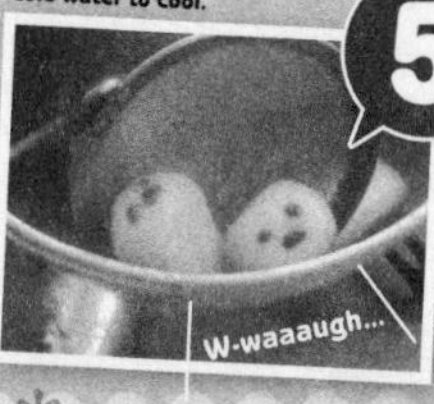

W-waaaugh...

6 Eat them with sweet soy sauce, strawberry sauce, or any way you'd like. ♪

Variation ☆

We put them in the old classic, red bean soup. ♪

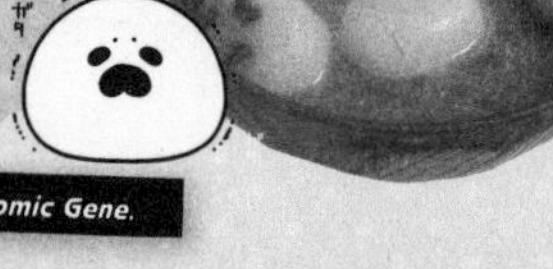

I'M DROWNING IN RED BEAN JAM...!
GATA
ガタ

A COMMENT FROM KOROMO-SENSEI ☆

After you laugh, their goodness sort of creeps up on you, doesn't it! If Mr. Polar Bear saw this recipe, I bet he'd make it right away.

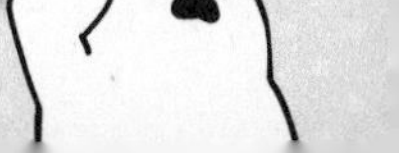

BISHI (SALUTE)
ビシッ

This article originally ran in the September 2016 issue of *Monthly Comic Gene*.

A POLAR BEAR in LOVE

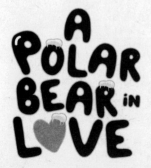

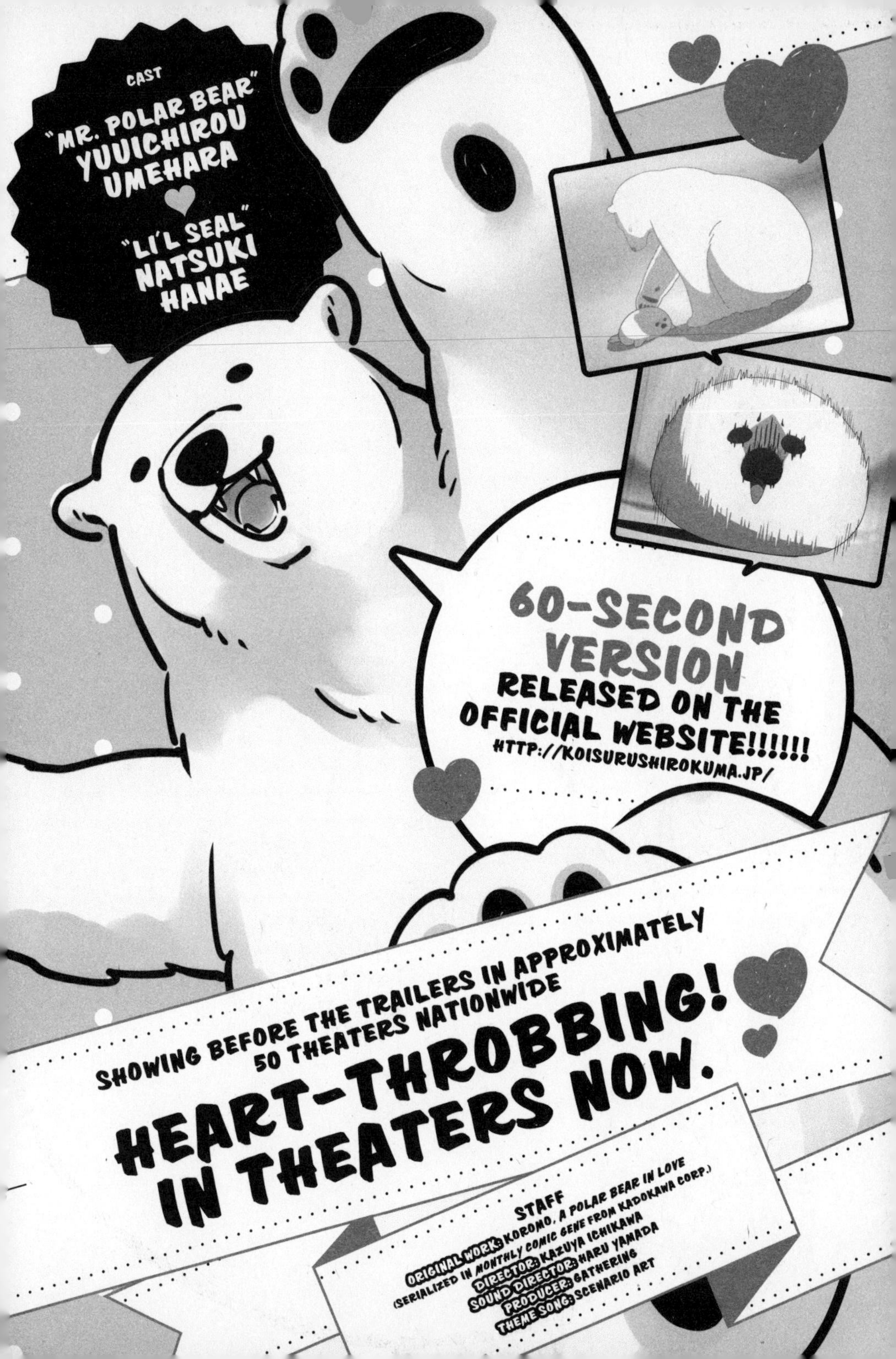
CAST
"MR. POLAR BEAR" YUUICHIROU UMEHARA
"LI'L SEAL" NATSUKI HANAE
60-SECOND VERSION
RELEASED ON THE OFFICIAL WEBSITE!!!!!!
HTTP://KOISURUSHIROKUMA.JP/
SHOWING BEFORE THE TRAILERS IN APPROXIMATELY 50 THEATERS NATIONWIDE
HEART-THROBBING! IN THEATERS NOW.
STAFF
ORIGINAL WORK: KOROMO, A POLAR BEAR IN LOVE
(SERIALIZED IN MONTHLY COMIC GENE FROM KADOKAWA CORP.)
DIRECTOR: KAZUYA ICHIKAWA
SOUND DIRECTOR: HARU YAMADA
PRODUCER: GATHERING
THEME SONG: SCENARIO ART

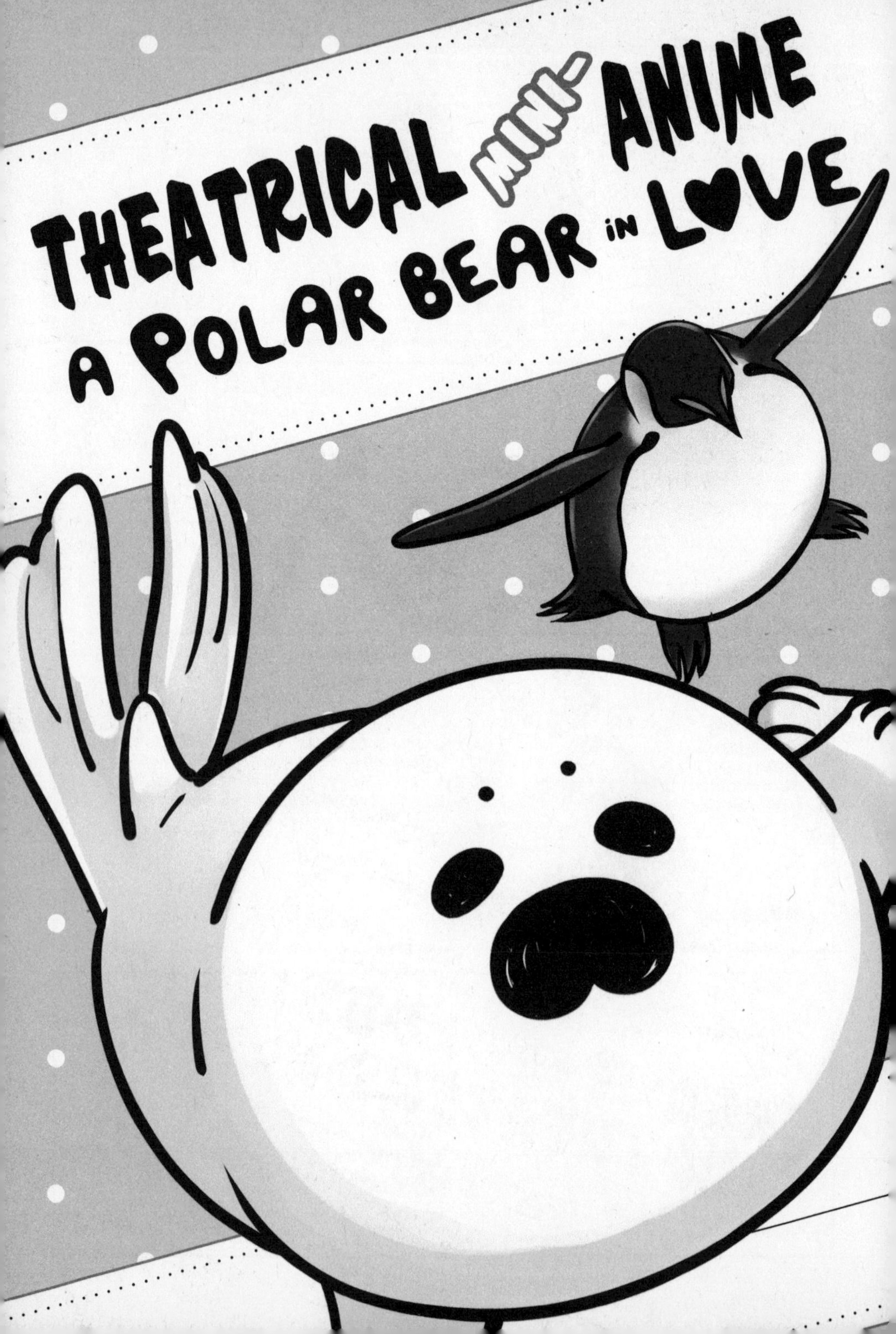
THEATRICAL MINI-ANIME
A POLAR BEAR IN LOVE

BEFORE THE COVER PHOTO WAS TAKEN

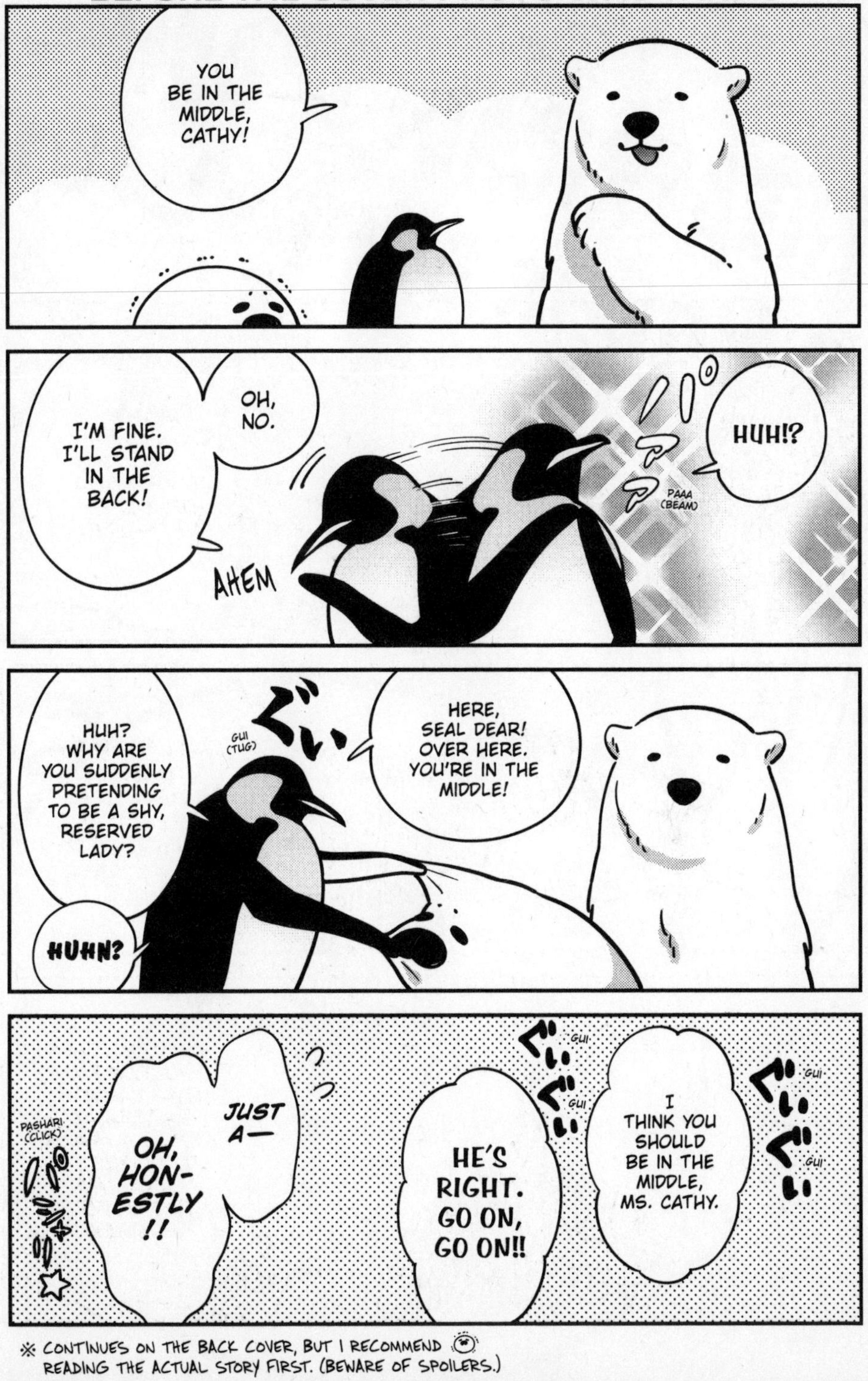
YOU BE IN THE MIDDLE, CATHY!
HUH!?
PAAA (BEAM)
OH, NO.
I'M FINE. I'LL STAND IN THE BACK!
AHEM
HERE, SEAL DEAR! OVER HERE. YOU'RE IN THE MIDDLE!
GUI (TUG)
HUH? WHY ARE YOU SUDDENLY PRETENDING TO BE A SHY, RESERVED LADY?
HUHN?
GUI
GUI
I THINK YOU SHOULD BE IN THE MIDDLE, MS. CATHY.
GUI
GUI
HE'S RIGHT. GO ON, GO ON!!
JUST A—
OH, HON-ESTLY!!
PASHARI (CLICK)

※ CONTINUES ON THE BACK COVER, BUT I RECOMMEND READING THE ACTUAL STORY FIRST. (BEWARE OF SPOILERS.)

CATHY AND SWEETIE

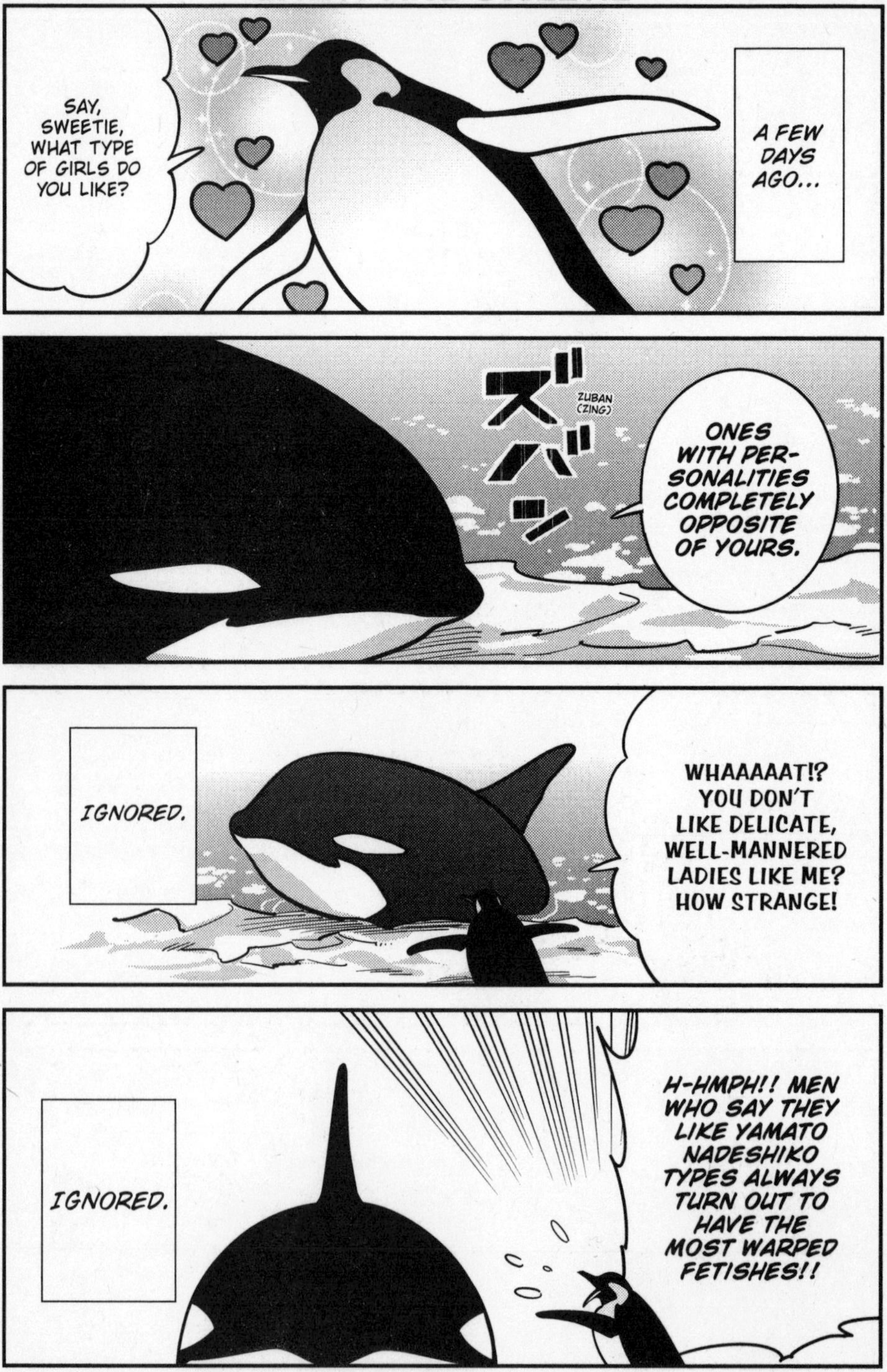
A FEW DAYS AGO...
SAY, SWEETIE, WHAT TYPE OF GIRLS DO YOU LIKE?
ONES WITH PER-SONALITIES COMPLETELY OPPOSITE OF YOURS.
ズバッ
ZUBAN (ZING)
WHAAAAAT!? YOU DON'T LIKE DELICATE, WELL-MANNERED LADIES LIKE ME? HOW STRANGE!
IGNORED.
H-HMPH!! MEN WHO SAY THEY LIKE YAMATO NADESHIKO TYPES ALWAYS TURN OUT TO HAVE THE MOST WARPED FETISHES!!
IGNORED.

AUTHOR'S NOTE

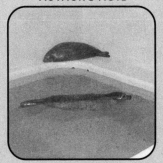

Koromo

**SWEET STEAMED
BUNS SHAPED
LIKE FRIED SHRIMP.
PHOTOGRAPHED
AT KAMOGAWA
SEA WORLD.**

TRANSLATION NOTES

PAGE 5

For clarification, the emperor penguin breeding cycle is hard on the *parents*, both male and female. The female's nutritional reserves are exhausted after she lays her egg, and after transferring the egg to the male's feet, she goes back to sea for two months or so to eat. The male goes without eating for sixty-two to seventy-five days, until the female returns and the chick hatches, and then it's his turn to go eat. The actual chicks don't seem to have a particularly hard time, relatively speaking.

PAGE 7

No guarantees on this one, but since Cathy is an emperor penguin, she may be named after Catherine the Great, empress of Russia from 1762 to 1796.

PAGE 143

"Mutsugorou" is the pen name of Masanori Hata, a Japanese zoologist, essayist, and filmmaker. He's best known in the West as the director and screenwriter of the movie *The Adventures of Milo and Otis*.

PAGE 148

This is actually a *kamakura*. *Kamakuras* are igloo-like huts made for "Little New Year" (the fifteenth day of the first lunar month) in areas of Japan that get heavy snowfall, particularly Akita and Niigata Prefectures. A water deity is enshrined in each hut, and people light lamps and eat snacks or light meals inside them.

PAGE 161

Yamato Nadeshiko is a poetic term for the classical ideal of womanhood in Japan, similar to "English Rose" in the UK. "Yamato" is another name for "Japan," and "Nadeshiko" is a type of wildflower. Yamato Nadeshiko types are generally graceful, quiet, modest, obedient, faithful, and industrious.

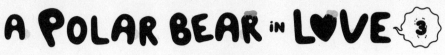

A POLAR BEAR in LOVE 3

Koromo

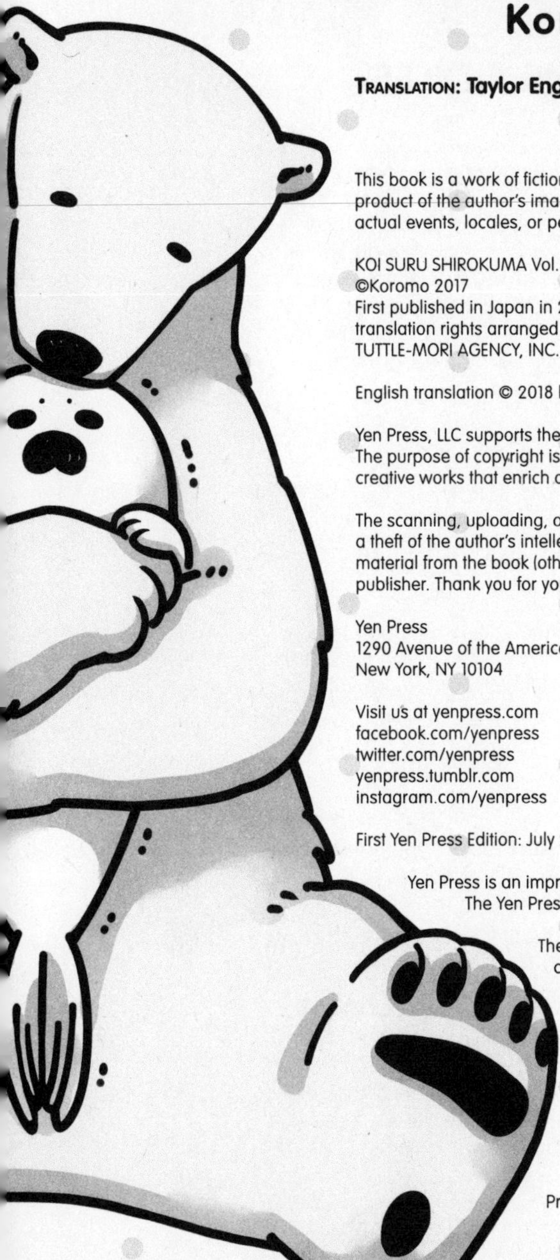

TRANSLATION: **Taylor Engel** ❤ LETTERING: **Lys Blakeslee**

KOI SURU SHIROKUMA Vol.3
©Koromo 2017
First published in Japan in 2017 by KADOKAWA CORPORATION, Tokyo. English translation rights arranged with KADOKAWA CORPORATION, Tokyo through TUTTLE-MORI AGENCY, INC., Tokyo.

English translation © 2018 by Yen Press, LLC

Yen Press
1290 Avenue of the Americas
New York, NY 10104

Visit us at yenpress.com
facebook.com/yenpress
twitter.com/yenpress
yenpress.tumblr.com
instagram.com/yenpress

First Yen Press Edition: July 2018

Yen Press is an imprint of Yen Press, LLC.
The Yen Press name and logo are trademarks of Yen Press, LLC.

The publisher is not responsible for websites (or their content) that are not owned by the publisher.

Library of Congress Control Number: 2017949438

ISBNs: 978-1-9753-2622-7 (paperback)
978-1-9753-5405-3 (ebook)

10 9 8 7 6 5 4 3 2 1

WOR

Printed in the United States of America